SPAIN & PORTUGAL
1998

John Muir Publications
Santa Fe, New Mexico

Other JMP travel guidebooks by Rick Steves
Asia Through the Back Door (with Bob Effertz)
Europe 101: History, Art, and Culture for the Traveler
(with Gene Openshaw)
Europe Through the Back Door
Mona Winks: Self-Guided Tours of Europe's Top Museums
(with Gene Openshaw)
Rick Steves' Best of Europe
Rick Steves' France, Belgium & the Netherlands (with Steve Smith)
Rick Steves' Germany, Austria & Switzerland
Rick Steves' Great Britain & Ireland
Rick Steves' Italy
Rick Steves' Russia & the Baltics (with Ian Watson)
Rick Steves' Scandinavia
Rick Steves' Phrase Books: German, Italian, French,
Spanish/Portuguese, and French/Italian/German

Gracías to ace researcher Steve Smith. Thanks also to Jules Wiersema for
research in and information on Barcelona.

John Muir Publications, P.O. Box 613, Santa Fe, NM 87504
Copyright © 1998, 1997, 1996, 1995 by Rick Steves
Cover copyright © 1998 by John Muir Publications
All rights reserved.

Printed in the United States of America
Second printing June 1998

Previously published as *2 to 22 Days in Spain and Portugal* © 1986, 1987,
1989, 1992, 1993, 1994

For the latest on Rick Steves' lectures, guidebooks, tours, and public
television series, contact Europe Through the Back Door, Box 2009,
Edmonds, WA 98020, tel. 425/771-8303, fax 425/771-0833, Web site:
www.ricksteves.com, or e-mail: rick@ricksteves.com.

ISSN 1084-4414
ISBN 1-56261-391-X

Europe Through the Back Door Editor Risa Laib
John Muir Publications Editors Krista Lyons-Gould, Kristin Shahane,
Nancy Gillan
Production Janine Lehmann
Design Linda Braun
Cover Design Cowgirls Design, Kathryn Lloyd-Strongin
Typesetting Cowgirls Design
Maps David C. Hoerlein
Printer Banta Company
Cover Photo Giralda Tower and Cathedral; Sevilla, Spain; copyright
©Blaine Harrington III

Distributed to the book trade by Publishers Group West
Berkeley, California

Europe

500 KM
300 MI

LAPLAND
ARCTIC CIRCLE
Trondheim
BOGNE FJORD
NORWAY
FINLAND
Bergen
Oslo
Helsinki
Turku
St. Petersburg
Stockholm
Tallinn
ESTONIA
RUSSIA
SWEDEN
BALTIC
LATVIA
Moscow
SCOTLAND
Edinburgh
DENMARK
SEA
Riga
LITHUANIA
IRELAND
IRE.
York
NORTH
Copenhagen
Vilnius
RUSS.
Dublin
DINGLE PENINSULA
ENGLAND
SEA
BELARUS
WALES
Lübeck
POLAND
Bath
London
Amsterdam
Berlin
Warsaw
Mont St. Michel
Bruges
NETH.
GERMANY
Krakow
Kiev
BRITTANY
NORMANDY
Brussels
BELG.
RHINE
Prague
UKRAINE
ATLANTIC
Paris
LUX.
MOSEL
ROM. ROAD
CZECH.
ALSACE
SLOVAK.
Colmar
Munich
MOLDOVA
OCEAN
FRANCE
SWITZ.
Bern
BAVARIA
Vienna
Budapest
LOIRE
BERN. OBER.
Salzburg
AUST.
ROMANIA
DORDOGNE
Chamonix
MT. BLANC
TIROL
HUNG.
BLACK
DOLO- MITES
SLOV.
Milan
CRO.
Belgrade
Bucharest
Carc.
PROVENCE
CINQUE TERRE
Venice
Aries
Florence
BOSNIA/ HERZ.
SEA
Nice
UMBRIA
SAN MARINO
SERBIA
Sofia
SPAIN
ANDORRA
MONACO
Rome
ADRIATIC
BULG.
Istanbul
Madrid
Barcelona
CORSICA
ITALY
ALB.
CAPPA- DOCIA
PORTUGAL
Toledo
SARDINIA
Naples
GREECE
TURKEY
Lisbon
AMALFI COAST
CORFU
AEGEAN
Ephesus
Seville
Gran.
MEDITERRANEAN
SICILY
Athens
ALGARVE
ANDALUSIA
PEL- PEL.
SEA
MOROCCO
ALGERIA
TUNISIA
SEA
CRETE

DCM

Top Destinations in Spain and Portugal

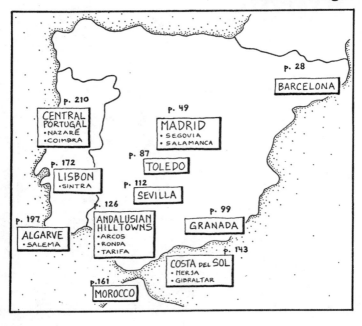

CONTENTS

INTRODUCTION

Like a grandpa bouncing a baby on his knee, Iberia is a mix of old and new, modern and traditional. Spain and Portugal can fill your travel days with traditional folk life, exotic foods, world-class art treasures, sunshine, friendly people, and castles where the winds of the past still howl. And Iberia (especially Portugal) is Europe's bargain basement.

This book breaks Spain and Portugal into their top big-city, small-town, and rural destinations. It then gives you all the information and opinions necessary to wring the maximum value out of your limited time and money in each of these destinations.

If you plan a month or less in Iberia and have a normal appetite for information, this lean and mean little book is all you need. If you're a travel info junkie (like me), this book sorts through the superlatives and provides a handy rack on which to hang your supplemental information.

Experiencing Spain and Portugal's culture, people, and natural wonders economically and hassle-free has been my goal for more than 20 years of traveling, tour guiding, and writing. With this book, I pass on to you the lessons I've learned, updated for 1998.

Rick Steves' Spain & Portugal is a tour guide in your pocket, with a balanced, comfortable mix of exciting cities and cozy towns, including an exotic taste of Morocco. It covers the predictable biggies and stirs in a healthy dose of Back Door intimacy. Along with seeing a bullfight, the Prado, and flamenco, you'll climb the church tower of a sun-parched Andalusian town, recharge your solar cells in an Algarve fishing village, and scramble the ramparts of a deserted Moorish castle. I've been selective, including only the most exciting sights. For example, there are countless whitewashed Andalusian hill towns; I recommend the best two.

The best is, of course, only my opinion. But after two busy decades of travel writing, lecturing, and tour guiding, I've developed a sixth sense of what tickles the traveler's fancy.

This Information Is Accurate and Up-to-Date

This book is updated every year. Most publishers of guide-books that cover a region from top to bottom can afford an update only every two or three years, and then the research is often by letter. Since this book is selective, covering only the places I think make the best month or so in Iberia, I can get it updated each summer. Even with annual updates, things change. But if you're traveling with the current edition of this book, I guarantee you're using the most up-to-date information available. Trust me, you'll regret trying to save a few bucks by traveling on old information. If you're packing an old book, you'll quickly learn the seriousness of your mistake . . . in Spain and Portugal. Your trip costs about $10 per waking hour. Your time is valuable. This guidebook saves lots of time.

Planning Your Trip

This book is organized by destinations. Each destination is covered as a mini-vacation on its own, filled with exciting sights and homey, affordable places to stay. In each chapter, you'll find:

Planning Your Time, a suggested schedule with thoughts on how best to use your limited time.

Orientation, including tourist information, city transportation, and an easy-to-read map designed to make the text clear and your arrival smooth.

Sights with ratings: ▲▲▲—Don't miss; ▲▲—Try hard to see; ▲—Worthwhile if you can make it; no rating—Worth knowing about.

Sleeping and Eating, with addresses and phone numbers of my favorite budget hotels and restaurants.

Transportation Connections to nearby destinations by train, bus, or car, with recommended roadside attractions for drivers.

The Appendix is a traveler's tool kit, with telephone tips, a climate chart, list of festivals, and cultural background.

Browse through this book, choose your favorite destinations, and link them up. Then have a great trip! You'll travel as a temporary local, getting the absolute most out of every mile, minute, and dollar. You won't waste time on mediocre sights because, unlike other guidebooks, I cover only the best. Since your major financial pitfall is lousy, expensive hotels, I've worked hard to assemble the best accommodations values for each stop. And, as you travel the route I know and love, I'm happy you'll be meeting some of my favorite Spanish and Portuguese people.

Trip Costs

Five components make up your trip cost: airfare, surface transportation, room and board, sightseeing, and shopping/entertainment/miscellany.

Airfare: Don't try to sort through the mess yourself. Get and use a good travel agent. A basic round-trip flight from the U.S.A. to Madrid or Lisbon should cost $700 to $1,000, depending on where you fly from and when. Always consider saving time and money by flying "open-jaws" (into one city and out of another, such as flying into Barcelona and out of Lisbon).

Surface Transportation: For a three-week whirlwind trip linking all of my recommended destinations, allow $350 per person for second-class trains and buses ($500 in first-class trains), or $500 per person (based on two people sharing) for a three-week car rental, tolls, gas, and insurance. Car rental is cheapest to arrange from home in the U.S.A. Train passes are normally available only outside of Europe. You may save money by simply buying your tickets as you go (see Transportation, below).

Room and Board: You can thrive in Iberia on $50 a day per person for room and board. A $50-a-day budget allows $5 for lunch, $15 for dinner, and $30 for lodging (based on two people splitting the cost of a $60 double room that includes breakfast). That's doable. Students and tightwads will do it on $30 ($15 per bed, $15 for meals and snacks). But budget sleeping and eating require the skills and information covered below (or more extensively in *Rick Steves' Europe Through the Back Door*).

Sightseeing: In big cities, figure $4 per major sight (Prado, Picasso Museum), $2 for minor ones (climbing church towers), and $30 for splurge experiences (bullfights, flamenco). An overall average of $10 a day works for most. Don't skimp here. After all, this category directly powers most of the experiences all the other expenses are designed to make possible.

Shopping/Entertainment/Miscellany: This can vary from nearly nothing to a small fortune. Figure $1 per coffee, beer, ice-cream cone, and postcard, and $10 to $20 for evening entertainment. Good budget travelers find that this category has little to do with assembling a trip full of lifelong and wonderful memories.

Exchange Rates

I list prices in *pesetas* and *escudos* throughout the book. Approximate exchange rates:

> 140 Spanish *pesetas* (ptas) = about $1; 100 ptas = about 70 cents.
> 170 Portuguese *escudos* = about $1; 100 *escudos* = about 60 cents.

The Portuguese use a dollar sign after the number of *escudos* (e.g., 170$00 or 170$). To figure rough prices in dollars, think of *pesetas* and *escudos* as pennies and cut 30 percent in Spain (3,000 ptas = about $21) and cut 40 percent in Portugal (5,000$00 = about $31).

Prices, Times, and Discounts

The prices in this book, as well as the hours and telephone numbers, are accurate as of mid-1997. Iberia is always changing, and I know you'll understand that this, like any other guidebook, starts to yellow even before it's printed.

In Europe—and in this book—you'll be using the 24-hour clock. After 12:00 noon, keep going—13:00, 14:00, and so on. For anything over 12, subtract 12 and add p.m. (14:00 is 2:00 p.m.).

This book lists peak-season hours for sightseeing attractions. Off-season, roughly October through April, expect shorter hours, more lunchtime breaks, and fewer activities. Confirm your sightseeing plans locally, especially when traveling between October and April.

Portuguese time is usually one hour earlier than Spanish time (due to daylight savings time), and Morocco can be up to two hours different from Spanish time. When traveling between countries, confirm local times of departure, and be flexible about arrival times.

While discounts for sightseeing and transportation are not listed in this book, seniors (60 and over), students (with International Student Identity Cards), and youths (under 18) often get discounts—but only by asking.

When to Go

Spring and fall offer the best combination of good weather, light crowds, long days, and plenty of tourist and cultural activities. Summer and winter travel both have their predictable pros and cons. July and August are most crowded and expensive in coastal areas, less crowded but uncomfortably hot and dusty in the interior. For weather specifics, see the climate chart in the Appendix. Whenever you anticipate crowds (as in July and August), call hotels in advance (call from one hotel to the next; your fluent receptionist can help you) and try to arrive early in the day.

Sightseeing Priorities

Depending on the length of your trip, here are my recommended priorities.

3 days:	Madrid, Toledo
5 days, add:	Lisbon
7 days, add:	Barcelona
10 days, add:	Andalucía, Sevilla
14 days, add:	Granada, Algarve
17 days, add:	Costa del Sol, Morocco
20 days, add:	Coimbra, Nazaré
22 days, add:	Salamanca, Segovia

Red Tape, Business Hours, and Banking

You currently need a passport but no visa and no shots to travel in Spain, Portugal, and Morocco.

For visitors, Iberia is a land of strange and frustrating schedules. Most businesses respect the afternoon siesta. When it's 100 degrees in the shade and you're wandering dusty, deserted streets looking for a bank to change money, you'll understand why.

Generally shops are open 9:00 to 13:00 and 15:00 or 16:00 to 19:00 or 20:00, longer in touristy places. On Saturday shops often open only in the morning, and are closed Sunday. The biggest museums stay open all day, most close for a siesta.

Bring a Visa or MasterCard with a pin number so you can use the same card to withdraw cash from ATM machines and to charge any expensive items. Both Spain and Portugal have easily available, easy-to-use 24 hour/day ATM machines (with English instructions). They'll save you time and money (on commission fees). I traveled painlessly throughout Spain and Portugal in 1997 with my Visa debit card (and my four-digit pin number). Get details at your bank, and bring a extra copy of your card just in case it gets de-magnetized or gobbled up by a machine. Bring traveler's checks as a backup.

Banks are generally open Monday through Friday from 9:00 to 14:00 in Spain and 8:30 to 15:00 in Portugal (often with a lunch break).

Whirlwind Three-Week Tour

Spanish banks charge acceptable commissions for changing traveler's checks. American Express offices (only in big cities) have a slightly less favorable rate, but change any type of traveler's check without a commission. Portugal's banks charge outrageous, unregulated commissions (around $8–$15). Shop around. Sometimes the hole-in-the-wall exchange offices offer better deals than the bank. Look for the rare American Express office. Better yet, have an ATM card handy.

Language Barrier

In Iberia, people in the tourist trade speak English but many locals don't. Here, more than in most places in Europe, a phrase book comes in handy, particularly if you want to interact with local people. You'll find that doors open quicker and with more smiles when you can speak a few words of the language.

Spanish is easier than Portuguese to learn and pronounce. Portuguese sounds like a French person speaking Spanish

Spain & Portugal's Best Three-Week Trip

Day	Plan	Sleep in
1	Arrive in Madrid	Madrid
2	Madrid	Madrid
3	El Escorial, Valley of Fallen, Segovia	Segovia
4	Segovia and Salamanca	Salamanca
5	Salamanca, Coimbra	Coimbra
6	Coimbra, Batalha, Fatima, Nazaré	Nazaré
7	Beach Day in Nazaré, Alcobaça side trip	Nazaré
8	Nazaré, Óbidos, Lisbon	Lisbon
9	Lisbon	Lisbon
10	Lisbon side trip to Belém and Sintra	Lisbon
11	Lisbon to the Algarve	Salema
12	Free beach day, Sagres	Salema
13	Across Algarve, Sevilla	Sevilla
14	Sevilla	Sevilla
15	Andalucía's Route of White Villages	Arcos
16	Arcos, Jerez, Tarifa	Tarifa
17	A day in Morocco	Tarifa
18	Gibraltar, Costa del Sol	Nerja
19	Nerja to Granada	Granada
20	Granada	Granada
21	Through La Mancha to Toledo	Toledo
22	Toledo	Toledo/Madrid/fly

While this itinerary is designed to be done by car, it can be done by train and bus (seven to eight bus days and four to five train days). For three weeks without a car, I'd modify it to start in Barcelona and finish in Lisbon: Barcelona; night train to Madrid area (Toledo, Segovia, El Escorial); night train to Granada; bus along Costa del Sol to Tarifa (Morocco), up to Arcos, Sevilla, Algarve; night train to Lisbon. This skips Coimbra and Salamanca and assumes you'll fly open-jaws into Barcelona and out of Lisbon. If catching the train back to Europe from Lisbon, you can sightsee your way there in three days (via Coimbra and Salamanca) or catch the night train to Madrid.

while bouncing on a pogo stick. In Portugal's big cities and along the Algarve, you can usually find someone who speaks English. Otherwise, Spanish, French, and sign language are helpful.

My Spanish and Portuguese phrase book, which includes a traveler's dictionary, will help you soar over the language barrier. A few useful Portuguese words are *bom día* (good morning), *obrigado/a* (thank you; women end the word with "a"), and *adeus* (goodbye). See the Survival Phrases sections of the Appendix for other useful words.

Travel Smart

Upon arrival in a new town, lay the groundwork for a smooth departure. Reread this book as you travel, and visit local tourist information offices. Buy a phone card and use it for reservations and confirmations. Carry TP throughout Iberia, bring along a water bottle, and linger in the shade.

Enjoy the friendliness of the local people. Ask questions. Most locals are eager to point you in their idea of the right direction. Wear your money belt, pack a pocket-size notepad to organize your thoughts, and practice the virtue of simplicity. Those who expect to travel smart, do.

Design an itinerary that enables you to hit the festivals, bullfights, and museums on the right days. As you read this book, note the problem days: Mondays, when many museums are closed, and Sundays, when public transportation is meager. Treat Saturdays as weekdays.

Plan ahead for banking, laundry, post-office chores, and picnics. Maximize rootedness by minimizing one-night stands. Mix intense and relaxed periods. Every trip (and every traveler) needs at least a few slack days. Pace yourself. Assume you will return.

Warning: Tourists are prime targets for thieves throughout Spain and Portugal, especially in Barcelona, Madrid, Sevilla, and Lisbon. While hotel rooms are generally safe and muggings are very rare, cars are commonly broken into, purses are snatched, and pockets are picked. Be on guard, wear a money belt, assume any commotion around you is a theft smoke screen, leave nothing of value in your car, and park carefully. When traveling by train, keep your rucksack in sight and get a *couchette* (bed in an attendant-monitored sleeping car) for safety on overnight trips.

Tourist Information

Your best first stop in a new city is the *Turismo* (tourist information office). Get a city map and advice on accommodations, public transportation (including bus and train schedules), special events, and recommendations for nightlife. Some Turismos have information on the entire country. When you visit a Turismo (abbreviated TI in this book), try to pick up maps for towns you'll be visiting later in your trip.

While the TI has listings of all lodgings and is eager to book you a room, use their room-finding service only as a last resort (bloated prices, fees, no opinions, and they take a cut from your host). Use the listings in this book and go direct.

The national tourist offices in the U.S.A. are a wealth of information. Before your trip, get their free general-information packet and request any specific information you want, such as city maps and schedules of upcoming festivals.

Spanish National Tourist Offices: 666 Fifth Ave., 35th floor, New York, NY 10103, tel. 212/265-8822, fax 212/265-8864, web site: www.okspain.org, 845 N. Michigan Ave., Chicago, IL 60611, tel. 312/642-1992, fax 312/642-9817; 1221 Breckell Ave., #1850, Miami, FL 33131, tel. 305/358-1992, fax 305/358-8223; 8383 Wilshire Blvd., #960, Beverly Hills, CA 90211, tel. 213/658-7188, fax 213/658-1061.

Portuguese National Tourist Office: 590 Fifth Ave., 4th floor, New York, NY 10036, tel. 212/354-4403, fax 212/764-6137, web site: www.portugal.org.

Recommended Guidebooks

You may want some supplemental travel guidebooks, especially if you are traveling beyond my recommended destinations. When you consider the improvement it will make in your $3,000 vacation, $25 or $35 for extra maps and books is money well spent. For several people traveling by car, the extra weight and expense are negligible.

Lonely Planet's *Spain* is thorough, well-researched, and packed with good maps and hotel recommendations for low-to-moderate-budget travelers (not updated annually, but published in 1997). Students and vagabonds will like the hip *Rough Guide: Spain* and *Rough Guide: Portugal* (written by insightful British researchers, but not updated annually) and the highly opinionated *Let's Go: Spain and Portugal* (by Harvard students, better hotel listings, updated annually, includes Morocco). If you're a backpacker with a train pass and an interest in the youth and night scene, get *Let's Go*. Older travelers like Frommer's Spain/ Morocco and Portugal guides even though they, like the Fodor guides, ignore alternatives that enable travelers to save money by dirtying their fingers in the local culture. The popular, skinny Michelin Green Guides to Spain and Portugal are excellent, especially if you're driving. They're known for their city and sightseeing maps, dry but concise and helpful information on all major sights, and good cultural and historical background. English editions are sold in Iberia. The well-written and thoughtful Cadogan guides to Spain and Portugal are excellent for "A" students on the road. The encyclopedic Blue Guides to Spain and Portugal are dry as the plains in Spain but just right for some.

Jan Morris' *Spain* provides a thoughtful warm-up for your sightseeing, and John Hopper's *The New Spaniards* provides an interesting look at Spain today. Juan Lalaguna's *Spain: A Traveler's History* is ideal for a readable background on this country's tumultuous history.

Rick Steves' Books and Videos

Rick Steves' Europe Through the Back Door (Santa Fe, N.M.: John Muir Publications, 1998) gives you budget travel tips on minimizing jet lag, packing light, planning your itinerary, traveling by car or train, finding budget beds without reservations, changing money, outsmarting thieves, avoiding rip-offs, hurdling the language barrier, staying healthy, taking great photographs, using your bidet, and much more. The book also includes chapters on 37 of my favorite "Back Doors."

Rick Steves' Country Guides are a series of eight guidebooks that cover Europe; Britain and Ireland; France, Belgium, and the Netherlands; Italy; Germany, Austria, and Switzerland; Scandinavia; and Russia and the Baltics, just as this one covers Spain and Portugal.

Europe 101: History and Art for the Traveler (with Gene Openshaw, Santa Fe, N.M.: John Muir Publications, 1996) gives you the story of Europe's peoples, history, and art, offering you a good preparation for the sights of Iberia from Roman times through the Inquisition and up to the Spanish Civil War. Written for smart people who were sleeping in their history and art classes before they knew they were going to Europe, *101* really helps Europe's sights come alive.

Mona Winks (Santa Fe, N.M.: John Muir Publications,

1996, also co-written with Gene Openshaw), provides fun, easy-to-follow, self-guided tours of Europe's top 20 museums. Madrid's Prado is the thickest tour in the book.

Rick Steves' Spanish/Portuguese Phrase Book (Santa Fe, N.M.: John Muir Publications, 1997) presents you with the words and survival phrases necessary to communicate your way through a smooth and inexpensive trip.

My television series, *Travels in Europe with Rick Steves*, includes four half-hour shows on Spain and Portugal. These may re-air on your local public television station, and they're also available as information-packed videotapes, along with my one-hour slide-show lecture on Spain and Portugal (call us at 425/771-8303 for our free newsletter/catalog). Two more Spain shows will be released with my fourth series in 1998.

Maps

The maps in this book, drawn by Dave Hoerlein, are concise and simple. Dave, who is well-traveled in Spain and Portugal, has designed the maps to help you locate recommended places and get to the TIs, where you'll find more in-depth maps (free or cheap) of the cities or regions.

Don't skimp on maps. Excellent Michelin maps are available (cheaper than in the U.S.A.) throughout Iberia in bookstores, newsstands, and gas stations. Train travelers can do fine with a simple rail map (such as the one that comes with your train pass) and city maps from the TIs. Drivers should invest in good 1:400,000 maps and learn the key to maximize the sightseeing value.

Transportation

By Car or Train?

Cars are best for three or more traveling together (especially families with small kids), those packing heavy, and those scouring the countryside. Trains and buses are best for solo travelers, blitz tourists, and city-to-city travelers.

Traveling by Bus and Train

Public transportation in Spain is quickly becoming as slick, modern, and efficient as in northern Europe. Portugal is straggling in train service but offers excellent bus

Cost of Public Transportation

1998 SPAIN FLEXIPASS

	1st class	2nd class
Any 3 days in 2 months	$190	$150
Extra rail days (max 7)	40	32

Kids 4 - 11 half fare. Pass holders pay a supplement (at the station) to ride the fast Talgo 200 and AVE trains. For just $41 - $73 extra, your pass can get you from Madrid or Barcelona to Paris, Zurich, or Milan on a "Night Talgo" sleeper train.

SPAIN RAIL & DRIVE PASS

Any 3 rail days and 3 car days in 2 months.

	1st class	extra car day
A-Economy car	$239	$55
B-Small car	249	75
C-Medium car	259	85
D-Small automatic	289	105

Prices are approximate per person for two traveling together. Solo travelers pay about $80 extra. The 3rd and 4th persons sharing the car buy only the railpass. Extra rail days (5 max.) cost $40.

PORTUGUESE FLEXIPASS

1st class: Any 4 days out of 15 for $99. Kids 4-11 half fare, under 4 free.

Iberia: Point-to-point 1-way 2nd class rail fares in $US. Add up fares for your itinerary to see whether a railpass will save you money.

---

transportation. The best public transportation option is to mix bus and train travel. Always verify bus or train schedules before your departure. Never leave a bus or train station without your next day's schedule options in hand. For advance planning, log onto mercurio.iet.unipi.it.

Trains: While you could save money by purchasing point-to-point tickets as you go, you may find the convenience of a railpass worth the extra cost. Both Spain and Portugal offer "flexi" railpasses that allow travel for a given number of days over a longer period of time. Spain also offers a rail-and-drive pass which, if used thoughtfully, gives you the ease of big-city train hops and the flexibility of a car for rural areas such as the Andalusian hill towns. A Eurailpass pays for itself only if you're traveling to Spain from the north (Paris to Madrid costs $135 second class). Remember, you'll be making a lot of connections by buses which are not covered by Eurail. Travelers under age 26 can buy cheap tickets in Wasteels offices (in most major train stations).

The long, second-class train rides from Madrid to Barcelona, Lisbon, Sevilla, and Granada cost about $50 each. First class costs 50 percent more.

First-class travelers are entitled to the use of comfortable "Intercity" lounges in train stations in Spain's major cities.

Most overnight trains have berths and beds that you can rent (not included in the cost of your train ticket or railpass). Sleeping berths *(coche-litera)* cost $18. A *coche-cama*, or bed in a classy quad compartment, costs $35; and a bed in a double costs $45. I go overnight whenever possible in Spain. Even with a train pass, reservations (for 600 ptas) are required on long Spanish train rides (over three hours). Reserve a seat for your departure as soon as you arrive in a town, either at the train station or at a RENFE office in big city centers.

RENFE (the acronym for the Spanish national train system) used to be "Relatively Exasperating, and Not For Everyone," but it is getting better. Spain categorizes trains this way:

The high-speed train called the **AVE (Alta Velocidad Española)** whisks travelers between Madrid and Sevilla in less than three hours. AVE is now 85 percent covered by the Eurailpass (Madrid to Sevilla costs Eurailers about $9). Franco left Spain a train system that didn't fit Europe's gauge. AVE trains run on European-gauge tracks.

The **Talgo** is fast, air-conditioned, and expensive. Talgo 200 is a train designed to run on AVE rails. **Intercity** and **Electro** trains fall just behind Talgo in speed, comfort, and expense. **Rapido, Tranvia, Semi-directo,** and **Expreso** trains are generally slower. **Cercania** are commuter trains for big-city workers and small-town tourists. **Regional** and **Correo** trains are slow, small-town milk runs. Trains get more expensive as they pick up speed, but all are cheaper per mile than their northern European counterparts.

In Spain, *salidas* means "departures" and *llegadas* is "arrivals"; in Portugal, *partidas* and *chegadas* are departures and arrivals, respectively. To decipher Portuguese train schedules, *diario* means "daily," *mudanca de comboio* means "change trains," *so* means "only," and *não* means "not." This is a typical quali-fier: "*Não se efectua aos sabados, domingos e feriados oficiais.*" Or "*So se effectua aos . . .*" ("only effective on . . . ").

In Spain, long-distance trains are priced differently according to their time of departure. Peak hours *(punta)* are most expensive, followed by *llano* and *valle* (quietest and cheapest times). Overnight trains (and buses) are usually less expensive than the daytime rides. On Spanish train schedules, "LMXJVSD" are the days of the week, starting with Monday. A train that runs "LMXJV-D" doesn't run on Saturdays. *Laborables* can mean Monday through Friday or Monday through Saturday. In either Spain or Portugal, to ask for a schedule at a ticket or information window, say "*Horario para _____-_____* (fill in names of cities), *por favor*." Most train stations have handy luggage lockers.

Buses: Always reserve long-distance buses ahead. Bus service on holidays, Saturdays, and especially Sundays can be dismal. Ask at the tourist office about travel agencies that sell bus tickets (and reserve seats) to save you time if the bus station is not central. Don't leave a bus station to explore a city without checking your departure options and making reservations if necessary. In the countryside, stop buses by waving. You can always stow your luggage under the bus.

Portugal has mostly slow, milk-run trains and an occasional Expreso. Off the main Lisbon–Porto–Coimbra train lines, buses are usually a better bet. In cases where buses and trains serve the same destination, the bus is often more efficient.

Bus schedules in Portugal are clearly posted at each major station. Look for "*Partidas*" (departures), not "*Chegadas*" (arrivals). They follow this standard format:

Destino	Partida	Chegada	Preço
Lisboa	14.15	16.35 (1)	1200$

If you see this schedule in Coimbra, your bus leaves Coimbra at 14:15 and arrives in Lisboa at 16:35. The times are listed with periods instead of colons. Exceptions are noted with a numeral. For instance, the "(1)" means you should look for a list of definitions at the end of the schedule. (1) could be: "*Excepto sabados e domingos*" (Except Saturdays and Sundays). More key Portuguese "fine print" words: Both *as* and *aos* mean "on." *De* means "from," as in "from this date to that date." *Feriado* means "holiday." *Directo* is "direct." *Ruta* buses make many stops. The posted schedules list most, but not all, destinations. If your intended destination isn't listed, check at the ticket/info window for the most complete schedule information. For longer trips your ticket may include an assigned seat.

Spain's bus system is more confusing than Portugal's because of its many different bus companies (though they're usually clustered within one building). The larger stations have an information desk with all the schedules. In smaller stations, check the destinations and schedules posted on each office window.

Iberian drivers and station personnel rarely speak English. Buses, even direct ones, often stop at stations for up to 30 minutes. In either Spain or Portugal, ask the driver "How many minutes here?" ("*¿Cuantos minutos aquí?*") so you can get out for a break. Some buses are entirely nonsmoking; others are nonsmoking in the front only. When you buy your ticket, ask for nonsmoking (*no fumadores* in Spanish, *não fumador* in Portuguese). It's usually pointless, since passengers ignore the signs, but it's a statement. Radios, taped music, and videos will accompany your ride. Bring earplugs for silence. Buses rarely have WCs but stop every two hours or so. Bus stations have WCs (rarely with TP) and cafés offering quick and cheap food.

Taxis

Most taxis are reliable and cheap. Drivers generally respond kindly to the request, "How much is it to ____, more or less?" (Spanish: "*¿Cuanto cuesta a* ____, *mas o menos?*" Portuguese: "*Quanto cuesta a* ____, *mais o menos?*"). Spanish taxis have more extra add-ons (luggage, nighttime, train-station pickup, and so on). Fine subway systems in Madrid and Barcelona make taxis unnecessary. Rounding the fare up to the nearest 50 ptas or *escudos* is adequate for a tip. City rides cost around $4. Keep a map in your hand so the cabbie knows (or thinks) you know where you're going.

Car Rental

It's cheapest to rent a car through your travel agent well before your departure. You'll want a weekly rate with unlimited mileage. Figure about $200 a week. For three weeks or longer, it's cheaper to lease; you'll save money on taxes and insurance.

Comparison shop through your agent. I normally rent a small economy model. For peace of mind, I splurge for the CDW insurance (Collision Damage Waiver, about $14 a day). A few "gold" credit cards cover CDW insurance; quiz your credit-card company on the worst-case scenario. With the luxury of CDW you'll enjoy Iberia's highways, knowing you can bring back the car in an unrecognizable shambles and just say, "S-s-s-sorry."

Driving

Driving in Iberia is great, although major roads can be clogged by caravans of slow-moving trucks. While the International Driver's License is officially required (cheap and easy to obtain from AAA; bring two photos and $10), many manage with only their U.S. driver's license.

The Spanish version of AAA is the Real Automobil Club. In Portugal it's the Automovil Clube de Portugal. Good maps are available and inexpensive throughout Iberia. Spanish tollways (*autopista*) can be very expensive.

Drive defensively. If you're involved in an accident, you will be blamed and in for a monumental headache. Seat belts are required by law. Expect to be stopped for a routine check by the police (be sure your car insurance form is up to date). There are plenty of speed traps. Tickets are issued and paid for on the spot. Portugal is statistically one of Europe's most dangerous places to drive. You'll see lots of ambulances on the road.

Gas and diesel prices are controlled and the same everywhere (around $3.50 a gallon for gas, less for diesel). *Gasolina* is either *normal* or *super* (unleaded is now widely available). Note that diesel is called *gasoleo*.

Get used to metric. A liter is about a quart, four to a gallon; a kilometer is six-tenths of a mile. Convert kilometers to miles by cutting them in half and adding back 10 percent of the original (120 km: 60 + 12 = 72 miles; 300 km: 150 + 30 = 180 miles).

Make a copy of your key for safety and convenience. Choose parking places carefully. Leave valuables in the trunk during the day and leave *nothing* worth stealing in the car overnight. While you should avoid parking lots with twinkly asphalt, thieves break car windows anywhere, even at stop lights. Police recommend leaving your car unlocked at night and the glove compartment open. If it's a hatchback, take the trunk cover off at night so thieves can look in without breaking in. Parking attendants all over Spain holler, "*Nada en el coche*"—"Nothing in the car." And they mean it. Ask at your hotel for advice on parking. In cities you can park safely but expensively in guarded lots.

Telephones and Mail

You cannot travel smartly in Iberia without using the telephones. A few tips will minimize frustration.

Coin-operated phones are rapidly being replaced by card-operated phones, making long-distance calling a breeze. Phone cards are normally purchased at a post office, newsstand, or *tabaco* shop. Upon entering Spain or Portugal, buy a card (*tarjeta telefónica* in Spanish, *cartão telefónico* in Portuguese). The smaller-value card is usually enough (two values available). Use your card to reserve hotels, confirm sightseeing plans, and call home. To use the card, simply insert it into the slot on the phone, wait for a dial tone and digital readout to show how much value remains on your card, and dial away—the cost of the call is automatically deducted from your card. Dial slowly and deliberately. Portuguese phone cards usually don't tell you your balance until after you dial, but they do thoughtfully beep for 15 seconds before dying. This gives you plenty of time to push the eject button (look at the directions on the phone beforehand) and slip in a new card.

Portuguese phones are even-tempered, but Spanish phones refuse to be rushed. After you "*inserta*" your "*tarjeta*" (phone card) into the Spanish phone, wait until the digital display says "*Marque numero*," then dial. Push the square "R" button to get a dial tone for a new call.

Dialing Direct: To dial long distance within a country, dial the area code before the number. The main telephone problems you're likely to have relate to the area codes. Spanish area codes begin with "9." Remember to use this "9" only if dialing long distance within Spain. To call my favorite Madrid hotel from Barcelona, dial 91 (Madrid's area code), then 521-2900 (local number). To call internationally, first dial the international access code (of the country you're calling from), the country code (of the country you're calling to), the area code (without its initial digit; for Spain, drop the 9; for Portugal, drop the 0), then the local number. To call the Madrid hotel from the U.S.A., dial 011 (U.S.A.'s international access code), 34 (Spain's country code), 1 (Madrid's area code without the initial 9), then 521-2900 (local number). To call my office from Spain, I dial 07 (Spain's international access code), 1 (U.S.A.'s country code), 425 (Edmonds' area code), then 771-8303. For a list of international access codes and country codes, see the Appendix. European time is six/nine hours ahead of the east/west coast of the U.S.A. Midnight in Seattle is breakfast in Madrid. Remember that if you're making hotel reservations from the U.S.A.

In Spain, if you ever hear a *"numero no exist"* recording after you dial, try the number again without the area code. Area code regions are huge (Tarifa, Jerez, and Arcos are in the same area). When calling between these cities, just dial the local number. When making an international call from Spain, dial 07 (Spain's international access code), and after you hear a high-pitched tone, continue dialing.

USA Direct Services: Calling the U.S.A. from any kind of phone is easy if you have an AT&T, MCI, or Sprint calling card. Each card company has a toll-free number in each European country which puts you in touch with an English-speaking operator who takes your card number and the number you want to call, puts you through, and bills your home phone number for the call (at the cheaper U.S.A. rate of about a dollar a minute, but you'll pay about $3 for the first minute plus a $2.50 service charge). You'll save money on calls of three minutes or more. Hanging up when you hear an answering machine is an expensive mistake—talk! Better yet, first use a small-value coin or a Spanish or Portuguese phone card to call home for five seconds—long enough to say "call me," or to make sure an answering machine is off so you can call back, using your USA Direct number to connect with a person. For a list of AT&T, MCI, and Sprint calling card operators, see the Appendix. Avoid using USA Direct for calls between European countries; it's much cheaper to call direct using coins or a Spanish or Portuguese phone card.

Mail: To arrange for mail delivery (allow ten days for a letter to arrive), reserve a few hotels along your route in advance and give their addresses to friends, or use American Express Company's mail services (available to anyone who has at least one American Express traveler's check). Phoning is so easy that I've dispensed with mail stops all together.

E-mail: E-mail is still rare among Iberian hoteliers. I've listed e-mail addresses when possible, but they're few and far between. You'll come across a few cyber-cafés only in the largest cities.

Sleeping

In the interest of smart use of your time, I favor hotels (and restaurants) handy to your sightseeing activities. Rather than list hotels scattered throughout a city, I describe my favorite two or three neighborhoods and recommend the best accommodations values in each, from $10 bunks to $120 doubles.

Spain and Portugal offer some of the best accommodations values in Europe. Most places are government-regulated with posted prices. While prices are low, street noise is high (Spaniards are notorious night owls). Always ask to see your room first. Check the price posted on the door, consider potential night-noise problems, ask for another room, or bargain the price down. You can request either *con vista* (with

---

Sleep Code

To give maximum information in a minimum of space, I use this code to describe accommodations listed in this book. Prices listed are per room, not per person. When there is a range of prices in one category, the price will fluctuate with the season. (Especially in resort areas, prices go way up in July and August. These seasons are posted at the hotel desk.) A 6 or 7 percent tax (which is not included in listed prices) will often be added to your bill. Breakfasts are rarely included in Spain and commonly included in Portugal.

S = Single room (or price for one person in a double).
D = Double or Twin. Double beds are usually big enough for non-romantic couples.
T = Triple (often a double bed with a single bed moved in).
Q = Quad (an extra child's bed is usually cheaper).
b = Private bathroom with toilet and shower or tub.
t = Private toilet only (the shower is down the hall).
s = Private shower or tub only (the toilet is down the hall).
CC = Accepts credit cards (Visa, MasterCard, American Express). If CC isn't mentioned, assume you'll need to pay in cash.
SE = Speaks English. This code is used only when it seems predictable that you'll encounter English-speaking staff.
NSE = Does not speak English. Used only when it's unlikely you'll encounter English-speaking staff.

According to this code, a couple staying at a "Db-5,500 ptas, CC:V, SE" hotel would pay a total of 5,500 *pesetas* (about $40) for a double room with a private bathroom. The hotel accepts Visa or Spanish cash in payment, and the staff speaks English.

view) or *tranquilo* (*calado* in Portuguese). In most cases the view comes with street noise. Meals may be required, and breakfast and showers can cost extra—always ask. All rooms have sinks with hot and cold water. Rooms with private bathrooms are often bigger and renovated, while the cheaper rooms without bathrooms often will be dingier and/or on the top floor. Any room without a bathroom has access to a bathroom on the corridor. Towels aren't routinely replaced every day; drip-dry and conserve. It's officially prohibited for hotels to use central heat before November 1 and after April 1 (unless it's unusually cold); prepare for cool evenings if you travel in spring and fall.

In most towns the best places to look for rooms are in the old and most interesting quarter, and/or near the main church, main square, and most sights. Don't judge places by their bleak and dirty entryways. Landlords, stuck with rent control, often stand firmly in the way of hardworking hoteliers who'd like to brighten their buildings up. Most of the year, prices are soft.

Types of Accommodations

Each country has its handy categories of accommodations. In Spain, government-regulated places have blue-and-white plaques outside their doors clearly marked F, CH, P, Hs, H, HsR, or HR. Despite the different names, all are basically hotels offering different services. I'll list them in ascending order of price and comfort. *Fonda* (F) is your basic simple inn, often with a small bar serving cheap meals. *Casa de Huéspedes* (CH) is a guest house without a bar. *Pensiónes* (P) are like CHs but serve meals. *Hostales* (Hs) have nothing to do with youth hostels. They are quite comfortable, are rated from one to three stars, and charge $30 to $60 for a double. *Hostal-Residencias* (HsR) and *Hotel-Residencias* (HR) are the same as Hs and H class, with no meals except breakfast. Hotels (H) are rated with one to five stars and go right up to world-class luxury places.

Any regulated place will have a complaint book (*libro de reclamaciones* in Spanish and *livro de reclamações* in Portuguese). A request for this book will generally solve any problem you have in a jiffy.

Portugal's accommodations system starts at the bottom with *Residencias*, *Albergarias*, and *Pensões* (one to four stars). These *pensiónes* are Portugal's best accommodation value— cheap ($30–50 doubles) and often tasteful, traditional, comfy, and family-run. Hotels (one to five stars) are more expensive ($40–150 doubles).

In both Spain and Portugal, you'll find rooms in private homes, usually in touristy areas where locals decide to open up a spare room and make a little money on the side. Ask for a *cama*, *habitacion*, or *casa particulare* in Spain, and a *quarto* in Portugal. They're cheap ($10–15 per bed without breakfast) and usually a good experience.

Spain and Portugal also have luxurious, government-sponsored, historic inns. These *paradores* (Spain) and *pousadas* (Portugal) are often renovated castles, palaces, or monasteries, many with great views and stately atmospheres. While they can be a good value (doubles from $80–150, reservations often necessary), I find many of them sterile, stuffy, and overly impressed with themselves, much like the tourists who stay there. I still list them where appropriate, as I enjoy wandering through them and having an occasional breakfast with real silver and too much service. But for a better value, sleep in what I call "poor-man's *paradores*"—elegant normal places that offer double the warmth and Old World intimacy for half the price.

Both Spain and Portugal have plenty of youth hostels and campgrounds, but, considering the great bargains on other accommodations, I don't think they're worth the trouble and don't cover them in this book. Hotels and *pensiónes* are easy to find, inexpensive, and when chosen properly, a fun part of the Spanish and Portuguese cultural experience. If you're on a starvation budget or just prefer camping or hosteling, plenty of information is available in appropriate guidebooks, through the National Tourist Office, and at local tourist information offices.

Making Reservations

While Easter, July, and August are often crowded, it is possible to travel at any time of year without reservations. But given the high stakes, erratic accommodations values, and the quality of the gems I've found for this book, I'd highly recommend calling ahead for rooms a day or two in advance as you travel. You might make a habit of calling between 9:00 and 10:00 on the day you plan to arrive, when the hotel knows who'll be checking out and just which rooms will be available. Use the telephone and the convenient telephone cards. Most hotels listed are accustomed to English-only speakers. A hotel receptionist will trust you and hold a room until 17:00 without a deposit, though some will ask for a credit-card number. Honor (or cancel by phone) your reservations. Long distance is cheap and easy from public phone booths. Don't let these people down—I promised you'd call and cancel if for some reason you won't show up. Don't needlessly confirm rooms through the tourist office; they'll take a commission.

If you know exactly which dates you need and really want a particular place, reserve a room well in advance before you leave home. To reserve from home, call, fax, or write the hotel. Phone and fax costs are reasonable, and simple English is usually fine. To fax, use the handy form in the Appendix. If you're writing, add the zip code and confirm the need and method for a deposit. A two-night stay in August would be "two nights, 16/8/98 to 18/8/98"—European hotel jargon uses your day of departure. You'll often receive a letter back requesting one night's deposit. A credit card will usually be accepted as a deposit, though you may need to send a signed traveler's check or a bank draft in the local currency. If your credit card is the deposit, you can pay with your card or cash when you arrive; if you don't show up, you'll be billed for one night. Reconfirm your reservations a day in advance for safety.

Eating in Spain

Spaniards eat to live, not vice versa. Their cuisine is hearty and served in big, inexpensive portions. You can get good $10 meals in restaurants.

Although not fancy, there is an endless variety of regional specialties. Two famous Spanish dishes are *paella* and *gazpacho*. *Paella* features saffron-flavored rice as a background for whatever the chef wants to mix in—seafood, sausage, chicken, peppers, and so on. *Gazpacho*, an Andalusian specialty, is a chilled soup of tomatoes, bread chunks, and spices—refreshing on a hot day. Spanish cooks love garlic and olive oil.

The Spanish eating schedule frustrates many visitors. Because most Spaniards work until 19:30, supper (*cena*) is usually served late, around 21:00 or 22:00. Lunch (*almuerzo*), also served late (13:00–16:00), is the largest meal of the day. Don't buck this system. No good restaurant serves meals at American hours.

The alternative to this late schedule, and my choice for a quick dinner, is to eat in *tapas* bars. *Tapas* are small portions, like appetizers, of all kinds of foods—seafood, salads, meat-filled pastries, deep-fried tasties, and on and on—normally displayed under glass at the bar (about $1). Prices can add up. Confirm the price before you order (point and ask *"¿Quanto cuesta un tapa?"*). *Pinchos* are bite-size portions (not always available), *tapas* are snack-size, and *raciónes* are larger portions of *tapas*—more like a full meal (about $3). Common *tapas* include *chorizo* (spicy sausage), *gambas* (shrimp), *calamares fritos* (fried squid rings), *jamón serrano* (cured ham), *queso manchego* (sheep cheese), and *tortilla española* (potato omelet). *Bocadillos* (sandwiches) are cheap and basic. A ham sandwich is just that—ham on bread, period. A *montado* is a half of a sandwich and a *pulga* is an even tinier sandwich.

For a budget meal in a restaurant, try a *plato combinado* (combination plate) which usually includes portions of one or two main dishes, a vegetable, and bread for a reasonable price; or the *menu del dia* (menu of the day), a substantial three-to-four-course meal that usually comes with a carafe of house wine. *Flan* (caramel custard) is the standard dessert. *Helado* (ice cream) is popular, as is *blanco y negro*, a vanilla-ice-cream-and-coffee float.

At a bar, the price of a *tapa*, beer, or coffee is cheapest if you eat or drink standing or sitting on a stool at the counter. You may pay a little more to eat sitting at a table and still more for an outdoor table. In the right place, a quiet coffee break on the town square is well worth the extra charge. But the cheapest seats sometimes get the best show. Sit at the bar and study your bartender—he's an artist.

When searching for a good bar, I look for the noisy places with ankle-deep piles of napkins and food debris on the floor, lots of locals, and the TV blaring. *Cheers*, broadcast almost nightly, is fun to watch in Spanish. Other popular television shows include bullfights and soccer games, as well as Spanish interpretations of soaps and silly game shows (you'll see Vanna Blanco).

Spain produces some excellent wine, both red (*tinto*) and white (*blanco*). Major wine regions include Valdepenas, Penedes, Rioja, and Ribera del Duero. Sherry, a fortified wine from the Jerez region, ranges from dry (*fino*) to sweet (*dulce*). *Cava* is Spain's answer to champagne. *Sangria* (red wine mixed with fruit juice) is popular and refreshing. To get a small draft beer, ask for a *caña*. Spain has good, cheap, boxed orange juice. For something completely different, try *horchata de chufa*, a sweet, milky beverage made from earth almonds.

For a quick and substantial breakfast, order *tortilla española* (potato omelet) with your *café solo* (black) or *café con leche* (with milk) in any café. The town market hall always has a colorful café filled with locals eating cheap breakfasts.

Eating in Portugal

The Portuguese meal schedule, while still late, is less cruel than Spain's. Lunch (*almoço*) is the big meal, served between noon and 14:00, while supper (*jantar*) is from 20:00 to 22:00. Perhaps as a result, *tapas* are not such a big deal. You'll eat well in restaurants for $8.

Eat seafood in Portugal. Fish soup (*sopa de peixe*) or shellfish soup (*sopa de mariscos*) is worth seeking out. *Caldo verde* is a popular vegetable soup. *Frango no churrasco* is roast chicken; ask for *piri-piri* sauce if you like it hot and spicy. *Porco a alentejana* is an interesting combination of pork and clams. *Meia dose* means half portion, while *prato do dia* is the daily special. For a quick snack, remember that cafés are usually cheaper than bars. *Sandes* (sandwiches) are everywhere. As in Spain, garlic and olive oil are big. The Portuguese breakfast (*pequeno almoço*) is just *café com leite* and a sweet roll, but due to the large expat English community, a full British "fry" is available in most touristy areas.

Portuguese wines are cheap and decent. *Vinho da casa* is the house wine. *Vinho verde* is a young light wine from the north that goes well with seafood. The Dão region produces the best red wines. And if you like port wine, what better place to sample it than its birthplace? Beer (*cerveja*) is also popular—for a small draft beer, ask for *uma imperial*. Freshly-squeezed orange juice (*sumo de laranja*), mineral water (*agua mineral*), and soft drinks are widely available.

Throughout Iberia, as a general rule, tips are included in the bill. Tipping beyond that is unnecessary, but leaving the coins from your change is a nice touch.

Stranger in a Strange Land

We travel all the way to Europe to enjoy differences—to become temporary locals. You'll experience frustrations. Certain truths that we find "God-given" or "self-evident," like cold beer, ice in drinks, bottomless cups of coffee, hot showers, body odor smelling bad, and bigger being better, are suddenly not so true. One of the benefits of travel is the eye-opening realization that there are logical, civil, and even better alternatives. A willingness to go local ensures that you'll enjoy a full dose of European hospitality.

If there is a negative aspect to the European image of Americans, it is that we are big, loud, aggressive, impolite, rich, and a bit naive. While Europeans look bemusedly at some of our Yankee excesses—and worriedly at others—they nearly always afford us individual travelers all the warmth we deserve.

Back Door Manners

While updating this book, I heard over and over again that my readers are considerate and fun to have as guests. Thank you for traveling as temporary locals who are sensitive to the culture. It's fun to follow you in my travels.

Send Me a Postcard, Drop Me a Line

If you enjoy a successful trip with the help of this book and would like to share your discoveries, please fill out and send the survey at the end of this book to me at Europe Through the Back Door, Box 2009, Edmonds, WA 98020. I personally read and value all feedback.

For our latest travel information, tap into our web site: www.ricksteves.com). Our e-mail address is rick@ricksteves.com. Anyone is welcome to request a free issue of our Back Door quarterly newsletter (it's free anyway).

Judging from all the positive feedback and happy postcards I receive from travelers who have used this book, it's safe to assume you're on your way to a great vacation—independently, inexpensively, and with the finesse of an experienced traveler. Thanks, and *buen viaje!*

BACK DOOR TRAVEL PHILOSOPHY
As Taught in *Rick Steves' Europe Through the Back Door*

Travel is intensified living—maximum thrills per minute and one of the last great sources of legal adventure. Travel is freedom. It's recess, and we need it.

Experiencing the real Europe requires catching it by surprise, going casual—"Through the Back Door."

Affording travel is a matter of priorities. (Make do with the old car.) You can travel—simply, safely, and comfortably—anywhere in Europe for $60 a day plus transportation costs. In many ways spending more money only builds a thicker wall between you and what you came to see. Europe is a cultural carnival, and time after time you'll find that its best acts are free and the best seats are the cheap ones.

A tight budget forces you to travel close to the ground, meeting and communicating with the people, not relying on service with a purchased smile. Never sacrifice sleep, nutrition, safety, or cleanliness in the name of budget. Simply enjoy the local-style alternatives to expensive hotels and restaurants.

Extroverts have more fun. If your trip is low on magic moments, kick yourself and make things happen. If you don't enjoy a place, maybe you don't know enough about it. Seek the truth. Recognize tourist traps. Give a culture the benefit of your open mind. See things as different but not better or worse. Any culture has much to share.

Of course travel, like the world, is a series of hills and valleys. Be fanatically positive and militantly optimistic. If something's not to your liking, change your liking. Travel is addicting. It can make you a happier American, as well as a citizen of the world. Our Earth is home to nearly 6 billion equally important people. It's humbling to travel and find that people don't envy Americans. They like us but, with all due respect, they wouldn't trade passports.

Globetrotting destroys ethnocentricity. It helps you understand and appreciate different cultures. Travel changes people. It broadens perspectives and teaches new ways to measure quality of life. Many travelers toss aside their hometown blinders. Their prized souvenirs are the strands of different cultures they decide to knit into their own character. The world is a cultural yarn shop and Back Door Travelers are weaving the ultimate tapestry. Come on, join in!

SPAIN

BARCELONA

Barcelona is Spain's second city and the capital of the proud and distinct region of Catalunya (Catalonia). With Franco's fascism now history, Catalunyan flags wave once again. The local language and culture are on a roll in Spain's most cosmopolitan and European corner.

Barcelona bubbles with life in its narrow Gothic Quarter alleys, along the grand boulevards, and throughout the chic, grid-planned new town. While Barcelona had an illustrious past as a Roman colony, Visigothic capital, 14th-century maritime power, and in more modern times, a top Mediterranean trading and manufacturing center, it's most enjoyable to throw out the history books and just drift through the city. If you're in the mood to surrender to a city's charms, let it be in Barcelona.

Planning Your Time

Sandwich Barcelona between flights or overnight train rides. There's little of earth-shaking importance within eight hours by train. It's as easy to fly into Barcelona as into Madrid, Lisbon, or Paris for most travelers from the U.S.A. Those renting a car can start here, sleep on the train to Madrid, and pick up the car after seeing the city.

On the shortest visit Barcelona is worth one night, one day, and an overnight train out. The Ramblas is two different streets by day and by night. Stroll it from top to bottom at night and again the next morning, grabbing breakfast on a stool in a café in the market. Wander the Gothic Quarter, see

Barcelona

the cathedral, and have lunch in Eixample (ay-SHAM-pla). The top two sights in town, Gaudí's Sacred Family Church and the Picasso Museum, are usually open until about 20:00. The illuminated fountains are a good finale for your day.

Of course, Barcelona in a day is a dash. To better appreciate the city's ample charm, spread your visit over two days.

Orientation (tel. code: 93)

Locate these orientation essentials on the map above: Barri Gòtic/Ramblas (Old Town), Eixample (fashionable modern town), Montjuïc (hill covered with sights and parks), and Sants Station (train to Madrid). The soul of Barcelona is in its compact core—the Barri Gòtic (Gothic Quarter) and the Ramblas (main boulevard). This is your strolling, shopping,

and people-watching nucleus. The city's sights are widely
scattered, but with a map and a willingness to figure out the
sleek subway system, all is manageable.

Tourist Information

There are three useful TI's in Barcelona: at the Sants train
station, the airport, and by far the best TI, on (actually,
under) Plaça de Catalunya across from Corte Inglés
(Monday–Saturday, 9:00–22:00, Sunday 9:00–21:00, tel.
93/304-3135; they even have a bank with fair rates, open until
20:30 Monday–Saturday). The Sants station's TI is located at
the access to platform 10 (weekdays 8:00–20:00, weekends
8:00–14:00, tel. 93/491-4431). Whichever TI you visit, get
the large city map and brochures on Gaudí, Miró, Dalí,
Picasso, and the Barri Gòtic. Ask for the free quarterly *Top
Tips Barcelona*, a comprehensive guide listing practical information (transportation, museum hours, restaurants) and
cultural information (history, festivals, and points of interest
grouped by neighborhood).

Arrival in Barcelona

By Train: Although many international trains use the França
Station, all domestic (and some international) trains use Sants
Station. Both França and Sants have subway stations: França's is
"Barceloneta" (2 blocks away), Sants' is "Sants Estacio" (under
the station). Both stations have baggage lockers. Sants station
has a good TI, a world of handy shops and eateries (including a
juice shop with a fascinating orange-juicer behind the TI), and
a classy "Club Intercity" lounge for first-class travelers (quiet,
plush, TV, shower, study tables, coffee bar). There is nothing
of interest within easy walking distance from the train station.
Catch the subway or a taxi to your hotel.

By Plane: Barcelona's El Prat de Llobregat Airport is 12
kilometers out of town and connected cheaply and quickly by
Aerobus (immediately in front of arrivals lobby, 4/hr, 20 min
to Plaça de Catalunya, buy 475-pta ticket from driver) or by
RENFE train (walk the tunnel overpass from airport to station,
2/hr, 20 min, 310 ptas, to Sants station and Plaça de Catalunya). A taxi to or from the airport costs about 3,000 ptas.
Airport information: tel. 93/478-5000. To avoid ten-hour train
trips, those continuing to Madrid or Sevilla should check the
reasonable flights from Barcelona.

Getting Around Barcelona

Barcelona's subway, among Europe's best, can be faster than a taxi and connects just about every place you'll visit. It has five color-coded lines (L1 is red, L2 is lilac, L3 is green, L4 is yellow, L5 is blue). Rides cost 135 ptas each. A T-2 Card gives you ten tickets for 720 ptas; a T-1 Card is a better deal, giving you ten tickets good for the bus or Metro (subway) for the same price. Pick up the TI's guide to public transport.

The handy Tourist Bus (Bus Turistic) shuttles tourists on an 18-stop circuit covering the must-sees, funicular, and *teleférico* (mid-June–mid-October, 9:00–21:30, buy tickets on bus). The one-day ticket (for 1,400 ptas) and two-day ticket (1,800 ptas) include some serious discounts on the city's major sights. Buses run every 20 minutes and take two hours to do the entire circuit.

Taxis are plentiful and honest, and they don't charge extra for evening rides. Rides start at 285 ptas. You can go from the Ramblas to the Sants station for 600 ptas (300 ptas extra for luggage).

Helpful Hints

Theft Alert: Barcelona, after recently illuminating many of its seedier streets, is not the pickpocket paradise it was a few years back, but it's good to be alert.

American Express: The AmExCo office doesn't charge a commission for cashing any brand of traveler's check (weekdays 9:30–18:00, Saturday 10:00–12:00, Paseo de Gracia 101, tel. 93/415-2371, Metro: Diagonal).

Monday Plans: Many sights, but not all, are closed on Monday. Instead, you can stroll the Ramblas, shop at El Corte Inglés, zip up the Columbus Monument, take a *golondrina* ride, visit Parc Güell, or tour the Sagrada Familia.

Language: Although Spanish is understood here (and the basic survival words are the same), Barcelona speaks a different language—Catalan. (Most place names in this chapter are listed in Catalan.) Here are the essential Catalunyan phrases:

Hello	*Hola*	Same as Spanish
Please	*Si us plau*	(see oos plow)
Thank you	*Gracies*	Virtually the same
Goodbye	*Adeu*	(ah-DAY-oo)
Exit	*Sordida*	Salida
Long live Catalunya!	*Visca Catalunya!*	(BEE-skah . . .)

Sights—The Ramblas

More than a Champs-Elysées, this grand boulevard called the
Ramblas takes you from rich at the top to rough at the port, a
20-minute walk. You'll find the grand opera house, ornate
churches, plain prostitutes, pickpockets, con men, artists, street
mimes, an outdoor bird market, elegant cafés, great shopping,
and people willing to charge more for a shoeshine than you
paid for the shoes. Sit on a white metal chair for 50 ptas and
observe. When Hans Christian Andersen saw this street more
than 100 years ago, he wrote that there could be no doubt that
Barcelona was a great city.

Rambla means "stream" in Arabic. The Ramblas was a
drainage ditch along the medieval wall that used to define what
is now called the Gothic Quarter. It has five separately named
segments, but addresses treat it as a mile-long boulevard.

Walking from Plaça de Catalunya downhill to the harbor,
the Ramblas highlights are:

▲**Plaça de Catalunya**—This vast central square is the
divider between old and new, and the hub for the Metro, bus,
and airport shuttle. Overlooking the square, the huge El
Corte Inglés department store offers everything from a travel
agency and haircuts to cheap souvenirs (10:00–21:30, closed
Sunday, supermarket in basement, ninth-floor terrace cafeteria with great city view—take elevator from west entrance,
tel. 93/302-1212). Four great boulevards start here: the
Ramblas, the fashionable Passeig de Gràcia, the cozier but
still fashionable parallel Rambla Catalunya, and the stubby,
shop-filled, pedestrian-only Portal de L'Angel.

▲▲**Mercat de Sant Josep** (a.k.a. La Boqueria)—This lively
produce market (8:00–20:00, best in the morning, closed Sunday) is an explosion of chicken legs, bags of live snails, stiff fish,
delicious oranges, sleeping dogs, and great bars for a cheap
breakfast (try a *tortilla española* and *café con leche*).

Gran Teatre del Liceu—Spain's only real opera house is
luscious but closed for a few years for renovation because of a
fire (tourable when it reopens).

Plaça Reial—This elegant, neoclassical square comes complete with old-fashioned taverns, a Sunday coin and stamp
market (10:00–14:00), and characters who don't need the
palm trees to be shady. Escudellers, a street 1 block toward
the water from the square, is lined with bars whose counters
are strewn with vampy ladies. The area is well policed, but if
you tried, you could get into trouble.

▲**Palau Güell**—This offers the only look at a Gaudí Art
Nouveau interior, and for me, it's the most enjoyable look at
Barcelona's organic architect. The interior is a theater
museum (300 ptas, usually open Monday–Saturday,
10:00–14:00, 16:00–20:00, Nou de la Rambla 3-5, tel. 93/317-
3974). Check the chimneys on the terrace—look for Gaudí's
la alcachofa (the artichoke) and the recent Olympic-rings chimney (with the outline of the 1992 Olympic mascot, Cobi, at
waist level on the white chimney).

Chinatown (Barri Xines)—Farther downhill, on the right-
hand side, is the world's only Chinatown with nothing even
remotely Chinese in or near it—a dingy, dangerous-after-dark
nightclub district with lots of street girls and a monument to
Dr. Fuller, the Canadian who discovered penicillin. Don't
venture in.

Columbus Monument (Monument a Colóm)—At the
harbor at the end of the Ramblas, this monument offers an
elevator-assisted view from its top (225 ptas, Monday–Saturday
9:00–21:00, Sunday 10:00–19:00; off-season 10:00–13:30,
15:30–18:30, closed Monday). It's interesting that Barcelona
would so honor the man whose discoveries ultimately led to its
downfall as a great trading power.

Maritime Museum (Museo Maritim)—This museum gives a
look at Barcelona's sea power before Columbus' discoveries
shifted the world's focus west. With fleets of seemingly unim-
portant replicas of old boats explained in Catalan and Spanish,
landlubbers find it pretty dull (800 ptas, Tuesday–Sunday
10:00–19:00, closed Monday).

Golondrinas—Little tourist boats make a half-hour tour of
the harbor every 20 to 30 minutes from 11:00 to 18:00 at the
foot of the Columbus Monument (300 ptas one-way to other
side of harbor, or 440 ptas round-trip). Consider this ride or
the harbor steps here for a picnic.

Maremagnum—This modern Spanish monstrosity of a mall
(with a cinema, aquarium, and restaurants) offers fine city
views. It's connected to the waterfront by a slick wood footbridge next to the golondrina boats.

Sights—Gothic Quarter (Barri Gòtic)
The Barri Gòtic is a bustling world of shops, bars, and
nightlife packed between hard-to-be-thrilled-about 14th- and
15th-century buildings. Except for the part closest to the
port, the area now feels safe, thanks to police and countless

Barcelona's Gothic Quarter

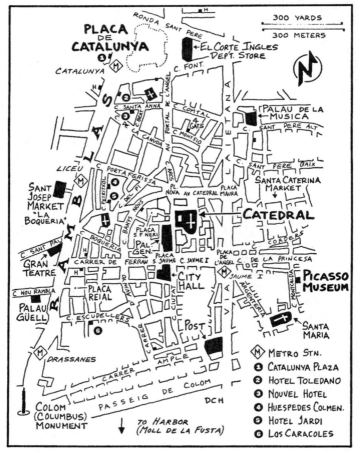

streetlights. There is a tangled grab-bag of undiscovered squares, grand squares, schoolyard plazas, art nouveau storefronts, baby flea-markets, musty antique shops, classy antique shops, and balconies with jungles behind wrought-iron bars. Go on a cultural scavenger hunt. Write a poem.

▲**Cathedral**—The colossal cathedral, a fine example of Catalan Gothic, was started in about 1300 and took 600 years to complete. Rather than stretching toward heaven, it makes a point to be simply massive (similar to the Gothic churches of Italy). The heavy choir (*coro*) in the middle confuses the dark and muddled interior. There's an admission fee to enter the *coro* from the back, but you can see everything for free from the front. Don't miss the cloister with its wispy garden and worthwhile little 50-pta museum (cathedral 8:00–13:30, 16:00–19:30; cloisters 8:45–13:15 and 16:00–18:45; museum 11:00–13:00; all closed Monday). The stirring and patriotic Sardana dances are held every weekend at the cathedral at 18:30 Saturday and noon on Sunday (and at Plaça St. Jaume at 18:30 Sunday). Drop into the courtyard of the Frederic Mares museum (down the small street running along the left side of the cathedral) for a tranquil break at its peaceful café.

Shoe Museum (Museo del Calzado)—Shoe-lovers can find this two-room shoe museum (with a we-try-harder attendant) on Plaça Sant Felip Neri, about a block beyond the outside door of the cloister (200 ptas, Tuesday–Sunday 11:00–14:00, closed Monday).

Royal Palace (Palau Reial)—The royal palace contains museums showing off Barcelona's Roman and medieval history, along with piles of medieval documents in the Arxiu de la Corona d'Aragon (Archives of the Kingdom of Aragon).

▲▲Picasso Museum—Far and away the best collection of Picasso's (1881–1973) work in Spain, this is a great chance to see his earliest sketches and paintings and better understand his genius (500 ptas, Tuesday–Saturday 10:00–20:00, Sunday 10:00–15:00, closed Monday; Montcada 15-19, Metro: Jaume; tel. 93/319-6310). He'd mastered the ability to paint realistically when just a teenager. Follow his progress as his skill increased geometrically—to cubism.

Textile and Garment Museum (Museu Textil i de la Indumentaria)—If fabrics from the fourth to 16th century leave you cold, have a *café con leche* on the museum's beautiful bourgeois patio (museum, 300 ptas; patio is within walls but outside museum, near Picasso Museum at Montcada 12-14).

▲Catalana Concert Hall (Palau de la Música Catalana)—This colorful hall is an extravagant burst of modernisme, with a floral ceramic ceiling, colored glass columns, and detailed mosaics. To get inside, you can either take a one-hour tour (200 ptas, Tuesday and Thursday 15:00–16:00 and Saturday 10:00–12:00, call to reserve, tel. 93/268-1000) or attend a concert (tickets as low as 600 ptas, cheapest tickets available

Modernisme

The Renaixenca (Catalan cultural revival) gave birth to Modernisme (Catalan Art Nouveau) at the end of the 19th century. Barcelona is the capital of modernisme. Its architecture broke with tradition and welcomed new technique and bold form. This free-flowing organic style experimented with glass, tile, iron, and brick as structural decoration rather than structural support.

Antonio Gaudí is the most famous moderniste artist. From four generations of metalworkers, a lineage of which he was quite proud, he incorporated his ironwork into his architecture and began to push the limits of structure and the concept of space in his designs.

Two other moderniste architects renowned for their unique style are Lluís Domènech i Muntaner and Josep Puig i Cadafalch. Take a stroll down the section of Passeig de Gràcia (between Consell de Cent and Arago) known as Mansana de Discordia, or "block of discord," where "decadent" works from these artists are displayed side by side, seemingly in an attempt to outdo each other.

Barcelona's Eixample neighborhood shimmies with the colorful, leafy, flowing, blooming shapes of modernisme in doorways, entrances, facades, and ceilings. Let yourself be mesmerized by the wild, sensuous, and mystical forms.

Moderniste Architects and Their Works

Gaudí

Casa Battlo, Paseo de Gràcia 43, Metro: Pg. de Gràcia

Casa Milà, Paseo de Gràcia 92, Metro: Diagonal

Casa Vincenz (done at age 26), c/Carolines 22, Metro: Fontana

Casa Calvet, c/Casp 48, Metro: Urquinaona

Parc Güell, Metro: Lesseps or Vallcarca

Palau Güell, Metro: Liceu, near Plaça de Catalunya

Sagrada Familia, Metro: Sagrada Familia

Domènech i Muntaner

Hospital de Sant Pau, Metro: Hospital Sant Pau

Palau de la Musica Catalana, Metro: Urquinaona

Casa Lleo Morera, Paseo de Gràcia 35, Metro: Pg. de Gràcia

Puig i Cadafalch

Quatre Gats, Montsio 3, Metro: Catalunya

Casa Amatller, Paseo de Gràcia 41, Metro: Pg. de Gràcia

Casa de les Punxes, Diagonal 416, Metro: Diagonal

for Sunday concerts at 11:00 or any show an hour before
showtime; Calle Sant Frances de Paula 2).

Sights—Gaudí's Art and Architecture

Barcelona is an architectural scrapbook of the galloping gables
and organic curves of hometown boy Antonio Gaudí. A devoted
Catalan and Catholic, his toil was for his soil. Completely
immersed in each project, he often lived on-site. He called Parc
Güell, La Pedrera, and the Sagrada Familia all home. For more
information on Gaudí, pick up a brochure at the tourist office.

▲**Sagrada Familia (Sacred Family) Church**—Gaudí's most
famous and persistent work is this unfinished landmark (800
ptas, daily 9:00–20:00, off-season 9:00–18:00, Metro:
Sagrada Familia, tel. 93/455-0247). From 1891 to 1925,
Gaudí worked on this monumental church of eight 100-
meter spires that will someday dance around a 160-meter
granddaddy spire. With the cranes, rusty forests of rebar,
and scaffolding requiring a powerful faith, it offers a fun look
at a living, growing, bigger-than-life building. Take the lift
(200 ptas) or the stairs (free) up to the dizzy lookout bridg-
ing two spires for a great city view and a gargoyle's-eye
perspective of the loopy church. If there's any building on
earth I'd like to see, it's the Sagrada Familia—finished. Judge
for yourself how the controversial current work fits in with
Gaudí's original formulation. The little on-site museum
displays physical models used for the church's construction
(daily 9:00–18:00).

▲**Palau Güell**—This is the best chance to enjoy a Gaudí
interior (see above under Ramblas). Curvy.

▲**Casa Milà (La Pedrera)**—This house and nearby Casa Battlo have Gaudí exteriors that laugh down on the crowds that
fill Passeig de Gràcia. Casa Milà, also called La Pedrera (The
Quarry), has a much-photographed roller coaster of melting-
ice-cream eaves. An elevator whisks you to the top where you
can wander under brick arches; enjoy the fascinating new
Espai Gaudí, a multimedia exhibit of models, photos, and
videos of Gaudí's works (in English); and frolic on the fanciful
rooftop (500 ptas, Tuesday–Saturday 10:00–20:00, Sunday
10:00–15:00, closed Monday, Passeig del Gràcia 92, Metro:
Diagonal). The entrance courtyard for the Fundacio Caixa de
Cataluyna, dreamily painted in pastels, is original and can be
seen free of charge.

Casa Battlo—Four blocks from Casa Milà (Passeig de Gràcia 43, Metro: Passeig de Gràcia), this house's roof has a cresting wave of tiles (or is it a dragon's back?). Check out the geometric facade of the house next door (#41) by the architect Puig i Cadafalch and the modernistic house (#35) by Lluís Domènechi Muntaner, designer of the Catalana Concert Hall. This Barcelonian version of keeping up with the Joneses led to the Passeig de Gràcia's local nickname, "the street of discord." If you're tempted to frame your photo from the middle of the street, be careful—Gaudí died under a streetcar!

Parc Güell—Gaudí fans find the artist's magic in this colorful park (free, daily 10:00–20:00) and small **Gaudí Museum** (200 ptas, museum open Sunday–Friday 10:00–14:00 and 16:00–18:00, closed Saturday, Metro: Vallarca but easier by bus #24 from Plaça de Catalunya; 1,000 ptas by taxi). Gaudí didn't intend this to be a park but a planned garden city. As a high-income housing project, it flopped. As a park . . . even after reminding myself that Gaudí's work is a careful rhythm of color, shapes, and space, I was disappointed.

Modern Art Museum (Museu d'Art Modern)—East of the França train station in Parc de la Ciutadella, this manageable museum exhibits Catalan sculpture, painting, glass, and furniture by Gaudí, Casas, Llimona, and others (300 ptas, Tuesday–Sunday 10:00–19:00, closed Monday).

Sights—Barcelona's Montjuïc

The Montjuïc (Mount of the Jews), overlooking Barcelona's hazy port, has always been a show-off. Ages ago it had the impressive fortress. In 1929, it hosted an International Fair from which most of today's sights originated. And in 1992, the Summer Olympics directed the world's attention to this pincushion of sightseeing attractions. Barcelona's skyway (Transbordador Aeri) is a temptation when you see it gliding fitfully across the harbor. It's often closed for safety reasons.

There are three ways to reach Montjuïc: on the Bus Turistic (see Getting Around Barcelona, above), bus #61 from Plaza España (135 ptas, every 10 minutes), or take the subway to Metro: Parallel and catch the funicular (250 ptas one-way, 350 ptas round-trip, 10:45–20:00, later in summer). All three options leave you at the *teleférico* which you can take to the Montjuïc castle (400 ptas one-way, 600 ptas round-trip), or walk uphill 20 minutes though the pleasant park.

Amusement Park (Parc d'Atraccions de Montjuïc)—Your best chance to eat, whirl, and hurl with local families (free, open daily in summers until late, access by the skyway or by Metro: Parallel, from which you can walk or ride the Montjuïc *teleférico*, which stops here on its way up to the fortress).

Castle of Montjuïc—This offers great city views and a military museum (200 ptas, Tuesday–Sunday 9:30–13:30, 15:30–19:30, closed Monday).

▲**Fountains (Fonts Lluminoses)**—Music, colored lights, and impressive amounts of water make an artistic and coordinated splash on summer Thursday, Friday, and Saturday nights (four 30-minute shows start on the half-hour, 22:00–23:30, walk toward huge towering National Palace from the Metro: Plaça Espanya).

Spanish Village (Poble Espanyol)—This tacky 5-acre model village uses fake traditional architecture from all over Spain as a shell to contain gift shops. Craftspeople do their clichétic thing only in the morning (9:00–19:30 but dead after 13:00, not worth the time or the 950 ptas). After-hours it becomes a popular local nightspot.

Torres de Avila—The music is loud and drinks are steep (900 ptas), but this modern building is remarkable. Designed by Mariscal, it features rotating walls, a glass elevator, glass floors, and a men's room with a circular pool table. It's just outside Poble Espanyol (Thursday–Sunday, 23:00–06:00).

▲**Catalonian Art Museum (Museo Nacional d'Art de Catalunya)**—Often called "the Prado of Romanesque art," this is a rare and world-class collection of Romanesque frescoes, statues, and paintings, much of it from remote Catalan village churches in the Pyrenees. Also see Gothic work and paintings by the great Spanish masters (500 ptas, Tuesday–Saturday 10:00–19:00, on Thursday until 21:00, Sunday 10:00–14:30, closed Monday, tel. 93/423-7199).

▲**Fundació Joan Miró**—For something a bit more up-to-date, this museum showcases the modern art talents of yet another Catalonian artist (600 ptas, 10:00–20:00, Sunday 10:30–14:30, Thursday until 21:30, closed Monday).

Sights—Eixample

Uptown Barcelona is a unique variation on the grid-planned cities you find all over. Barcelona snipped off the building corners to create light and spacious eight-sided squares at every intersection (and difficulty in finding signs of crossroads). Wide sidewalks, hardy shade trees, chic shops, and plenty of art nouveau fun (by Gaudí and company) make the Eixample a refreshing break from the Old Town. For the best Eixample example, ramble Rambla Catalunya (unrelated to the more famous Ramblas) and pass through Passeig de Gràcia (Metro: Passeig de Gràcia).

The 19th century brought to Barcelona great economic and demographic growth. By the mid-1800s, the city was busting out of its medieval walls. A new modern section was planned to follow a grid-like layout and bring the city's focus uptown with the intersection of three major thoroughfares: Gran Via, Diagonal, and the Meridiana. Deemed the Eixample, or "Enlargement," this progressive plan would carry Barcelona well into the 20th century.

The plan envisioned a city in which everything was accessible to everyone. Each 20-block square district would have its own hospital and large park, each 10-block-square area would have its own market and general services, each 5-block-square grid, called a *barri*, would house its own schools and day-care centers. The hollow space found inside each "block" of apartments would form a neighborhood park.

While many details were never realized, the Eixample was an urban success. Although construction was ongoing, grids were laid at the project's inception. Individuals bought plots where they built—adhering to the height, width, and depth limitations—as they pleased. The turn of the century produced the most ornate structures, many in the newly developed moderniste style. The bourgeoisie positioned themselves as close to the center as possible. For this reason, the best buildings are near the Passeig de Gràcia.

Before the age of elevators, the bourgeoisie lavishly decorated only the lower floors. Glass windows, brass handrails, and marble steps adorn the *principal* (ground floor). As you ascend, the steps get lower and narrower, and the lustrous marble is replaced by splintering wood.

Sarria and Gràcia (north of where Passeig de Gràcia turns into Gran de Gràcia) were both independent villages outside of the city. Many Barcelonans had summer homes there. Now both neighborhoods, incorporated into modern-day Barcelona, maintain their separate identities and fiestas. The charming Plaza Rovira i Trias marks the Old Town center of Gràcia.

Sleeping in Barcelona
(140 ptas = about $1, tel. code: 93)
Sleep Code: **S**=Single, **D**=Double/Twin, **T**=Triple, **Q**=Quad, **b**=bathroom, **t**=toilet only, **s**=shower only, **CC**=Credit Card (Visa, MasterCard, Amex), **SE**=Speaks English, **NSE**=No English.

Barcelona is Spain's most expensive city. Still, it has reasonable rooms. Your big decision is which neighborhood. A few places raise their rates for "high season," which, for business hotels, is outside of summer, on weekdays, and during conventions. Since dumpy, cheap hotels cater only to tourists, their high season is summer. Most prices listed do not include the 7 percent tax or the optional breakfast.

Sleeping near the Ramblas and in the Gothic Quarter
(zip code: 08002)
(These accommodations are listed in roughly geographical order downhill from Plaça de Catalunya.)

Catalunya Plaza is a business hotel with all the air-con, minibar comforts (Sb-13,000 ptas, Db-15,000 ptas, CC:VMA, on the plaza at Plaça de Catalunya 7, tel. 93/317-7171, fax 93/317-7855, SE).

Hotel Barcelona is another big American-style hotel with soft prices (Sb-13,000 ptas, Db-17,000 ptas, with a sun-roof terrace, 1 block away at Caspe 1-13, tel. 93/302-5858, fax 93/301-8674).

Hotel Toledano's elevator takes you high above the noise and into the *zona bella vista*. Request a view balcony to overlook the Ramblas. This small and folksy hotel is run by the helpful English-speaking owner Juan Sanz and his son Albert (Sb-3,900 ptas, Db-6,900 ptas, Tb-8,600 ptas, Qb-9,600 ptas, cheaper off-season, TV with BBC in every room, CC:VMA, Rambla de Canaletas 138, tel. 93/301-0872, fax 93/412-3142, e-mail: Toledano@idgrup.ibernet.com). Juan runs **Hostal Residencia Capitol** one floor above, which is cheaper and appropriate for backpackers (S-2,900 ptas, D-4,600 ptas, Db-5,200 ptas; you can share six-bedded rooms for hostel prices).

The **Hotel Lloret** is a big, Old World, dark place right on the Ramblas. Its worn rooms have almost all been renovated with air-conditioning (S-3,500 ptas, Sb-4,800 ptas, Db-6,800 ptas, extra bed-1,000 ptas, continental buffet breakfast-450 ptas, choose between a Ramblas balcony with street noise or *tranquilo* in the back, elevator dominates the stairwell, CC:VMA, Rambla de Canaletas 125, tel. 93/317-3366, fax 93/301-9283, SE). If you want to immerse yourself in the Ramblas, do it here.

Huéspedes Santa Ana, nearby on Carrer de Santa Ana, a wonderful pedestrian street 1 block down the Ramblas, is plain, clean, and quiet (S-2,600 ptas, D-4,200 ptas, Db-5,200 ptas, T-4,800 ptas, Carrer de Santa Ana 23, tel. 93/301-2246). The friendly owner, Maria, plans lots of renovations, but the rooms will remain small and cramped.

Nouvel Hotel, an elegant Victorian-style building on the same great street, has very comfortable rooms (Sb-8,000 ptas, Db without balcony-10,800 ptas, Db with balcony-12,800 ptas, huge Db suite-19,600 ptas, air-con and royal, CC:VMA, Carrer de Santa Ana 18, tel. 93/301-8274, fax 93/301-8370, SE).

Sister hotels straddling the same street and run by one company, with shiny, modern bathrooms, all the comforts, and similar prices (Sb-5,400 ptas, Db-8,800 ptas with breakfast, CC:VMA), but in buildings that feel more concrete than Victorian, are **Hotel Cataluña** (elevator, Carrer de Santa Ana 24, tel. 93/301-9120, fax 93/302-7870) and **Hotel Cortes** (Carrer de Santa Ana 25, elevator, tel. 93/317-9112, fax 93/302-7870). **Hostal Campi**, big, musty, and ramshackle, is a few doors off the Ramblas (D-3,500 ptas, Db-4,600 ptas, no elevator, Canuda 4, tel. 93/301-3545, NSE).

Hostal Residencia Lausanne, housed in an art nouveau building, has recently been renovated. The friendly owner, Javier, promotes a worldly, harmonious setting (S-2,500 ptas, D-3,500 ptas, Ds-4,500 ptas, Db-6,000 ptas, a few great triples and quads, outdoor terrace, TV room, Avenida Portal de l'Angel 24, tel. 93/302-1139, SE).

Hostal Residencia Rembrandt, on a lively pedestrian street between the Ramblas and the cathedral, has a southern-Spain garden-patio feel and bad beds (S-2,700 ptas, Sb-3,500 ptas, D-4,000 ptas, Db-5,500 ptas, breakfast-350 ptas, Portaferrisa 23, tel. & fax 93/318-1011, SE). Join the locals on their evening pilgrimage (18:00–20:00) to nearby Petritxol, a street brimming with art galleries and *churros* shops.

Huéspedes Colmenero is very clean and family-run on a great, safe but noisy alley, with seven cute rooms and tiny balconies. Rosa speaks French but no English and offers the best cheap rooms in the Old Town (S-3,000 ptas, D-4,000 ptas,

Db-5,500 ptas, 1,000 ptas more if staying only one night; two streets toward the cathedral from the Ramblas at Petritxol 12, tel. 93/302-6634, fax: what's that?).

Hotel Jardi is a hard-working, clean, plain place on the happiest little square in the Gothic Quarter. Room prices vary according to newness, view, and balconies (in the old wing: D-5,000–5,500 ptas, T-5,600–6,500 ptas; in the new wing: Sb-6,000 ptas, Db-7,000 ptas, Tb-8,500 ptas, continental breakfast-650 ptas, no elevator, CC:VMA, halfway between the Ramblas and the cathedral on Plaça Sant Josep Oriol #1, tel. 93/301-5900, fax 93/318-3664, NSE). Rooms with balconies enjoy a classic plaza setting.

To sleep safely and quietly—but deeper—in the Gothic Quarter, these two new, modern neighbors keep businesspeople happy with TV, telephone, and air-con: **Hotel Adagio** (Sb-6,600 ptas, Db-8,250 ptas, Tb-9,900 ptas, saggy beds, includes breakfast, elevator, CC:VMA, Fernan 21, tel. 93/318-9061, fax 93/318-3724) and across the street, the **Hotel California** (Sb-5,500 ptas, Db-8,000 ptas, Tb-11,000 ptas, includes breakfast, CC:VMA, Raurich 14, tel. 93/317-7766, fax 93/317-5474). The California lacks an elevator but has bigger and brighter halls and bathrooms.

Sleeping in Eixample
(zip code: 08008)
For a more elegant and boulevardian neighborhood, sleep north of Gran Vía Cortes Catalanes in Eixample, a ten-minute walk from the Ramblas action.

There's nothing noncommittal about **Hotel Residencia Neutral**. With 35 cheery rooms, classy public rooms, mosaic floors, high ceilings, and a passion for cleanliness, it's the best Eixample value (tiny Sb-3,000 ptas, big Sb-4,400 ptas, Ds-4,500 ptas, Db-5,800 ptas, Ts-5,100 ptas, Tb-6,200 ptas, CC:VM, elegantly located 2 blocks north of Gran Vía at Rambla Catalunya 42, 08007 Barcelona, tel. 93/487-6390.

Hostal Residencia Windsor, newly refurbished, is peaceful, polished, and a decent value (S-3,200 ptas, Sb-4,000 ptas, Ds-5,600 ptas, Db-6,700 ptas, elevator, some balconies, Rambla Catalunya 84, tel. 93/215-1198, SE).

Pensión Fani is a budget cheapie. It's dark, quiet, and basic (S-2,000 ptas, D-4,500 ptas, elevator, Valencia 278, second floor, tel. 93/215-3645 and 93/215-3044).

Hostels

Hostal de Joves is clean and well-run (1,400 ptas per person with breakfast if you're under 26, 1,500 ptas otherwise, communal kitchen, Passeig de Pujades 29, next to Parc de la Ciutadella and Metro: Arc de Triomf, tel. 93/300-3104; open 7:00–10:00 and 15:00–24:00). **Hostal Mare de Deu de Montserrat** is much cheerier than Hostal de Joves and worth the extra commute time (1,600 ptas with a hostel card, or 1,800 ptas without, for bed and breakfast if you're under 26, 2,200 ptas otherwise, dinner available, sheets-350 ptas, Passeig Mare de Deu del Coll 41, near Parc Güell, Metro: Vallcarca, follow Republica Argentina exit, tel. 93/210-5151, fax 93/210-0798). **Hostal Pere Tarres** is also good and accepts nonmembers who are willing to pay a bit more (1,450 ptas with breakfast, Calle Numancia 149, near the Sants station and Metro: Les Corts, tel. 93/410-2309).

Eating in Barcelona

Barcelona, the capital of Catalonian cuisine, offers a tremendous variety of colorful places to eat. The harbor area, especially Barceloneta, is famous for fish. The best *tapas* bars are in the Gothic Quarter and around the Picasso Museum. Many restaurants are closed in August when the owners, like you, are on vacation.

Eating in the Gothic Quarter

Los Caracoles, at Escudellers 14, a block off the Plaça Reial in red-light bar country, is a huge and trendy Spanish wine cellar dripping in atmosphere (pricey, daily 13:00–24:00, Metro: Drassanes, tel. 93/302-3185). You'll eat better on a budget at the very popular and neighboring **La Fonda** (Escudellers 10, tel. 93/301-7515). A fine place for local-style food in a local-style setting is **Restaurant Agut** (inexpensive, closed in July or August, huge servings, Calle Gignas 16, tel. 93/315-1709). **El Portalon**, in the bowels of the Gothic Quarter (between Ramblas and the cathedral), is a fair value (closed Sunday, Calle Banys Nous 20).

Taverna Basca Irati has great *tapas* in a bustling atmosphere full of locals (Calle Cardenal Casanyes 17, Metro: Liceu, tel. 93/302-3084).

Els Quatre Gats, Picasso's hangout, is popular with locals. Before it was founded in 1897, the idea of a café for artists was mocked as a place where only *quatre gats* ("four cats," meaning nobody) would come (Monday–Saturday 8:30–01:30, Sunday 17:00–01:30, CC:VMA, Montsio 3, tel. 93/302-4140).

Eating near Plaza Catalunya

Self Naturista is a bright and cheery buffet that will make vegetarians and health-food-lovers feel right at home. Others may find a few unidentifiable plates and drinks (11:30–22:00, closed Sunday, near several recommended hotels, just off the top of Ramblas at Carrer de Santa Ana 13). Another vegetarian choice is **Bio Center** (9:00–23:00, closed Sunday, Pintor Fortuny 25, Metro: Catalunya, tel. 93/301-4583).

Julivert Meu teams up regional specialties like *pan con tomate* (bread with tomato and olive oil), *jamón serrano* (cured ham), and *escalivadas* (grilled vegetables) in a rustic interior (Monday–Saturday 13:00–01:00, Sunday 13:00–16:00 and 20:00–01:00, Bonsuccés 7, Metro: Catalunya, tel. 93/318-0343).

Eating Elsewhere in Barcelona

In the Eixample, at **La Bodegueta**, have a *carajillos* (coffee with rum) and a *flauta* (sandwich on flute-thin baguette) in this authentic below-street-level bodega (Monday–Saturday 8:00–01:30, Sunday 7:00–13:00, Rambla Catalunya 100, at intersection with Provenza, Metro: Diagonal, tel. 93/215-4894) or slip into the classy **Quasi Queviures** for upscale *tapas*, sandwiches or the whole nine yards (Passeig de Gracia 24).

El Café de Internet provides an easy way to munch a sandwich while sending e-mail messages to mom (600 ptas for a half-hour, Monday–Saturday 10:00–24:00, closed Sunday, Gran Vía 656, Metro: Passeig de Gràcia, tel. 93/302-1154, web site: www.cafeinternet.es).

Café de L'Ópera, one of Barcelona's mainstays, serves a great *café con leche* (daily 9:00–02:30, La Rambla 74, tel. 93/317-7585).

Egipte, with its old sewing-machine tables, high ceilings, and rooms separated by tall French doors, simmers with charisma. Try the *pebrots amb bacalao*—cod-stuffed red bell peppers over rice (daily 13:00–01:00, Jerusalem 3, behind the Boqueria, Metro: Liceu, tel. 93/317-7480).

For a quick meal, pick up a healthy sandwich at **Pans & Company**. This Catalan chain puts the food back in fast food. Its sister establishment, **Pastafiore**, dishes up salads and pasta at a fair price (500–800 ptas). Both are a lifesaver on Sunday, when many restaurants are closed (daily 8:00–24:00, opens at 9:00 on Sunday, located on Plaza Urquinaona, Provenza, La Rambla, Portal de l'Angel, and just about everywhere else).

Tapas and Tascas

A regional joke sums up eating habits in Catalunya. A person from Madrid takes a Catalan friend on a lengthy run of *tapas* bars. At each stop they sample lots of munchies. Hours later, the night ends and the Madrileño, stuffed to the gills, says to the Catalan, "Good, no?" The Catalan replies, "Not bad. But when do we eat?"

Tapas may not be standard fare in Catalunya but Barcelona boasts some of the region's finest "dive bars," called *tascas*. These colorful, historic bars are unlike anything else you'll see in Barcelona. You're most likely to enjoy local crowds from 22:00 until the wee hours. For the most fun and flavorful route through the Gothic Quarter, go to the Plaza de la Merce (Metro: Drassanes), then follow the small street that runs along the right side of the church (Carrer Merce), stopping at whichever *tascas* look fun. Consider these: **La Jarra** is known for its tender *jamón canario* (baked ham) and salty potatoes. **El Corral** makes one of the neighborhood's best *chorizo al diablo* (hell sausage), which you sauté yourself. It's great with the regional specialty *pan con tomate*. Across the street **La Plata** keeps things wonderfully simple, serving extremely cheap plates of sardines and small glasses of keg wine. You can smell **Las Campanas'** fragrant sausage a block away, whew . . . Or try *fuet*, a mini-salami from nearby **Vic**. After a stop at **El Born**, a former *pescaderia* (fish market), have a chat with the parrot at **Bar la Choza del Sopas. Miramelindo** and **Berimbao** are all well worth a stop for their ambience and specialty drinks (*mojitos* and *caiparinas*). At the end of Carrer Merce, **Bar Vendimia** serves up tasty clams and mussels. The street paralleling Carrer Merce, Carrer Ample, has ample additional bar-hopping possibilities in more refined confines.

In the Gothic Quarter, **Cavateca Vinoteca** is a great *cava* bar, bubbling with Spain's sparkling wine (Verdaguer i Callis 10, near the Palau de la Música Catalana, tel. 93/310-0938).

Transportation Connections—Barcelona

By train to: Lisbon (2/day, 20 hrs with change in Madrid), **Madrid** (6/day, 7–9 hrs, $50 with a *couchette*), **Paris** (3/day,

11–15 hrs, $70 night-train reservation required), **Sevilla** (6/day, 9 hrs), **Málaga** (3/day, 14 hrs), **Nice** (1/day, 12 hrs, change in Cerbere). Train info: tel. 93/490-0202.

By bus to: Madrid (6/day, 8 hrs, half the price of a train ticket).

NEAR BARCELONA: CADAQUES AND MONTSERRAT

Cadaques

Since the late 1800s, Cadaques has served as a haven for intellectuals and artists alike. Salvador Dalí, raised in nearby Figueres, brought international fame to this sleepy Catalan port in the 1920s. He and his wife, Gala, set up home and studio at the adjacent Port Lligat. Cadaques inspired surrealists such as Eluard, Magritte, Duchamp, Man Ray, Buñuel, and García Lorca. Even Picasso was drawn to this enchanting coastal *cala* (cove), painting some of his cubist works here.

From the moment you descend into the town, taking in whitewashed buildings and deep blue waters, you're struck by the tranquility and beauty of Cadaques. Have a glass of *vino tinto* or *cremat* (a traditional brandy and coffee drink served flambé style) at one of the seaside cafés and let the lapping waves, brilliant sun, and gentle breeze subtly rejuvenate you.

From Cadaques, any Dalí fan will want to side-trip about an hour west to the Museu Dalí in Figueres (daily 9:00–20:00, off-season 10:30–18:00 and closed Monday, three SARFA buses per day from Cadaques, tel. 972/51-19-76).

To see a few Dalís right in Cadaques, visit the small Museu Perrot-Moore (summer 11:00–13:00 and 16:00–20:00, Calle Vigilant, tel. 972/25-82-31). The tourist office at Carrer Cotxe 2, is open daily (11:00–13:00 and 16:00–19:00, tel. 972/25-83-15).

Sleeping and Eating: Hotel La Residencia, owned by Dalí's first manager, Captain Moore, is a pleasant, modern hotel strewn with art and sporting a sunny garden patio. Sculptures, prints, paintings, and photos (in addition to Dalí wall covering and upholstery) line the corridors and fill the rooms (Db-8,500 ptas, Avenida Caritat Serinyana 1, tel. 972/25-83-12, fax 972/25-80-13). The nondescript **Hostal Marina** (D-4,500 ptas, Ds-5,500 ptas, Db-8,000 ptas, breakfast 450 ptas, Riera 3, tel. 972/25-81-99) and **Hostal Cristina**

(S-3,500 ptas, D-4,500 ptas, breakfast 500 ptas, La Riera s/n, tel. 972/25-81-38) are clean and conveniently located in the main plaza, around the corner from the tourist office and across from the beach. For a fine dinner, try **Casa Anita** down a narrow street from La Residencia. Sitting with other diners around a big table, you'll enjoy house specialties like *calamars a la planxa* and homemade *helado* (ice cream). Muscatel from a glass *porron* finishes off the tasty meal and unique experience (Juan and family, tel. 972/25-84-71).

Connections: From Barcelona, there are frequent departures from the RENFE station at Metro: Passeig de Gracia.

Montserrat

Montserrat is a popular day trip from Barcelona (53 km). Hymns ascribe this "serrated mountain" to little angels who carved the rocks with golden saws. Geologists blame 10 million years of nature at work. While the area was completely covered by water, winds deposited pebbles that mixed with other materials on the sea floor. Underwater mountains formed and were later exposed and left at the mercy of erosion.

Montserrat's top attraction is its basilica with the Black Virgin icon (La Moreneta, open to visitors 6:00–20:00). The Montserrat Escolania, or choir school, is considered to be the oldest music school in Europe. Fifty young boys, who live and study in the monastery itself, make up this choir, which performs daily at 13:00 and 18:45. And the Museu de Montserrat offers prehistoric tools, religious art, ancient artifacts, and a few paintings by great artists such as El Greco and Caravaggio.

Connections: The Ferrocarriles Catalanes trains leave hourly for Montserrat from Barcelona's Plaça Espanya (1 hr with transfer). Get off at Aeri de Montserrat stop at the base of the mountain where the funicular awaits (1,750-pta round-trip includes funicular).

MADRID

Today's Madrid is upbeat and vibrant, enjoying a kind of post-Franco renaissance. You'll feel it. Even the statue-maker beggars have a twinkle in their eyes.

Madrid is the hub of Spain. This modern capital—Europe's highest, at over 2,000 feet—has a population of more than 4 million and is young by European standards. Only 400 years ago, King Philip II decided to move the capital of his empire from Toledo to Madrid. One hundred years ago Madrid had only 400,000 people, so nine-tenths of the city is modern sprawl, surrounding an intact, easy-to-navigate historic center.

Dive headlong into the grandeur and intimate charm of Madrid. The lavish Royal Palace, with its gilded rooms and frescoed ceilings, rivals Versailles. The Prado has Europe's top collection of paintings. The city's huge Retiro Park invites you for a shady siesta and a hopscotch through a mosaic of lovers, families, skateboarders, pets walking their masters, and expert bench-sitters. Make time for Madrid's elegant shops and people-friendly pedestrian zones. Enjoy the shade in an arcade. On Sundays, cheer for the bull at a bullfight or bargain like mad at a mega-flea market. Lively Madrid has enough street singing, barhopping, and people-watching vitality to give any visitor a boost of youth.

Planning Your Time
Madrid's top two sights, the Prado and the palace, are worth a day. If you hit the city on a Sunday, allot another day for the

flea market and a bullfight. Ideally, give Madrid two days (outside of Sunday events) and spend them this way:

Day 1: Breakfast of *churros*, as recommended below, before a
brisk, good-morning-Madrid walk for 20 minutes from Puerta
del Sol to the Prado; 9:00 to noon in the Prado; lunch at La
Plaza; take an afternoon siesta in the Retiro Park or lap up the
modern art at Reina Sofia *(Guernica)* and/or the Thyssen-
Bornemisza Museum; early evening *paseo, tapas* for dinner
around Plaza Santa Ana.

Day 2: Breakfast and browse through San Miguel market, tour
Royal Palace, lunch near Plaza Mayor; afternoon free for other
sights, shopping, or side trip to El Escorial (open until 19:00).
Note that the Prado, the T-B Museum, and El Escorial are
closed on Monday.

Orientation (tel. code: 91)

The historic center can easily be covered on foot. No major
sight is more than a 20-minute walk from the Puerta del Sol,
Madrid's central square. Your time will be divided between the
city's two major sights—the palace and the Prado—and its
barhopping, car-honking, contemporary scene.

The Puerta del Sol is at the dead center of Madrid and of
Spain itself; notice the "kilometer zero" marker, from which all
of Spain is surveyed, at the police station (southwest corner).
The Royal Palace to the west and the Prado Museum and
Retiro Park to the east frame Madrid's historic center.

Southwest of Puerta del Sol is a 17th-century district with
the slow-down-and-smell-the-cobbles Plaza Mayor and plenty
of relics from pre-industrial Spain.

North of Puerta del Sol runs the Gran Vía, and between
the two are lively pedestrian shopping streets. The Gran Vía,
bubbling with business, expensive shops, and cinemas, leads
down to the impressively modern Plaza de España. North of
the Gran Vía is the gritty Malasana quarter, with its colorful
small houses, shoemakers' shops, sleazy-looking *hombres*, milk
vendors, bars, and hip night scene.

Tourist Information

Madrid has four handy Turismos: one on the Plaza Mayor at #3
(open 10:00–20:00, Saturday 10:00–14:00, closed Sunday; tel.
91/366-5477); another near the Prado Museum, across from the
front door of the giant Palace Hotel (weekdays 8:00–20:00,

Madrid

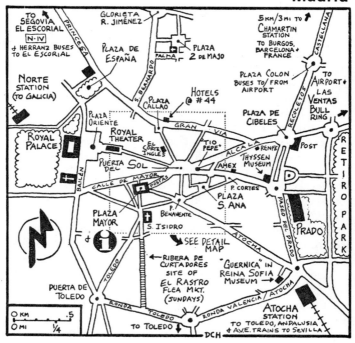

Saturday 9:00–13:00, Duque de Medinaceli 2, tel. 91/429-4951); and smaller offices at the Chamartin train station (same hours, tel. 91/315-9976) and at the airport (weekdays 9:00–19:00, Saturday 9:00–13:00, tel. 91/305-8656). Confirm your sightseeing plans and pick up a map and *Enjoy Madrid*, the free monthly city guide. (The TI's free guide to city events, *En Madrid*, is not as good as the easy-to-decipher weekly entertainment guide, *Guía del Ocio*, on sale at streetside newsstands for 125 ptas.) If interested, ask at the TI about bullfights and *Zarzuela* (the local light opera). The free and amazingly informative *Mapa de Comunicaciones España* lists all the Turismos, *paradores*, RENFE train information telephone numbers, and highway SOS numbers, with a road map of Spain. If you're heading to other destinations in this book, see if the Madrid TI has free maps and brochures. Many small-town Turismos keep erratic hours and run out of these pamphlets, so get what you can here. Get bus schedules, too, to avoid unnecessary trips to the various bus stations.

Arrival in Madrid

By Train: The two main rail stations, Atocha and Chamartin, are both on subway lines with easy access to downtown Madrid. Each station has all the services, though there is no TI at Atocha. In Spain, train rides longer than about three hours require reservations, even if you have a Eurailpass. To avoid needless running around, arrange your departure upon arrival.

Chamartin handles most international trains, and Atocha runs AVE trains to Sevilla. Both stations offer *largo recorrido* (long-distance) trains as well as *cercanias* (local trains to nearby destinations). Atocha is more clearly split into two halves (local and long-distance trains) with separate schedules; this is initially confusing if you're in the wrong side of building. Atocha also has two helpful (necessary) customer-service offices called Atencion al Cliente (daily 7:00–23:00), one office for each half of the building. The Chamartin station is less confusing. Its customer-service office is called Atencion al Viajero (behind the ticket windows, in the middle of the building) and the helpful TI is opposite track 20. Club AVE in Atocha (upstairs) is a lounge reserved solely for AVE ticketholders. Club Intercity in Chamartin is less exclusive— you can get in if you have a first-class railpass or sleeper reservation, or Intercity or Talgo ticket.

Both train stations have Metro stops named after themselves (i.e., Metro: Chamartin). Note that there are two Atocha Metro stops in Madrid. The train station's Metro station is "Atocha RENFE." If you're traveling between Chamartin and Atocha, use the Cercanias trains (free with a railpass); it's far quicker than the subway.

At the downtown RENFE office, you can get train information, reservations, and tickets (Monday–Friday 9:30–20:00, credit cards accepted, best to go in person, 2 blocks north of the Prado museum at Calle Alcala 44, tel. 91/328-9020).

By Bus: Madrid's three key bus stations are all connected by Metro: La Sepulvedana (handles Segovia and Avila, Metro: Principe Pio), the brand-new Estación sur Autobuses (covers Toledo, Metro: Menendez-Alvaro), and Estación Herranz (serves El Escorial, Metro: Moncloa). For details, see Transportation Connections at the end of this chapter.

By Plane: Madrid's Barajas Airport, 10 miles east of downtown, comes well-equipped to help new arrivals. It has a 24-hour bank with fair rates, an ATM, a TI, a telephone office where you can buy a phone card, a RENFE desk for rail information, a pharmacy, on-the-spot car-rental agencies, and easy public transportation into town. Airport info: tel. 91/305-8343.

Use your phone card to call and confirm your hotel and the price, then take the yellow bus into Madrid (to Plaza Colón, 4/hr, 30 min, 375 ptas). From Plaza Colón, take the subway to your hotel (walk up the stairs and face the blue "URBIS" sign high on a building—the subway stop, M. Serrano, is 50 yards to your right). If you take a taxi (easily available from the airport bus station at Plaza Colon), insist on the meter. For a taxi to or from the airport, allow at least 2,500 ptas. To get a rough idea of the price before you hop in, ask "*¿Cuanto cuesta a Madrid, mas o menos?*" (How much is it to Madrid, more or less?)

Getting Around Madrid

By Subway and Bus: Madrid's subway is simple, cheap (130 ptas/ride, buy the ten-ride ticket for 660 ptas), and speedy (outside of rush hour you'll go about seven stops in ten minutes). The city's broad streets can be hot and exhausting. A subway trip of even a stop or two can save time and energy. Pick up a free map (*Plano del Metro*) at most stations. Navigate by subway stops (shown on city maps). To transfer, follow signs to the next subway line (numbered and color-coded). End stops are used to indicate directions. Insert your ticket in the turnstile; retrieve it as you pass through. Green *Salida* signs point to the exit.

City buses, while not so easy, can be useful. If interested, get a bus map at the TI or the info booth on Puerta del Sol. Tickets are 130 ptas (buy on bus) or 660 ptas for ten tickets, called a *bonobus* (buy at kiosks or tobacco shops). Bus and Metro tickets aren't interchangeable.

By Taxi: Taxis are reasonable, but you'll go faster and cheaper by subway.

Helpful Hints

The American Express office at Plaza Cortes 2 (Metro: Sevilla) is a handy place to cash any kind of traveler's checks at a decent rate with no commission (Monday–Friday 9:00–17:30, Saturday 9:00–12:00, tel. 91/577-4000). They also sell AVE train tickets, but can't help you with AVE reservations if you have a train pass. The U.S. Embassy is at Serrano 75 (tel. 91/577-4000) and the Canadian Embassy is at Nuñez de Balboa 35 (tel. 91/431-4300). The grand department store, El Corte Inglés (Monday–Saturday 10:00–21:30, just off Puerta del Sol) has a travel agency and gives free Madrid maps (at the information desk, just inside the door at northwest intersection of Preciados and Tetuan). The telephone office, centrally located at Gran Vía 30, has metered phones and accepts credit cards for charges over 500 ptas (daily 10:00–23:00).

Theft Alert: Be wary of pickpockets, anywhere, anytime, but particularly on Puerta del Sol (main square), the subway, and crowded streets. On my last trip, half the American couples I met had experienced a pickpocket attempt. Wear your money belt. In crowds, keep your daybag in front of you. Some thieves "accidentally" spill ketchup on your clothes, then pick your pocket as they help you clean up. Fortunately, violent crime against tourists is very rare.

Museum Pass: If you plan to visit the Prado, Reina Sofia, and Thyssen-Bornemisza museums, buy the Paseo del Arte pass (1,050 ptas, available at all three museums and valid for one year). Remember, the Prado and Reina Sofia are free Saturday afternoon and Sunday.

Monday Plans: If you're in Madrid on a Monday (when most museums are closed), you can see Picasso's *Guernica* (Centro Reina Sofia), rent a boat at Retiro Park, tour the nearby botanical gardens, visit the Royal Palace, shop, or café-hop.

Sights—Madrid

▲▲▲**Prado Museum**—The Prado is my favorite collection of paintings anywhere. With more than 3,000 canvases, including entire rooms of masterpieces by Velázquez, Goya, El Greco, and Bosch, it's overwhelming. Take a tour or buy a guidebook (or bring me along by ripping out and packing the Prado chapter from *Mona Winks*). Focus on the Flemish and northern (Bosch, Dürer, Rubens), the Italian (Fra Angelico, Raphael, Botticelli, Titian), and the Spanish art (El Greco, Velázquez, Goya).

Follow Goya through his cheery *(The Parasol)*, political *(The Third of May)*, and dark *(Saturn Devouring His Children)* stages. In each stage, Goya asserted his independence from artistic conventions. Even the standard court portraits from his "first" stage reflect his politically liberal viewpoint, subtly showing the vanity and stupidity of his subjects by the looks in their goony eyes.

Heart of Madrid

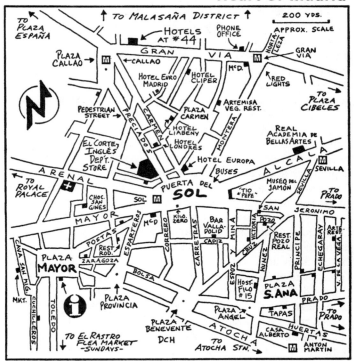

His political stage, with paintings like *The Third of May*, depicting a massacre of Spaniards by Napoleon's troops, makes him one of the first artists with a social conscience. Finally, in his gloomy "dark stage," Goya probed the inner world of fears and nightmares, anticipating the 20th-century preoccupation with dreams. Also don't miss Bosch's *The Garden of Earthly Delights*. Most art is grouped by painters, and any guard can point you in the right direction if you say "*¿Dónde está . . . ?*" and the painter's name as Españoled as you can (e.g., Titian is "*Ticiano*" and Bosch is "*El Bosco*"). The Prado is quietest at lunchtime from 14:00–16:00 (500 ptas, free Saturday after 14:30 and Sunday; Tuesday–Saturday 9:00–19:00, Sunday 9:00–14:00, closed Monday; Paseo de Prado, Metro: Banco de España or Atocha—each a 20-minute walk from the museum, tel. 91/420-2836).

▲▲**Centro Reina Sofia**—This exceptional modern art museum is most famous for Picasso's *Guernica*, a massive painting showing the horror of modern war. It deserves much study. Franco's death ended the work's exile in America, and now it reigns as Spain's national piece of art. The museum also houses an easy-to-enjoy collection of other modern artists whom Picasso influenced so much, from Dalí to Miró (500 ptas, free Saturday after 14:30 and Sunday; open 10:00–21:00, Sunday 10:00–14:30, closed Tuesday; Santa Isabel 52, Metro: Atocha, across from the Atocha train station, look for the exterior glass elevators, tel. 91/467-5062).

▲▲**Thyssen-Bornemisza Museum**—This stunning new museum displays the impressive collection of Baron Thyssen, a wealthy German married to a former Miss Spain. Art-lovers appreciate how the good baron's art complements the Prado's collection. For a fine walk through art history, start on the top floor and do the rooms in numerical order. While it's basically minor works by major artists and major works by minor artists (the real big guns are over at the Prado), the Thyssen is stronger in Impressionism and 20th-century art. Located across from the Prado at Paseo del Prado 8 in the Palacio de Villahermosa (600 ptas, 10:00–19:00, closed Monday, Metro: Banco de España or Atocha, tel. 91/369-0151).

▲▲**Plaza Mayor and Medieval Madrid**—The Plaza Mayor, a vast, cobbled, traffic-free chunk of 17th-century Spain, is just a short walk from the Puerta del Sol. Each side of the square is uniform, as if a grand palace were turned inside out. Throughout Spain, lesser *plazas mayores* provide peaceful pools for the river of Spanish life. A stamp-and-coin market bustles here on Sundays from 10:00 to 14:00, and on any day it's a colorful and affordable place to enjoy a cup of coffee. The TI is at #3.

Medieval Madrid is now a rather sterile tangle of narrow streets bounded by the Royal Palace, Plaza Mayor, Teatro Real, and Plaza Puerta de Moros. The uninviting old Plaza de la Villa was the center of Madrid before Madrid was the center of Spain. The most enjoyable action in this area is contained in a glass-and-iron cage called the Mercado de San Miguel (produce market, closed Sunday) next to the Plaza Mayor. Drop by for the morning flurry and pull up a stool for breakfast (Metro: Opera).

▲▲▲**Royal Palace (Palacio Real)**—Europe's third-greatest palace (after Versailles and Vienna) is packed with tourists and royal antiques. You can wander on your own through its clock-filled, lavish interior, or join a free English tour. Tours start whenever a group of ten to 20 gathers; if you just missed one, try to catch up with it (950 ptas admission, Monday–Saturday 9:30–18:00, Sunday 9:00–15:00, closes one hour earlier in winter, very crowded in summer, arrive early or late, Metro: Opera, tel. 91/542-0059). The Palace is free on Wednesday. Your ticket includes the impressive armory and the pharmacy, both on the courtyard. The nearby **Museo de Carruajes Reales**, with its excellent collection of royal carriages, should reopen in 1998 after extensive renovation; confirm at the TI or Palace. The adjacent, newly consecrated **Catedral de la Almudena** is refreshingly clean, modern, and utilitarian (free, Monday–Saturday 10:00–13:00 and 18:00–20:00, Sunday 10:00–14:00).

▲▲**Zarzuela**—For a delightful look at Spanish light opera that even English-speakers can enjoy, try an evening of Zarzuela. Guitar-strumming Napoleons in red capes, buxom women with masks and fans, castanets and stomping feet, aficionados singing along from the cheap seats where the acoustics are best, Spanish-speaking pharaohs, melodramatic spotlights, the people's opera—that's Zarzuela. The TI's monthly guide has a special Zarzuela listing.

▲▲**El Rastro**—Europe's biggest flea market is a field day for shoppers, people-watchers, and thieves (Sundays and holidays 9:00–15:00, best before 12:00). Thousands of stalls titillate more than a million browsers. If you brake for garage sales, you'll pull a U-turn for El Rastro—you can buy or sell nearly anything here. Start at the Plaza Mayor and head south, or take the subway to Tirso de Molina. Hang on to your wallet. Munch on a *relleno* or *pepito* (meat-filled pastry). Europe's biggest stamp market thrives simultaneously on the Plaza Mayor.

Chapel San Antonio de la Florida—Goya's tomb stares up at a splendid cupola filled with his own frescoes (free, Tuesday–Friday 10:00–14:00 and 16:00–20:00, weekends 10:00–14:00, closed Monday; Paseo de la Florida 5, Metro: Principe Pio, tel. 91/547-0722).

▲▲**Retiro Park**—Siesta in this 350-acre green and breezy escape from the city. These peaceful gardens offer great picnicking and people-watching. Walk to the big lake (El Estanque) where you can rent a rowboat (450 ptas for 45 min), or wander through the Palacio de Crystal. A grand boulevard of statues leads to the Prado. The Botanical Garden (Jardín Botánico) nearby is a pleasant extension of Retiro

Park to the southwest (250 ptas, daily 10:00–sunset, Plaza de
Murillo 2, Metro: Atocha or Retiro).

▲▲▲**Bullfight**—Madrid's Plaza de Toros hosts Spain's top
bullfights on most Sundays and holidays from Easter through
October and nearly every day mid-May through early June.
Top fights sell out in advance. Fights usually start punctually
at 19:00. Tickets range from 1,000 to 6,000 ptas. There are
no bad seats; paying more gets you in the shade and/or closer
to the gore (*filas* 8, 9, and 10 tend to be closest to the action).
Booking offices add 20 percent and don't sell the cheap seats
(Calle de la Victoria 3, tel. 91/521-1213, or Plaça del
Carmen 1, tel. 91/531-2732). To save money, buy your ticket
at the bullring. Tickets go on sale the day of the fight at
10:00; 10 percent of the seats are kept available to be sold
two hours before the fight (Calle Alcala 231, Metro: Ventas,
tel. 91/356-2200). The **bullfighting museum** (*Museo
Taurino*) is next to the bullring (250 ptas, Monday–Friday
9:30–14:30, Calle Alcala 237, tel. 91/725-1857). See the
Appendix for more on the "art" of bullfighting.

▲**Royal Tapestry Factory** (**Real Fabrica de Tapices**)—
Have a look at the traditional making of tapestries (250 ptas,
Monday–Friday 9:00–12:30, closed August, cheap tours in
Spanish only, Calle Fuenterrabia 2, Metro: Menendez Pelayo,
tel. 91/551-3400).

▲*Paseo*—The people of Madrid (Madrileños) take afternoon
siestas because so much goes on in the evenings. The nightly
paseo is Madrid on parade. Young and old, everyone's outside
taking a stroll, "cruising" without cars, seeing and being seen.
Gran Vía, Calle de Preciados, and the Paseo del Prado are
particularly active scenes.

Parque de Atracciones—For a colorful amusement-park
scene, complete with Venetian canals, dancing, eating, games,
free shows, and top-notch people-watching, try Parque de
Atracciones (open most afternoons and evenings from noon
until around midnight, only Saturday and Sunday in off-
season, Metro: Batan, tel. 91/463-2900 for exact times). This
fair and Spain's best zoo (daily 10:00–20:30, dolphin shows, tel.
91/711-9950) are in the vast Casa de Campo Park just west of
the Royal Palace.

Shopping—Shoppers can focus on the colorful pedestrian area
between Gran Vía and Puerta del Sol. The giant Spanish
department store El Corte Inglés, is a block off Puerta del Sol

and a handy place to pick up just about anything you may need (Monday–Saturday 10:00–21:00, closed Sunday, free maps at info desk, supermarket in basement).

Sleeping in Madrid
(140 ptas = about $1, tel. code: 91)
Sleep Code: **S**=Single, **D**=Double/Twin, **T**=Triple, **Q**=Quad, **b**=bathroom, **t**=toilet only, **s**=shower only, **CC**=Credit Card (Visa, MasterCard, Amex), **SE**=Speaks English, **NSE**=No English. Breakfast is not included unless noted. In Madrid, the 7 percent IVA tax is generally, but not always, included in the price.

Madrid has plenty of centrally located budget hotels and *pensiónes*. You'll have no trouble finding a decent double for $30 to $60. The city is most crowded in July and August, but prices are the same throughout the year and it's almost always easy to find a place. The accommodations I've listed are all within a few minutes' walk of Puerta del Sol. Competition is stiff. Those on a budget can bargain. Nighttime Madrid's economy is brisk. Even decent areas are littered with shady-looking people after dark. Just don't invite them in.

Sleeping in the Pedestrian Zone Between Puerta del Sol and Gran Vía
(zip code: 28013)
Predictable and away from the seediness, these are good values for those wanting to spend a little more. Especially for these hotels, call first to see if the price is firm. Their formal prices may be inflated and some offer weekend deals. Use Metro: Sol for these five hotels.

Hotel Europa has red-carpet charm: a quiet courtyard, a royal salon, plush halls, polished wood floors, and squeaky-clean rooms with balconies overlooking the pedestrian zone or an inner courtyard. All rooms have TVs (CNN) and big, modern bathrooms (Sb-6,100 ptas, Db-8,200 ptas, Tb-11,100 ptas, elevator, easy phone reservations with no deposit, CC:VM, Calle del Carmen 4, tel. 91/521-2900, fax 91/521-4696, very helpful staff SE). They have a 1,400-ptas-a-day parking deal and plan on having air-conditioning by 1998. Have breakfast next door at Kenia cafeteria.

Hotel Londres is a business-class hotel: dark, stark, air-conditioned, and a little smoky (Db-9,000 ptas, renovated

Db-10,500 ptas, CC:VM, elevator, don't trust their safes; Galdo 2, tel. 91/531-4105, fax 91/531-4101, some English spoken). **Hotel Euromadrid** is dull, with a concrete character rather than charm. It's all air-conditioned, with private bathrooms, TVs, and an elevator (Sb-6,500 ptas, Db-8,500 ptas, Tb-9,600 ptas, buffet breakfast included, CC:VMA, Mesonero Romanos 7, tel. 91/521-7200, fax 91/521-4582, SE). Nearby, the **Hotel Cliper** is faded-elegant, with a better combination of friendliness and character and comfortable rooms on a fairly quiet street (Sb-5,200 ptas, Db-8,000 ptas, includes breakfast, some rooms with air-con, CC:VMA, Chincilla 6, near Plaza Carmen, tel. 91/531-1700, fax 91/531-1707, SE).

The huge **Hotel Liabeny** feels classy and new, with spacious rooms and all the comforts (Sb-13,500 ptas, Db-19,000 ptas, plus 7 percent IVA tax, air-con, parking and buffet breakfast each 1,500 ptas/day, attached restaurant and bar, CC:VMA, off Plaza Carmen at Salud 3, tel. 91/531-9000, fax 91/532-7421, SE, web site: www.apunte.es/liabeny, e-mail: liabeny@apunte.es).

Sleeping at Gran Vía #44
(zip code: 28013)

The pulse (and noise) of today's Madrid is best felt along the Gran Vía. This main drag in the heart of the city stays awake all night. Despite the dreary pile of prostitutes just a block north, there's a certain urban decency about it. My choices (all at Gran Vía #44, entrance between the Lladro shop and the Lotería) are across from Plaza del Callão, a colorful 4 blocks of pedestrian malls up from the Puerta del Sol. Although many rooms are high above the traffic noise, I'd request *tranquilo* for a brick-wall view on the back side. The Café & Te next door provides a classy way to breakfast. The Callão Metro stop is at your doorstep, and the handy Gran Vía stop (direct to Atocha) is 2 blocks away. The first two listings are especially popular; call well in advance to reserve.

Hostal Residencia Valencia is bright, cheery, and professional. The friendly manager, Antonio Ramirez, speaks English (Sb-4,000 ptas, big Sb-4,500 ptas, Ds-5,300 ptas, Db-5,800 ptas, CC:VM, fifth floor, tel. 91/522-1115, fax 91/522-1113). Also a good value but a bit smoky and with less character is friendly **Hostal Residencia Continental** (Sb-3,600 ptas, Db-5,000 ptas, CC:VMA, fourth floor, tel. 91/521-4640, fax 91/521-4649, SE).

Hostal Residencia Miami is clean and quiet, with lovely, well-lit rooms, padded doors, and plastic-flower decor throughout. It's like staying at your eccentric aunt's in Miami Beach. The bubbly landlady, Sra. Sanz, and her too-careful husband, who dresses up each day for work here, speak no English (S-2,500 ptas–3,000 ptas, D-3,500 ptas, Db-4,500 ptas, closed August—if they take reservations in August, they are booking you elsewhere, eighth floor, tel. 91/521-1464).

Across the hall, **Hostal Alibel**, like Miami with less sugar, rents eight big, airy, quiet rooms (D-3,500 ptas, Ds-4,200 ptas, Db-4,500 ptas, tel. 91/521-0051, NSE). Downstairs, **Hostal Josefina** has creaky vinyl floors and junkyard doors but strong beds in museum-warehouse rooms and a pleasant owner (S-2,700 ptas, Sb-3,000 ptas, Ds-4,000 ptas, Ts-6,000 ptas, seventh floor, tel. 91/521-8131 and 91/531-0466, NSE).

Sleeping on or near Plaza Santa Ana (zip code: 28012)

The Plaza Santa Ana area has plenty of small, cheap places. While well-worn and noisy at night, it has an almost Parisian ambience, with colorful bars and very central location (three minutes from Puerta del Sol's "Tío Pepe" sign; walk down Calle San Jeronimo and turn right on Principe). At most of these hotels, fluent Spanish is spoken, toilets and showers are usually down the hall, and there's no heat during winter. Metro: Sol.

In the beautifully tiled Plaza Santa Ana 15 building, on the corner of the square closest to Puerta del Sol and all the good *tapas* bars, and up a dark wooden staircase (flick on the light) are three of my favorites: **Hostal la Rosa**, on the third floor, has pleasant rooms and shiny wood floors. If you can stay on her good side, Encarnita is a kick. She speaks no English (and is sure you speak Spanish). For 900 ptas you can use her washing machine (S-1,800 ptas, Ss-2,000 ptas, small D-2,800 ptas, D/double bed-3,000 ptas, D/twins-3,400 ptas, Ds-4,400 ptas, T-4,000 ptas, Ts-5,200 ptas, Qs-6,000 ptas, Quint/s-7,000 ptas, tel. 91/532-5805). **Hostal Filo** is squeaky clean with a nervous but helpful management and 20 rooms hiding in a confusing floor plan (S-2,000 ptas, Ss-3,000 ptas, D-3,500 ptas, Ds-4,500 ptas, T-4,500 ptas, Ts-5,000 ptas, closed in August, second floor, tel. 91/522-4056). **Hostal Delvi** is simple, clean, and friendly (S-1,800 ptas, D-2,500 ptas,

Ds-3,500 ptas, Ts-4,500 ptas, third floor, tel. 91/522-5998,
Marie NSE). Marie promises these discounted prices to those
with this book.

The cheapest beds are across the street at **Hostal
Lucense** (S-1,500 ptas, D-2,300 ptas, Ds-3,000 ptas, T-3,500
ptas, 200 ptas per shower, Nuñez de Arce 15, tel. 91/522-
4888, run by Sr. and Sra. Muñoz, both interesting characters,
Sr. SE) and **Casa Huéspedes Poza** (same prices and owners,
Nuñez de Arce 9, tel. 91/222-4871). Hopeless romantics
might enjoy playing corkscrew up the rickety cut-glass
elevator to the very simple yet homey **Pensión La
Valenciana**'s old and funky rooms, with springy beds. All
rooms have balconies, three of them overlooking the square
(S-1,500 ptas, D-3,500 ptas, Principe 27, fourth floor,
right on Plaza Santa Ana next to the theater with flags, tel.
91/429-6317, NSE). Because of these three places, I list no
Madrid youth hostels.

Hostal R. Veracruz II, 2 blocks north of Puerta del Sol, is
a tranquil oasis with spotless, well-maintained rooms (Sb-3,500
ptas, Db-4,900 ptas, Tb-6,600 ptas, elevator, air-con, CC:VM,
Victoria 1, third floor, 28012 Madrid, tel. 91/522-7635, fax
91/522-6749, NSE).

Splurges: To be on the same square and spend in a day
what others spend in a week, luxuriate in **Hotel Reina
Victoria** (Sb-20,500 ptas, Db-27,000 ptas, includes breakfast,
CC:VM, Plaza Santa Ana 14, tel. 91/531-4500, fax 91/522-
0307, SE). For a royal, air-conditioned breather and some
cheap entertainment, spit out your gum, step into its lobby,
grab a sofa, and watch the bellboys push the beggars back out
of the revolving doors. **Suite Prado**, 2 blocks south of Plaza
Santa Ana, is expensive but a better value, offering attractive,
air-conditioned suites with a homier feel (Sb/suite-16,000 ptas,
Db/suite-20,000 ptas, cheaper off-season, suites have fridges
and comfy sitting rooms, CC:VMA, Manuel Fernandez y
Gonzalez 10, at the intersection with Venture de la Vega,
28014 Madrid, tel. 91/420-2318, fax 91/420-0559, SE).

Sleeping Elsewhere in Central Madrid
Just off the Plaza Mayor, **Hostal Montalvo** is sprawling,
family-run, comfortable, and just east of the elegant Plaza
Mayor on a quiet, traffic-free street (S-2,700 ptas, Sb-3,700
ptas, D-4,000 ptas, Db-5,000 ptas, Tb-7,300 ptas, elevator,

call a tomorrow

CC:VM, Zaragoza 6, 28012 Madrid, third floor, Metro: Opera, tel. 91/365-5910, some English spoken).

Halfway between the Prado Museum and the Plaza Santa Ana in a quiet, stately neighborhood lie two gems and one suitable hotel, all in the same building with an elevator. At #34 Cervantes (28014 Madrid, Metro: Anton Martin), you'll find the spotless, friendly and comfortable **Hotel Cervantes** (Sb-4,500 ptas, Db-6,000 ptas, CC:VM, third floor, tel. 91/429-2745, NSE), and the equally polished and friendly **Hotel Gonzalo** (Sb-3,800 ptas, Db-5,000 ptas, second floor, tel. 91/429-2714, CC:VM, NSE). The **Hotel Cobrero** is less welcoming, but clean and perfectly sleepable (Sb-3,700, Db-4,700, first floor, tel. 91/429-4171, NSE).

Eating in Madrid

In Spain only Barcelona rivals Madrid for taste-bud thrills. You have two basic dining choices: an atmospheric sit-down meal in a well-chosen restaurant, or a meal of *tapas* (appetizers) in a bar or (more likely) in several bars. Many restaurants are closed in August.

Eating in the Pedestrian Zone Between Puerta del Sol and Gran Vía

Restaurante Puerto Rico has fine food, good prices, and few tourists. Try it now before the menu has English translations (13:00–16:30 and 20:30–24:00, closed Sunday, Chinchilla 2, off Gran Vía on same street as Hotel Cliper, tel. 91/532-2040). Carnivores will devour the grilled meats at **El Gaucho** (Tetuan 34) while vegetarians will prefer the fare and rare nonsmoking ambience at **Artemisa II** at Tres Cruces 4, just off Plaza Carmen (closed Sunday night, CC:VMA, tel. 91/521-8721).

Eating Between the Puerta del Sol and Plaza Santa Ana

For an inexpensive, local-style dinner within 2 blocks of the Puerta del Sol, consider **Restaurante Pozo Real.** It's friendly and popular with locals, with quiet tables in the back (daily 9:00–24:30, Calle del Pozo 6, tel. 91/521-7951). Madrid's best pastry shop is next door (closed Monday). The vegetarian **Artemesia I** offers tasty meals in smoke-free comfort (daily 13:30–16:00 and 21:00–midnight, non-veggie options available, CC:VMA, Via de la Vega 4 off San Jeronimo, tel. 91/429-5092).

Tapas: For maximum fun, people, and atmosphere, go mobile and do the "*tapa* tango"—a local tradition of going from one bar to the next, munching, drinking, and socializing. *Tapas* are toothpick appetizers, salads, and deep-fried foods served in most bars. Madrid is Spain's *tapa* capital. Grab a toothpick and stab something strange—but establish the prices first. Some items are very pricey, and most bars offer larger *raciónes* rather than smaller *tapas*. *Un pincho* is a bite-sized serving (not always available), *una tapa* is a bit more, and *una ración* is half a meal. Say "*un bocadillo*" and it comes on bread as a sandwich. *Caña* is a glass of draft beer.

Prowl the area between Puerta del Sol and Plaza Santa Ana. There's no ideal route, but the little streets (in this book's map) between Puerta del Sol, San Jeronimo, and Plaza Santa Ana hold tasty surprises. From Puerta del Sol, head east to Carrera de San Jeronimo 6 for your first stop: the **Museo del Jamón** (Museum of Ham)—tastefully decorated, unless you're a pig. This frenetic, cheap, stand-up bar is an assembly line of fast and deliciously simple *bocadillos* and *raciónes*. Options are shown in photographs with prices. Just point and eat (daily 9:00–24:00, sit-down restaurant upstairs). Shrimp-lovers, head up the street to tiny **La Casa del Abuelo**, at Victoria 12, where sizzling, expensive little *gambas* go down great with the house wine (daily 11:00–15:30 and 18:00–23:30). Fan out from there, walking each little street within 100 yards. On outdoor restaurant row, the **La Ria** *tapas* bar (Pasaje Matheu 5), has cheap plates of ten mussels—toss the shells on the floor as you smack your lips. Follow Nuñez de Arce up to Plaza Santa Ana, where (on the far side) several upscale *cervecerías*, relaxing and comfortable spots for *tapas*, spill onto the sidewalk. The more civil **Casa Alberto**, a block south of Plaza Santa Ana at the end of Calle Principe, is a classy, tasty *tapas* bar (11:00–01:00, closed Sunday evening and all day Monday, Huertas 18); it's hard to stop at just one *canape de salmon ahumado* (smoked salmon appetizer). The popular dining room in the back has a different, pricier menu (lunch starts at 13:30, dinner at 21:00).

Plaza Santa Ana offers a great late-night scene. Just off the plaza, a tiny alley called Manuel Fernandez y Gonzalez offers plenty of distractions. Try the tiled **Los Gabrieles, Viva Madrid**, or **La Toscana**. As the night progresses, head over to Calle Huertas for more proof that this city never sleeps. Beware the potent concoctions at **La Lupe**.

Eating near the Plaza Mayor

At **Restaurante Rodriguez**, the food's not fancy but hearty (San Cristobal 15, 1 block toward Puerta del Sol from Plaza Mayor, tel. 91/231-1136). Many Americans are drawn to Hemingway's favorite, **Sobrino del Botín** (daily 13:00–16:00 and 20:00–24:00, Cuchilleros 17 near Plaza Mayor, tel. 91/366-4217). Touristy and pricey, it's the last place he'd go now. Those in need of a dirt-cheap but tasty *bocadillo* line up at the **Casa Rua** on Plaza Mayor's southwest corner. Picnic shoppers forage at the San Miguel market (below).

Fast Food, Picnics, and Breakfast

Fast Food: For an easy, light, cheap meal, try **Rodilla**, on the northeast corner of Puerta del Sol at #13 (daily 8:30–20:30). **Pans & Company**, a chain with shops throughout Madrid, offers healthy, tasty sandwiches. Skip the soppy salads (daily 9:00–24:00, Plaza Callão 3, Gran Vía 30, and many more).

Picnics: The department store **El Corte Inglés** has a well-stocked deli, but its produce is sold only in large quantities (10:00–21:00, closed Sundays). A perfect place to assemble a cheap picnic is downtown Madrid's neighborhood market, **Mercado de San Miguel** (9:00–14:00 and 16:00–19:00, closed Saturday afternoon and Sunday; from the Plaza Mayor, face the colorful building and exit from the upper left-hand corner). How about breakfast surrounded by early morning shoppers in the market's café? Get a couple of oranges to go.

Churros con chocolate **for breakfast:** If you like hash browns and eggs in American greasy-spoon joints, you must try the Spanish equivalent: greasy, cigar-shaped fritters dipped in pudding-like chocolate at **Bar Valladolid** (open daily from 7:00, Sunday from 8:00, 2 blocks off the Tío Pepe end of Puerta del Sol, south on Espoz y Mina, turn right on Calle de Cadiz). It's the changing of the guard, as workers of the night finish their day by downing a cognac, and workers of the day start theirs by dipping *churros* into chocolate. (One serving is often plenty for two.) With luck, the *churros* machine in the back will be cooking. Throw your napkin on the floor like you own the place. For something with less grease and more substance, ask for a *tortilla española* (potato omelet), *zumo de naranja* (orange juice), and *café con leche*.

The classier **Chocolatería San Ginés** is another Madrid magnet for *churros* and chocolate (Pasadizo de San Ginés 5, off Calle Arenal near Disco "Joy," tel. 93/365-6546).

Transportation Connections—Madrid

By train to: Toledo (9/day, 75 min, from Madrid Atocha), **Segovia** (9/day, 2 hrs, from Chamartin and 6/day from Atocha), **Ávila** (10/day, 1 hr, from Chamartin and Atocha), **Salamanca** (3/day, 3 hrs, from Chamartin), **Barcelona** (5/day, 8 hrs, from Chamartin and Atocha), **Granada** (3/day including an overnight, 6–9 hrs, from Chamartin and Atocha), **Sevilla** (12/day, 9 hrs, or 3 hrs by AVE, from Atocha), **Córdoba** (11 AVE trains/day, 2 hrs, from Chamartin and Atocha), **Lisbon** (2/day, 8–10 hrs, including an overnight, from Chamartin), **Paris** (5/day, 12–16 hrs, two direct overnights, from Chamartin). Train information: tel. 91/328-9020.

Spain's new AVE bullet train opens up some good itinerary options. Pick up the brochure at the station. Prices vary with times and class. The basic Madrid–Sevilla fare is 9,200 ptas (1,500 ptas less on the almost-as-fast Talgo). AVE is now 85 percent covered by Eurail (so the Madrid–Sevilla–Madrid round-trip costs Eurailers about 2,400 ptas). So far AVE only covers Madrid–Córdoba–Sevilla. Consider this exciting day trip from Madrid: 7:30 depart, 9:15–12:40 in Cordoba, 13:30–21:00 in Sevilla, 23:30 back in Madrid. Reserve each AVE segment.

By bus to: Segovia (hrly, 90 min) and **Ávila** (3/day, 2 hrs), both destinations handled by La Sepulvedana; go to the bus station at Paseo de la Florida 11 (tel. 91/530-4800) past the Hotel Florida Norte (Metro: Principe Pio). To catch a bus to **Toledo** (2/hr, 75 min), go to the brand-new Estación sur Autobuses (Metro: Menendez-Alvaro).

By bus, train, and car to El Escorial: Buses leave from the Intercambiador bus station at Madrid's Metro stop Monocloa (as you exit the Metro, follow signs to "Autobuses" and Calle Princesa) and drop you in the El Escorial center (hrly, 1 hr, Autocares Herranz, tel. 91/890-4100). One bus a day is designed to let travelers do the Valley of the Fallen as a side trip from El Escorial; the bus leaves El Escorial at 15:15 (15-min trip) and leaves Valley of the Fallen at 17:30. Trains run to El Escorial but let you off a 20-minute walk (or a shuttle-bus ride, 2/hr) from the monastery and city center.

By car, visiting El Escorial and Valley of the Fallen on the way to Segovia is easy (except on Monday, when both sights are closed).

Avoid driving in Madrid. Rent your car when you're ready to leave. To save money, make car rental arrangements through your travel agent before you leave home. In Madrid try Europcar (San Leonardo 8, tel. 91/541-8892, airport: tel. 91/305-4420), Hertz (Gran Vía 88, tel. 91/542-5803, airport: tel. 91/305-8452), or Avis (Gran Vía 60, tel. 91/548-4203, airport: tel. 91/305-4273). Ask if your car can be delivered free to your hotel.

NORTHWEST OF MADRID:
EL ESCORIAL, VALLEY OF THE FALLEN, SEGOVIA, SALAMANCA

Don't slip into and out of Madrid by train before considering several fine side trips northwest of Spain's capital city.

Spain has a lavish, brutal, and complicated history. An hour from Madrid, tour the imposing and fascinating palace of El Escorial, headquarters of the Spanish Inquisition. Nearby, at the awesome Valley of the Fallen, pay tribute to the countless victims of Spain's bloody Civil War.

Segovia, with its remarkable Roman aqueduct and romantic castle, is also an easy side trip from Madrid. Farther out, you can walk the perfectly preserved medieval walls of Ávila. And, at Salamanca, enjoy Spain's best town square, swirling in a frisky college-town ambience.

Planning Your Time

See El Escorial and the Valley of the Fallen together in less than a day. By car, do them en route to Segovia; by bus, make it a day trip from Madrid.

Segovia is worth a half-day of sightseeing and is a joy at night. Ávila is not without charm, but merits only a quick stop to marvel at its medieval walls, if you're driving and in the neighborhood.

Salamanca, with its art, university, and Spain's greatest Plaza Mayor, is worth a day and a night but is stuck out in the tules. On a three-week Barcelona–Lisbon "open-jaws" itinerary, I'd hook south from Madrid and skip Salamanca. If you're doing a circular trip, Salamanca is a natural stop halfway between Portugal and Madrid.

Madrid Area

In total, these sights are worth a maximum of three days if you're in Iberia for less than a month. If you're in Spain for just a week, I'd still squeeze in a look at El Escorial and the Valley of the Fallen.

EL ESCORIAL

The Monasterio de San Lorenzo de El Escorial is a symbol of power rather than elegance. This 16th-century palace, 30 miles northwest of Madrid, gives us a better feel for the Counter-Reformation and the Inquisition than any other building. Built at a time when Catholic Spain felt threatened by Protestant "heretics," its construction dominated the Spanish economy for 20 years (1563–1584). Because of this bully in the national budget, Spain has almost nothing else to show from this most powerful period of her history. The giant, gloomy building (gray-black stone, 2,600 windows, 1,200 doors, over 100 miles of passages, 200 yards long, 150 yards wide, 1,600 overwhelmed tourists) looks more like a prison than a palace. Four hundred years ago, the enigmatic and introverted King Philip II ruled his bulky empire and

directed the Inquisition from here. To 16th-century followers
of Luther, this place epitomized the evil of Catholicism.
Today it's a time capsule of Spain's "Golden Age," packed
with history, art, and Inquisition ghosts.

El Escorial looks confusing at first, but you simply follow
the arrows and signs in one continuous walk-through. Guides
in each room can answer basic questions. The side entrance
(off Grimaldi) is the best place to start. This is the general
order you'll follow (though some rooms are sure to be closed
for renovation). The small **Museo de Arquitectura** has easy-
to-appreciate models of the palace and the machinery used to
construct it. The **Museo de Pintura**, packed with big paintings in small rooms, features works by Titian, Veronese,
Rubens, Bosch, van Dyck, and van der Weyden. The **king's
apartments** are notable for their austerity, with a bed so small
you wonder where today's king-size beds came from. Stairs
take you down into the **Pantéon**, the gilded resting place of 23
kings and queens, four centuries worth of Spanish monarchy.
The nine-chambered Pantéon de los Infantes holds the
remains of various royal children and relatives. Paintings by
Ribera, El Greco, Titian, and Velázquez elegantly decorate the
salas capitulares (chapter rooms). The **cloister** (which may be
partially closed) glows with bright, newly restored paintings by
Tibaldi.

Follow the signs to the **church.** The altar is spectacular
when illuminated (put 100 ptas in the small box near the
church entrance, just before the gated doors), but the highlight is Cellini's marble sculpture *The Cruxifixion* (to the left
as you enter).

Last comes the *biblioteca*, the library (have your ticket
handy). Try not to rush this room. The ceiling is a burst of
color, and the meshed bookcases feature illustrated books. At
the far end of the room, the elaborate model of the solar system
looks like a giant gyroscope, revolving unmistakably around the
earth. Notice the misshapen North America.

Admission to the palace is 850 ptas (Tuesday–Sunday
10:00–18:00 from April–September, enter before ticket office
closes at 16:00, closed Monday, closes an hour earlier off-
season, tel. 925/890-5011). A tour is included if you pay 950 ptas
for admission, but the tour is limited to the apartments and
mausoleum only; tours are available only from 10:00–12:30 and
16:00–18:00, and English tours occur only if at least 30 people

gather. You'll find scanty but sufficient captions in English within the palace. For more information, skip the tour and get the *Visitor's Guide: Monastery of San Lorenzo El Real de El Escorial* (900 ptas, available at any of several shops in the palace). It follows the general route you'll take and is better than the cheaper but overly comprehensive book-length *Official Guide* (600 ptas).

If you arrive at El Escorial by bus, walk from the bus stop a half-block up Florida Blanca to the TI at #10 (weekdays 10:00–14:00 and 15:00–17:00, Saturday 10:00–14:00, closed Sunday, tel. 91/890-1554). Another block up Florida Blanca brings you to a crossroad. To your right are two pleasant, stair-stepped plazas (Jacinto Benavente and San Lorenzo), dotted with trees and cafés. To your left, the street called Grimaldi takes you downhill to the side (and easiest) entrance to the palace.

El Escorial town is worth a browse. To shop for a picnic, stop by the Mercado Publico on Calle del Rey 9, a four-minute walk from the palace (9:00–14:00, closed Sunday). For a change from Spanish fare, try pizza at **Tavolata Reale** (near El Escorial entrance, tel. 91/809-4591) or **Restaurante China Hong Kong** (Calle San Anton 6, tel. 91/896-1894).

Transportation Connections—El Escorial

From Madrid: Buses leave from the Intercambiador bus station at Madrid's Metro stop Monocloa (as you exit the Metro, follow signs to "Autobuses" and Calle Princesa) and drop you in the El Escorial center (12/day, 1 hr, Autocares Herranz, tel. 925/890-4100).

The train isn't a good choice. Although trains leave twice hourly from Madrid's Atocha station, you're dropped a 20-minute walk (or shuttle-bus ride, 2/hr) from El Escorial center and monastery.

Consider combining a day trip to El Escorial and the Valley of the Fallen. The bus company Autocares Herranz offers one round-trip bus connection every afternoon (except Monday, when sights are closed) for tourists interested in seeing the Valley of the Fallen from El Escorial (see Valley of the Fallen, below).

Before you leave El Escorial by bus to return to Madrid, you'll need to stop at the bar on Calle del Rey, just around the corner from the bus stop, to get "confirmed" (no charge) even if you already have a round-trip ticket.

VALLEY OF THE FALLEN (EL VALLE DE LOS CAÍDOS)

Eight kilometers from El Escorial, high in the Guadarrama Mountains, a 150-yard-tall granite cross marks an immense and powerful underground monument to the victims of Spain's 20th-century nightmare—its Civil War (1936–1939).

The stairs that lead to the imposing monument are grouped in sets of tens, meant to symbolize the Ten Commandments (including "Thou shalt not kill"—hmm). The emotional *Pieta* draped over the entrance was sculpted by Juan de Avalos, the same artist who created the dramatic figures of the four evangelists at the base of the cross.

A solemn silence and a stony chill fill the "basilica," larger (860 feet long) than St. Peter's, as Spaniards pass under the huge, forbidding angels of fascism to visit the grave of General Franco. The term "basilica" normally designates a church built over the remains of a saint, not a fascist dictator. Franco's prisoners, the enemies of the right, dug this memorial out of solid rock.

The sides of the monument are lined with 16th-century Brussels tapestries of the Apocalypse and side chapels containing alabaster copies of the most famous Virgin Mary statues in Spain.

Interred behind the high altar and side chapels are the remains of the approximately 50,000 people, both Republicanos and Franco's Nacionalistas, who lost their lives in the war. Regrettably the urns are not visible, so it is Franco who takes center stage. His grave, strewn with flowers, lies behind the high altar. In front of the altar is the grave of José Antonio, the founder of Spanish fascism. Between these fascists' graves is the statue of a crucified Christ. The seeping stones seem to weep.

On your way out, stare into the eyes of those angels with swords and two right wings and think about all the "heroes" who keep dying "for God and country," at the request of the latter (650 ptas, Tuesday–Sunday 9:30–19:00, closed Monday).

The expansive view from the monument's terrace includes the peaceful, forested valley and sometimes snow-streaked mountains. A funicular climbs to the base of the cross and a better view (350 ptas round-trip, 11:00–13:30 and 16:00–18:30). Near the parking lot (and bus stop) are a small snack bar and picnic tables.

Without a car, the easiest way to get to the Valley of the Fallen is from El Escorial by an Autocares Herranz bus (1/day,

15 min, leaves El Escorial at 15:15, leaves the Valley of the Fallen at 17:30, 870-pta round-trip includes admission to the site). Buy your ticket in El Escorial at the bar on Calle del Rey, just around the corner from the bus stop (the bus driver will point the way).

SEGOVIA

Fifty miles from Madrid, this town of 55,000 boasts a great Roman aqueduct, a cathedral, and a castle. Segovia is a medieval "ship" ready for your inspection. Start at the stern— the aqueduct—and stroll up Calle de Cervantes to the prickly Gothic masts of the cathedral. Explore the tangle of narrow streets around Plaza Mayor, then descend to the Alcázar at the bow.

Orientation (tel. code: 921)

Tourist Information: The two helpful tourist offices, at Plaza Mayor 10 (tel. 921/46-03-34) and on Plaza del Azoguejo, under the aqueduct (tel. 921/44-03-02), are open at the same time (daily 9:00–14:00 and 17:00–20:00, shorter hours off-season).

Arrival in Segovia: The station is a 30-minute walk from the center. Take a city bus from the train station to get to Plaza Mayor (2/hr, 100 ptas, leaving from the same side of the street as the station—confirm by asking, "*¿Para Plaza Mayor?*"). Taxis are a reasonable option (500 ptas). If you arrive by bus, it's a 15-minute walk to the center (turn left out of the bus station and continue straight across the roundabout onto Calle Ladrera). Day-trippers can store luggage at the train station but not at the bus station. Drivers can park their cars overnight for free in the park facing the Alcázar (gate closes at about 21:00).

Helpful Hints: The Telefónica phone office has handy metered phone booths (Monday–Saturday 10:00–14:00 and 17:00–21:30, closed Sunday, accepts credit cards for charges over 500 ptas, on Plaza de los Huertos). If you buy handicrafts such as tablecloths from street vendors, make sure the item you're buying is the one you actually get; some unscrupulous vendors substitute inferior goods at the last minute.

Sights—Segovia

▲**Roman Aqueduct**—Built by the Romans, who ruled Spain for more than 500 years, this 2,000-year-old acueducto

Segovia

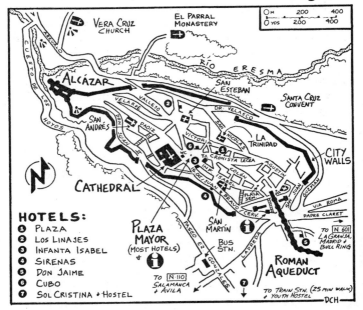

Romano is 2,500 feet long and 100 feet high, has 118 arches, was made without any mortar, and still works. It's considered Segovia's backup plumbing. From underneath the aqueduct, climb the steps off Plaza Azoguejo for an overhead view.

▲**Cathedral**—Segovia's cathedral was Spain's last major Gothic building. Embellished to the hilt with pinnacles and flying buttresses, the exterior is a great example of the final overripe stage of Gothic called "Flamboyant." The dark, spacious, and elegantly simple interior provides a delightful contrast (cathedral is free, 250 ptas for the small but interesting museum and cloister, daily 9:00–19:00, off-season it closes from 13:00–15:00 and at 18:00).

▲▲**Alcázar**—This Disneyesque rebuilt exaggeration of the old castle, which burned down 100 years ago, is fun to explore and worthwhile for the view of Segovia from the tower (375 ptas, daily 10:00–19:00; off-season until 18:00, get the 25-pta English brochure). Don't miss the Throne Room (Sala del Solio), where Columbus came to get his fantasy financed.

Strolling—Roman and Romanesque Segovia was made for

roamin'. Rub shoulders with Segovian yuppies parading up and down Calle Juan Bravo. For subtler charm, wander the back streets, away from the trinket shops and ladies selling lace. Segovia has a wealth of 12th- and 13th-century Romanesque churches (usually open during mass, often around 8:00 and 19:30, ask at TI). Look Catholic and drop in. The San Justo church has well-preserved frescoes (free, Tuesday–Saturday 12:00–14:00 and 16:00–19:00, off-season until 18:00, near base of aqueduct, a couple of blocks from Plaza Azoguejo, in the newer side of town).

▲**Vera Cruz Church**—This 12-sided, 13th-century Romanesque church was built by the Knights Templar and used to house a piece of the "true cross" (175 ptas, 10:30–13:30 and 15:30–19:00, closed Monday; off-season until 18:00, closed in November, outside of town beyond the castle, about 20 minutes walk from main square). There's a postcard city view from here, and more views follow as you continue around Segovia on the small road below the castle labeled *ruta turística panoramica.*

▲**La Granja Palace**—This "Little Versailles," 10 kilometers south of Segovia, is much smaller and happier than El Escorial. The palace and gardens were built by the homesick French King Philip V, grandson of Louis XIV. It's a must for tapestry-lovers. Fountain displays send local crowds into a frenzy at 17:30 on most summer Wednesdays, Saturdays, Sundays, and holidays (confirm schedule at Segovia TI). Entry to the palace includes a required 45-minute guided tour, usually in Spanish (650 ptas, Tuesday–Sunday 10:00–18:00, closed Monday; off-season hours: Tuesday–Saturday 10:00–13:30 and 15:00–17:00, Sunday 10:00–14:00; tel. 921/47-00-19). Eight buses a day make the 30-minute trip from Segovia.

Sleeping in Segovia
(140 ptas = about $1, tel. code: 921, zip code 40001)
Sleep Code: **S**=Single, **D**=Double/Twin, **T**=Triple, **Q**=Quad, **b**=bathroom, **t**=toilet only, **s**=shower only, **CC**=Credit Card (**V**isa, **M**asterCard, **A**mex), **SE**=Speaks English, **NSE**=No English.

The best places are on or near the central Plaza Mayor. This is where the city action is: the cheapest and best bars, most touristic and *típico* eateries, and the tourist office. Segovia is crowded on weekends and in July and August, so arrive early or call ahead. The 7 percent IVA tax is not included in the price and neither is breakfast.

Hostal Plaza is just off Plaza Mayor toward the aqueduct. You'll find *serioso* management and long, snaky corridors, but the rooms are clean and cozy (S-3,000 ptas, one Sb-4,800 ptas, D-4,000 ptas, Db-6,500 ptas, Tb-7,100 ptas, CC:VM, Cronista Lecea 11, tel. 921/46-03-03, fax 921/46-03-05, NSE).

Hotel Los Linajes is ultra-classy, with rusticity mixed into its newly poured concrete. This poor-man's *parador* is a few blocks beyond the Plaza Mayor, with commanding views and modern niceties (Sb-7,200 ptas, Db-10,500 ptas, Tb-12,500 ptas, cheaper off-season, breakfast-775 ptas, parking, elevator, CC:VMA, Dr. Velasco 9, tel. 921/46-04-75, fax 921/46-04-79). From Plaza Mayor, take Escuderos downhill; at the five-way intersection, angle right on Dr. Velasco. Drivers, follow brown signs from aqueduct.

Hotel Infanta Isabel, right on Plaza Mayor, is the ritziest hotel in the Old Town. It's friendly, elegant, and pricey, but cheaper off-season (Sb-7,500 ptas, Db-10,500–13,000 ptas depending on room size, elevator, CC:VMA, tel. 921/46-13-00, fax 921/43-32-40, SE).

A place I don't like that fills a void in Segovia is the big, stuffy, hotelesque **Hotel Sirenas** (Sb-7,000 ptas, Db-8,000 ptas, cheaper off-season, air-con, elevator, CC:VM, 3 blocks down from the Plaza Mayor at Calle Juan Bravo 30, tel. 921/46-26-63 fax 921/46-26-57, NSE).

Hostal Don Jaime, near the base of the aqueduct, is shiny-new, well-maintained, and friendly (S-2,800 ptas, Db-5,000 ptas, Tb-6,300 ptas, Qb-7,000 ptas, CC:VM, Ochoa Ondategui 8, from TI at aqueduct, cross under the aqueduct and angle right uphill on a side street for 2 blocks, tel. 921/44-47-87, NSE).

Right on Plaza Mayor at #4 is a tiny and dark but clean enough place (look hard for the "Hospedaje Habitaciones" sign). The **Hospedaje Cubo** has four simple, sinkless but tidy rooms; ask for a room *con ventana* to avoid the window-less room (S-1,200 ptas, D-2,700 ptas, T-4,000 ptas, ask first at next-door Turuta Bar if rooms are available before climbing the stairs to Plaza Mayor 4, tel. 921/46-09-17, NSE). **Pensión Ferri**, around the corner, is a last resort (S-1,600 ptas, D-2,300 ptas, shower-300 ptas, Escuderos 10, one-half block off Plaza Mayor, tel. 921/46-09-57, NSE).

Across from the train station is the **Hostal Sol Cristina** (S-2,500 ptas, D-3,800 ptas, Db-5,000 ptas, T-5,000 ptas, Tb-7,500 ptas, Calle Obispo Quesada 40, tel. 921/42-75-13, NSE), and its nearby twin, **Hostal Residencia Sol Cristina-Dos** (same prices, same phone number).

The **Segovia Youth Hostel** is a great hostel—easygoing, comfortable, clean, friendly, and very cheap (open July and August only, Paseo Conde de Sepulveda between the train and bus stations, tel. 921/42-00-27).

Eating in Segovia

Look for Segovia's culinary claim to fame, roast suckling pig (*cochinillo asado*: 21 days of mother's milk, into the oven, and onto your plate). It's worth a splurge here or in Toledo or Salamanca. While you're at it, try *sopa Castellana*, soup mixed with eggs, ham, and garlic bread.

The **Mesón de Candido**, one of the top restaurants in Castile, is worth the splurge if you'd like to spend 3,500 ptas on a memorable dinner (daily 12:00–16:00 and 20:00–23:00, Plaza del Azoguejo 3, under the aqueduct, tel. 921/42-81-03 for reservations).

Just off the Plaza Mayor, serving *típico* regional specialties, is the touristy **La Oficina** (daily 10:00–16:00 and 20:00–23:30, off-season closed Monday; quarter pig-3,500 ptas, whole pig-13,000 ptas, English menu; Cronista Lecea 10, tel. 921/46-02-86). **Narizotas** is a more modern place, attracting locals and tourists with 1,800-pta *platos combinados* (daily 13:00–16:00 and 20:00–23:30, Plaza de Medina del Campo 1, tel. 921/46-26-79).

The cheapest bars and eateries line Calle de Infanta Isabel, just off the Plaza Mayor. For nightlife, the bars on Plaza Mayor, Calle de Infanta Isabel, and Calle Isabel la Católica are packed.

Breakfast at the cafeteria bar **Korppus** (Plaza del Corpus 1, a block down C. I. Católica from the Plaza Mayor, look for blue awnings). There's no real supermarket in the Old Town, but an outdoor produce market thrives on Plaza de los Huertos (Thursday 8:00–14:00).

Transportation Connections—Segovia

By train to: Madrid (9/day, 2 hrs, Chamartin and Atocha stations). If day-tripping from Madrid, look for the Cercanias (commuter train) ticket window and departure board in the Madrid train station and get a return schedule. Train info: tel. 921/42-07-74.

By bus to: La Granja (8/day, 30 min), Ávila (3/day, 45 min), **Salamanca** (3/day, 3–4 hrs, transfer in Labajos; consider busing from Segovia to Ávila for a visit and then continue to Salamanca by bus or train), **Madrid** (hrly, 90 min; departs from Madrid's La Sepulvedana bus station, Metro: Principe Pio, just past the Hotel Florida Norte, Paseo de la Florida 11, tel. 921/530-4800).

ÁVILA

A popular side trip from Madrid, the birthplace of St. Teresa is famous only for its perfectly preserved medieval walls. You can climb onto them through the gardens of the *parador*. Ávila's Old Town is charming, with several fine churches and monasteries. Pick up a box of the famous local sweets called *yemas*— like a soft-boiled egg yolk cooled and sugared.

Ávila is well connected to **Segovia** (3 buses/day, 45 min), **Madrid** (10 trains/day, 2 hrs, both Chamartin and Atocha stations), and **Salamanca** (5 trains/day, 2 hrs; 3 buses/day, 2 hrs). By car, it's easy and worth a look if you're driving from Segovia or Madrid to Salamanca.

SALAMANCA

This sunny sandstone city boasts Spain's grandest plaza, its oldest university, and a fascinating history all swaddled in a strolling, college-town ambience.

Salamanca is a youthful and untouristy Toledo. The city is a series of monuments and clusters of cloisters. The many students help keep prices down. *Paseo* with the local crowd down Rua Mayor and through Plaza Mayor. The young people congregate until late in the night, chanting and cheering, talking and singing. When I asked a local woman why young men all alone on the Plaza Mayor suddenly break into song, she said, "Doesn't it happen where you live?"

Orientation (tel. code: 923)

Tourist Information: The more convenient Turismo is on the Plaza Mayor (under the arch, on the right as you face the clock; Monday–Saturday 9:00–14:00, 16:30–18:30, Sunday from 10:00; tel. 923/21-83-42). The other TI, covering Salamanca and the

Castille region, is in the Casa de las Conchas on Rua Mayor (similar hours, tel. 923/26-85-71). Temporary TIs also spring up in July and August at the train and bus stations.

Arrival in Salamanca: From Salamanca's train and bus stations it's a 20-minute walk or an easy bus ride to Plaza Mayor. From the train station, turn left out of the station and walk down to the ring road, cross it at Plaza España, then angle slightly left up Calle Azafranal. Bus #1 from the train station lets you off at Plaza Mercado (the market), next to Plaza Mayor.

From the bus station, turn right and walk down Avenue Filiberto Villalobos; take a left on the ring road and the first right on Ramon y Cajal. Bus #4 takes you to the city center; the closest stop is on Gran Vía, about 4 blocks from Plaza Mayor (ask a fellow passenger, "*¿Para Plaza Mayor?*"). Taxis to the center cost around 500 ptas.

Helpful Hints: The RENFE office, near Plaza Mayor, sells train tickets and *couchette* reservations (Monday–Friday 9:00–14:00 and 17:00–19:00, cash only, Plaza de Libertad 10, NSE but helpful). Some travel agencies, such as Viajes Salamanca next to the Turismo, sell city-to-city bus tickets.

Sights—Salamanca

▲**Plaza Mayor**—Built in 1755, this ultimate Spanish plaza is a fine place to nurse a cup of coffee and watch the world go by. The town hall, with the clock, grandly overlooks the square, and the Arch of the Toro (built into the eastern wall) leads to the covered market. Imagine the excitement of the days, just 100 years ago, when bullfights were held in the square. How about coffee at the town's oldest café, Café Novelty?

▲▲**Cathedrals, Old and New**—These cool-on-a-hot-day cathedrals are both richly ornamented and they share buttresses. You get to the old through the new. Before entering the new church, check out the ornate Plateresque facade (Spain's version of Flamboyant Gothic).

The "new" cathedral was begun in 1513 and finished in 1733, with Renaissance and Baroque parts added later (free and lackluster). The recorded music helps. The *coro*, or choir, blocks up half of the church, but its wood carving is sumptuous; look up to see the elaborate organ.

The entrance to the old cathedral (12th-century Romanesque) is near the rear of the new one (300 ptas, daily 10:00–13:30 and 16:00–19:30). Sit in a front pew to study the

Salamanca

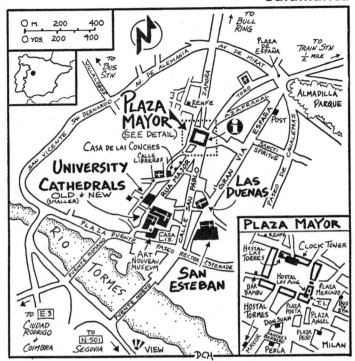

53 altarpiece scenes from Mary's life (by the Italian Florentino, 1445), and the dramatic Last Judgment fresco above it—notice Jesus sending condemned souls into the literal jaws of hell.

Then head into the cloister and explore the chapels, notable for their unusual tombs, ornate altarpieces, and ceilings with leering faces. Capilla San Bartolome de Los Anajas has a gorgeously carved 16th-century alabaster tomb and wooden Moorish organ.

▲▲**University**—Salamanca University, the oldest in Spain (1230), was one of Europe's leading centers of learning for 400 years. Columbus came here for travel tips. Today many Americans enjoy its excellent summer program. The old lecture halls around the cloister, where many of Spain's Golden Age heroes studied, are open to the public (300 ptas, Monday–Saturday 9:30–13:00 and 16:00–19:00, Sunday

10:00–13:00, the free English info sheet is full of details; enter from Patio de Escuela, off Calle Libreros). Some of the rooms are still used by the university for prestigious academic ceremonies.

In the Hall of Fray Luis de León, the tables and benches are made of narrow wooden beams, whittled down by centuries of studious doodling. The professor spoke from the church-threatening *catedra*, or pulpit. It was here that free-thinking Fray Luis de León, after the Inquisition jailed and tortured him for five years, returned to his place and started his first post-imprisonment lecture with, "As we were saying yesterday . . . "

The altarpiece in the chapel depicts professors swearing to Mary's virginity (how did they know?), and the library upstairs is definitely worth the climb. Check out the cloister's ceiling outside the library for home-decorating ideas.

The entrance portal of the university is a great example of Spain's Plateresque style—masonry so intricate it looks like silverwork. The people studying the facade aren't art fans. They're trying to find a tiny frog on a skull that students looked to for good luck.

As you leave the university, you'll see the statue of Fray Luis de León. Behind him, to your left (his right), is the entrance to a peaceful courtyard containing the Museum of the University, notable for Gallego's fanciful 16th-century *Sky of Salamanca* (included in university admission, closes one hour earlier).

▲**Museo Art Nouveau y Art Deco**—Located in the Casa Lis, this new museum is a refreshing change of pace with its beautifully-displayed collection of stained glass, jewelry, and statues (Calle Gibraltar 14, between the cathedrals and the river, tel. 923/12-14-25).

Casa de las Conches—The aptly named "House of Shells," dating from the 15th century, is a landmark on Rua Mayor (free, Monday–Friday 9:00–21:00, weekends 10:00–14:00 and 16:00–19:00). Go upstairs for a close-up view of the powerful towers of the 17th-century Clerecia church. The church, worth a look, is open sporadic afternoons.

Church of San Esteban—Dedicated to St. Stephen (Esteban) the martyr, this complex contains a cloister, pantheon of tombs, museum, sacristy, and church. Before you enter, notice the Plateresque facade and its bas-relief of the stoning of St. Stephen. The crucifixion above is by Cellini. Once inside, follow the free English pamphlet and arrows. Upstairs you'll find the museum (with illustrated 16th-century choir books at the far end) and the entrance to the choir. The church is overwhelmed by a Churriguera altarpiece, a textbook example of the style named after him. Quietly ponder the gold-plated cottage cheese, as tourists retch and say "too much" in their mother tongue (200 ptas, daily 9:00–13:30 and 16:00–19:30).

Convento de las Dueñas—Next door, the much simpler *convento* is a joy. It consists of a double-decker cloister with a small museum of religious art. Check out the stone meanies exuberantly decorating the capitals on the cloister's upper deck (200 ptas, daily 10:30–13:00 and 16:15–19:00). The nuns sell sweets daily except Sunday (375 ptas for a box).

Flea Market—Salamanca's Rastro turns Plaza del Puente (near the Roman bridge) into a huge garage sale every Sunday (9:00–14:00).

Honorable Mention—Romantics will enjoy the low-slung Roman bridge, much of it original, spanning the Rio Tormes. The ancient (pre-Roman) headless bull, blindly guarding the entrance to the bridge, is a symbol of the city. Nearby, at the Parque Fluvial, you can rent rowboats.

Sleeping in Salamanca
(140 ptas = about $1, tel. code: 923)
Sleep Code: **S**=Single, **D**=Double/Twin, **T**=Triple, **Q**=Quad, **b**=bathroom, **t**=toilet only, **s**=shower only, **CC**=Credit Card (Visa, MasterCard, Amex), **SE**=Speaks English, **NSE**=No English.

Salamanca, being a student town, has plenty of good eating and sleeping values. All my listings are on or within a three-minute walk of the Plaza Mayor; directions are given from the Plaza Mayor, assuming you are facing the building with the clock (e.g., 3 o'clock is 90 degrees to your right as you face the clock). The 7 percent IVA tax is included only in the prices charged by the cheaper hotels.

Hostal Los Angeles, at about 3 o'clock, has simple but cared-for rooms, with a few overlooking the square. Stand on the balcony and inhale the essence of Spain (S-1,800 ptas, D-2,800 ptas, T-4,000 ptas, Plaza Mayor 10, 37002 Salamanca, tel. 923/21-81-66, Louis and Sabina NSE). To try for a view, ask, "*Con vista, por favor.*" If that fails, avoid the windowless room by asking, "*Con ventana*" (window).

Hotel Las Torres offers a regal on-the-square option. The rooms are comfortable and the glass elevator is *muy* modern (Sb-9,000 ptas, Db-12,000 ptas, CC:VMA, Plaza Mayor 47, under the clock, 37002 Salamanca, tel. 923/21-21-00, fax 923/21-21-01, SE). Rooms with views cost the same as rooms without views.

Hotel Don Juan, just off Plaza Mayor, has classy, comfy rooms and an attached restaurant (Sb-6,500 ptas, Db-9,000 ptas, Tb-12,000 ptas, cheaper off-season, elevator, air-con, double-paned windows, CC:VM, exit Plaza Mayor at about 5 o'clock, turn right, Quintana 6, 37001 Salamanca, tel. 923/26-14-73, fax 923/26-24-75, SE).

Hotel Milan is your best normal-hotel-budget bet, with a friendly yet professional atmosphere, a TV lounge, and quiet, bright rooms (Sb-3,700 ptas, Db-5,500 ptas, elevator, CC:VM, leave the Plaza Mayor about 5 o'clock and go left around fancy hotel to Plaza del Angel 5, 37001 Salamanca, tel. 923/21-75-18, fax 923/21-96-97, NSE).

The clean and homey **Hostal La Perla Salmantina** is a cozy gem in an ideal, quiet location (D-3,500 ptas, Ds-4,000 ptas, Db-4,800 ptas, exit Plaza Mayor at about 6 o'clock and walk down the Rua Mayor, then left to Sánchez Barbero 7, 37001 Salamanca, tel. & fax 923/21-76-56, NSE).

The handy **Hostal Tormes** is a student-type residence with big, clean, spartan rooms on the pedestrian street connecting the Plaza Mayor and the university (S-1,700 ptas, D-3,000 ptas, Db-3,800 ptas, Tb-4,800 ptas, shower-200 ptas, Rua Mayor 20, 37008 Salamanca, tel. 923/21-96-83, NSE).

Hostal Plaza Mayor has 19 rooms with bath and a good location just southwest of Plaza Mayor (Sb-4,000 ptas, Db-6,500 ptas, Plaza del Corrillo 20, attached restaurant, tel. 923/26-20-20, fax 923/21-75-48).

Eating in Salamanca

There are plenty of good, inexpensive restaurants between the Plaza Mayor and the Gran Vía and as you leave the Plaza Mayor toward the Rua Mayor. Just wander and eat at your own discovery or try **Café Novelty** (Plaza Mayor's oldest coffee shop) or any of several places on Calle Bermejeros, such as **Taberna de Pilatos** (at #5, 13:00–15:00 and 21:00–03:00, closed Sunday).

Restaurante Isidro has a super assortment of seafood and meat dishes (daily 13:00–16:30 and 20:00–23:00, menu of the day-1,100 ptas, Pozo Amarillo 19, about a block north of the covered market, close to Plaza Mayor, tel. 923/26-28-48). **Restaurante Dulcinea** is a classier, pricier version of the Isidro (menu of the day-1,400–1,950 ptas, Pozo Amarillo 5, tel. 923/21-78-43).

The **Mandala** is popular with the younger crowd for its tasty *tapas*, attractive setting, and good prices (daily 8:00–24:00, Calle Serranos 9–11, from Casa de las Conches, follow Rua Antigua alongside Clerecia church for 2 blocks, tel. 923/12-33-42). Wash down your *tapas* or *plato combinado* with a *batido* (milkshake).

Tops for *tapas* in Salamanca is the **Café Chinitas**, one of several *tapas* bars lining Calle Van Dyck. It's a 15-minute walk from Plaza Mayor, but its prices and selection are great. On a hot day, the iced *gazpacho* (spicy tomato juice) is a spiritual experience. It's offered daily in summer; otherwise, hope for an "*Hay Gazpacho*" sign (daily 8:00–01:00, Van Dyck 14-16, from Plaza Mayor, follow Toro north as it changes its name to Maria Auxiliadora; after you cross Avenida de Portugal, take the third left, tel. 923/25-02-93). Runner-up, and far more central, is the **Bar Bambu**, offering lots of cheap, good *tapas* just off the southwest corner of Plaza Mayor (daily 9:00–01:30, Calle Prior 4, pass the Burger King and immediately head downstairs). Overlooking the Plaza Mayor, the **Cervantes Bar** (near the TI) serves great *tapas* and meals to a mainly local crowd of all ages.

Salamanca's high student population supports a vast array of trendy hangouts. Current hotspots include **Cum Laude** (across from Bar Bambu) and the amazing **De Laval Genoves Submarino,** where the interior looks and feels like an actual submarine (Calle San Justo 27-31, five-minute walk east of Plaza Mayor). Other good, centrally-located *tapas* bars can be found at **El Candil** (on Ventura Ruiz Aguilera) and **La Covachuela**, where the waiter will amaze you with coin tricks (in the Portales de San Antonio; establish prices before ordering).

The covered *mercado* on Plaza Mercado (8:00–14:00, closed Sunday) is ideal for picnic gatherers. And if you always wanted seconds at communion, buy a bag of giant communion wafers, a local specialty called *obleas*.

Transportation Connections—Salamanca
By train to: Madrid (3/day, 3 hrs, Madrid's Chamartin station), **Ávila** (3/day, 1.5 hrs; also 3 buses/day), **Barcelona**

(1/day, 10 hrs; also 1 bus/day), **Coimbra** (1/day, 6 hrs, departure about 5:00; taxis are available at any hour at Plaza Mercado to get you to the station, for about 600 ptas). Train information: tel. 923/12-02-02.

By bus to: Segovia (3/day, 34 hrs, transfer in Labajos or Ávila), **Ciudad Rodrigo** (7/day, 1 hr). Bus info: tel. 923/23-22-66.

CIUDAD RODRIGO

(Worth a visit only if you're traveling from Salamanca to Coimbra.) This rough-and-tumble old town of 16,000 people caps a hill overlooking the Río Agueda. Spend an hour wandering among the Renaissance mansions that line its streets and exploring its cathedral and Plaza Mayor. Have lunch or a snack at **El Sanatorio** (Plaza Mayor 14). The *tapas* are cheap, the crowd is local, and the walls are a Ciudad Rodrigo scrapbook, including some bullfighting that makes the Three Stooges look demure.

Ciudad Rodrigo's cathedral has some entertaining carvings in the choir and some pretty racy work in its cloisters. Who said, "When you've seen one Gothic church, you've seen 'em all"?

The tourist information office is just inside the old wall near the cathedral (tel. 923/46-05-61). The Plaza Mayor is a 2-block walk from there.

Ciudad Rodrigo is a convenient stop on the Salamanca–Coimbra drive. Buses connect Salamanca and Ciudad Rodrigo with surprising efficiency in about an hour. From there you can connect (with less ease) to Coimbra.

Route Tips for Drivers

Madrid to El Escorial to Valley of the Fallen to Segovia
(50 miles): Taxi to your car-rental office (or ask if they'll deliver the car to your hotel). Pick up the car by 8:30 and ask directions to highway A6. Follow "A6-Valladolid" signs to the clearly marked exit on M505 to El Escorial. Get to El Escorial by 9:30 to beat the crowds. The nearby **Silla de Felipe** (Philip's Seat) is a rocky viewpoint where the king would come to admire his palace being built.

From El Escorial, follow "C600-Valle de los Caídos" signs to the Valley of the Fallen. You'll see the huge cross marking it in the distance. After the tollbooth, follow "Basilica" signs to the parking place (toilets, tacky souvenirs, and cafeteria). As you leave, turn left to Guadarrama on C600, go under the highway, and follow signs to Puerto de Navacerrada. From there, you climb past flocks of sheep, over a 6,000-foot-high mountain pass (Pto. de Navacerrada) into old Castile, through La Granja to Segovia. (Segovia is much more important than La Granja, but garden-lovers enjoy a quick La Granja stop.)

At the Segovia aqueduct, turn into the Old Town (the side where the aqueduct adjoins the crenelated fortress walls) and park on or as close to the Plaza Mayor as possible. To be legal—and they do issue expensive tickets—pick up a cheap permit from the tobacco shop just down C.I. Católica (90-min maximum 9:00–20:00, free 20:00–9:00). You should be safe on the square.

Segovia to Salamanca (100 miles): Leave Segovia by driving around the town's circular road, which offers good views from below the Alcázar. Then follow the signs for Ávila (road N110). Notice the fine town view from the three crosses at the crest of the first hill. Just after the abandoned ghost church at Villacastin, turn onto N501 at the huge Puerta de San Vicente (cathedral and Turismo are just inside). The Salamanca road leads around the famous Ávila walls to the right. The best wall view is from the signposted Cuatro Postes, a mile northwest of town. Salamanca (N501) is clearly marked, about an hour's drive away.

A few miles before Salamanca, you might want to stop at the huge bull on the right of the road. There's a little dirt path leading right up to it. The closer you get, the more you realize it isn't real. Bad boys climb it for a goofy photo, but I wouldn't. There's a great photo opportunity, complete with river reflection, at the edge of Salamanca (at the light before the first bridge).

Parking in Salamanca is terrible. You can park dangerously over the river or along the Paseo de Canaliejas for free. I found a meter near my hotel (along Calle Palominos) and kept it fed (100 ptas for two hours, 9:00–14:00 and 16:00–20:00, free Saturday and Sunday afternoon). Leave nothing of value in your car.

TOLEDO

An hour to the south of Madrid, Toledo teems with tourists, souvenirs, and great art by day, delicious roast suckling pig, echoes of El Greco, and medieval magic by night. Incredibly well-preserved and full of cultural wonder, the entire city has been declared a national historical monument.

Spain's historic capital is 2,000 years of tangled history—Roman, Visigothic, Moorish, and Christian—crowded onto a high, rocky perch protected on three sides by the Tejo River. It's so well preserved that the Spanish government has forbidden any modern exteriors. The rich mix of Jewish, Moorish, and Christian heritages makes it one of Europe's art capitals.

Toledo was a Visigothic capital back in 554 and Spain's political capital until 1561, when it reached its natural limits of growth as defined by the Tejo River Gorge. Though the king moved to more spacious Madrid, Toledo remains the historic, artistic, and spiritual center of Spain. In spite of tremendous tourist crowds, Toledo just sits on its history and remains much as it was when El Greco called it home and painted it 400 years ago. If you like El Greco, you'll love Toledo.

Planning Your Time
To properly see Toledo's museums (great El Greco), cathedral (best in Spain), and medieval atmosphere (best after dark), you'll need two nights and a day. Toledo is well-connected by train and bus to Madrid and miserable by car. Try to do it outside of car-rental time.

Toledo

Orientation (tel. code: 925)

Lassoed into a tight tangle of streets by the sharp bend of the Tejo River (called the Tagus where it hits the Atlantic, in Lisbon), Toledo has the most confusing medieval street plan in Spain. But it's a small town of only 50,000 people, major sights are well signposted, and most locals will politely point you in the right direction.

Orient yourself with a walk (at least mentally) past Toledo's main sights. Starting in the central Plaza Zocódover, walk southwest along the Calle de Comércio. After passing the cathedral on your left, follow the signs to Santo Tomé and the cluster of other sights. This walk shows you that the visitor's city lies basically along one small but central street. Still, I routinely get completely turned around. Knowing that the town is bounded by the river on three sides and is very small, I wander happily lost. When it's time to get somewhere, I pull out the map or ask, "*¿Dónde está Plaza Zocódover?*"

Tourist Information

The TI is just outside the north wall (Monday–Friday 9:00–18:00, Saturday 9:00–19:00, Sunday 9:00–15:00, tel. 925/22-08-43). The readable local guide, *Toledo, Its Art and Its History* (small version-700 ptas, sold all over town), explains all the sights (which generally provide no on-site information) and gives you a photo to point at and say, "*¿Dónde está . . . ?*" Most sights are closed on Monday.

Arrival in Toledo

The train station, a 30-minute hike from the town center, is easily connected to Plaza Zocódover by buses #5 and #6 (110 ptas, pay on bus) or taxi (400 ptas). If you're walking, turn right as you leave the station, cross the bridge, pass the bus station, go straight through the roundabout, and continue uphill to the TI and north gate (Puerta Bisagra). The bus station, closer to town, is also served by buses #5 and #6 (110 ptas), but it's easier to walk (15 min).

Sights—Toledo

▲▲**El Greco's Art**—Born on Crete and trained in Venice, Domenikos Theotocopoulos (tongue-tied friends just called him "The Greek") came to Spain to get a job decorating El Escorial. He failed there but succeeded in Toledo, where he spent the last 37 years of his life. He mixed all three regional influences into his palette. From his Greek homeland, he absorbed the solemn, abstract style of icons. In Venice he learned the bold use of color and dramatic style of the later Renaissance. These styles were then fused in the fires of fanatic Spanish-Catholic devotion.

Not bound by the realism so important to his 16th-century contemporaries, El Greco painted dramatic visions of striking colors and figures, with bodies unnatural and elongated as though stretched between heaven and earth. He painted souls, not faces. His work, on display at virtually every sight in Toledo, seems as fresh as contemporary art, thoroughly modern in its disregard of realism.

▲▲▲**Cathedral**—Holy Toledo! Spain's leading Catholic city has a magnificent cathedral. Shoehorned into this crowded city, its exterior is hard to appreciate. But the interior is so lofty, rich, and vast that it grabs you by the vocal chords and all you can do is whisper, "Wow." Walk through this holy redwood forest. Find any old pillar to sit under and imagine when the light bulbs were candles and the tourists were pilgrims—before the "No Photo" signs, when every window provided spiritual as well as physical light. The cathedral is basically Gothic, but took more than 200 years to build (1226–1493). So you'll see a mix of styles—Gothic, Renaissance, and Baroque—elaborate wrought-iron work, lavish woodcarving, window after colorful window of 500-year-old stained glass, and a sacristy with a collection of paintings that would put any museum on the map.

Don't miss the unique Transparente. In the 1700s, a hole was cut into the ceiling to let a sunbeam brighten the mass. Melding this big hole into the Gothic church presented a challenge that resulted in a Baroque masterpiece. Study this riot of angels doing flip-flops, babies breathing thin air, bottoms of feet, and gilded sunbursts. It makes you hope no one falls down. I like it, as, I guess, did the long-dead cardinal whose hat hangs from the edge of the hole (choosing the place in the cathedral in which their hat will hang till it rots is a perk only cardinals enjoy).

If you're there between 9:30 and 9:45, you can peek into the otherwise locked Mozarabic Chapel (Capilla Mozarabe) to witness the Visigothic mass, the oldest surviving Christian ritual in Western Europe. You're welcome to partake in this impressive example of peaceful coexistence of faiths, but once the door closes, you're a Visigoth for 30 minutes.

While the basic cathedral is free, seeing the great art requires a ticket. The cathedral's sacristy has more than 20 El Grecos; masterpieces by Goya, Titian, Rubens, Velázquez, and Bellini; and a carved St. Francis that seems to live. The choir (*coro*) is elaborately carved inside and out. Notice the scenes from the conquest of Granada. The treasury's biggie is the 10-foot-high, 430-pound, very decorated something-or-other (by Arfe), which is carried through Toledo in the Corpus Christi parade. It's made of gold and silver, much of which arrived on Columbus' first load home. The chapter house (Sala Capitular) has a rich gilt ceiling, interesting Bible-storytelling frescoes, and a pictorial review of hundreds of years of Toledo archbishops (500 ptas, sacristy open Monday–Saturday 10:30–13:00 and 15:30–19:00, Sunday 10:30–13:30 and 16:00–19:00; closes an hour earlier off-season).

This confusing collage of great Spanish art deserves a guided tour. Hire a private guide (or freeload), or at least follow

Toledo's Plaza Zocódover

N

PENSION SEGOVIA

SILLERIA

TO PUERTA NUEVA BISAGRA

ARMAS

PLAZA

ZOCODOVER

HOTEL MARAVILLA

ARCH

TO SANTA CRUZ MUSEUM

CALLE TOLEDO OHIO

CALLE COMERCIO

CAFE #38

SIERPE

CALLE

BARRIO REY

CAFE TELESFORO

McDONALDS

BAR PARILLA

TO CATEDRAL + EL GRECO'S HOUSE

MAGDALENA CHURCH

HOTEL CARLOS V

CUESTA CARLOS V

ALCÁZAR

JUAN LAB.

HOSTAL NUEVO LABRADOR

PENSION LUMBRERAS

* NOT TO SCALE- PLAZA ZOC. TO PENSION LUMBRERAS IS A 5 MIN. WALK

DCH

a local guidebook. Fernando Garrido, a guide and interpreter who runs a jewelry shop in the cathedral cloister (at the entrance, where you buy cathedral tickets), gives an excellent one-hour tour for 10,000 ptas. He's a kind of Rodrigo Danger-field, with a wealth of information (tel. 925/22-40-07). Say "*Buenos días*" to him and check out his shop. If you can't afford his tour on your own, try assembling a group.

▲▲**Santa Cruz Museum**—This great Renaissance hospital build-ing holds 18 El Grecos in a stately, classical, music-filled setting (200 ptas, Monday 10:00–14:00 and 16:00–18:30, Tuesday–Saturday 10:00–18:30, Sunday 10:00–14:00, Cervantes 3).

▲**Alcázar**—A huge, former imperial residence dominating the Toledo skyline, Alcázar became a kind of right-wing Alamo of Spain's Civil War when a force of Franco's Nationalists (and hundreds of hostages) were besieged for two months. Finally, after many fierce but futile Republican attacks, Franco sent in an army that took Toledo and freed the Alcázar. The place was rebuilt and glorified under Franco. Today you can see its Civil War exhibits, giving you an interesting—and right-wing—look at the horrors of Spain's recent past (125 ptas, Tuesday–Sunday 10:00–13:30 and 16:00–18:30, closed Monday; closes an hour earlier off-season).

▲**Santo Tomé**—A simple chapel with El Greco's most loved painting. The powerful *Burial of the Count of Orgaz* couples heaven and earth in a way only The Greek could. It feels so right to see a painting left where the artist put it 400 years ago. Don't rush this. Sit down—let it perform. Each face is a detailed portrait. Notice El Greco himself eyeballing you (seventh figure in from the left). The boy in the foreground is El Greco's son (150 ptas, daily 10:00–13:45 and 15:30–18:45, closes an hour earlier off-season).

▲**El Greco's House**—It wasn't really El Greco's, but it really is a house, giving you an interesting look at the interior of a traditionally furnished Renaissance home. You'll see El Greco's masterful *View of Toledo* and portraits of the apostles (400 ptas, 10:00–14:00 and 16:00–18:00, closed Sunday afternoon and Monday, Samuel Levi 3).

Sinagoga del Transito (Museo Sefardi)—This best surviving slice of Toledo's Jewish past, built in 1366, is next to El Greco's House on Calle de los Reyes Católicos (same price and hours as the House).

Synagogue of Santa Maria Blanca—This synagogue-turned-church with Moorish arches is an eclectic but harmonious gem (150 ptas, daily 10:00–14:00 and 15:30–19:00, closes an hour earlier off-season, Reyes Católicos 2-4).

Shopping

Toledo probably sells as many souvenirs as any city in Spain. This is the place to buy medieval-looking swords, armor, maces, three-legged stools, and other nouveau antiques. It's also Spain's damascene center, where for centuries craftspeople have inlaid black steelware with gold, silver, and copper wire. At Calle Ciudad 19, near the cathedral and Plaza Ayuntamiento, you can see swords and knives being made in the workshop of English-speaking Mariano Zamorano. Judging by what's left of his hand, his knives are among the best. El Martes, Toledo's colorful outdoor market, bustles on Calle de Cervantes, Tuesday from 9:00–14:00.

Sleeping in Toledo
(140 ptas = about $1, tel. code: 925)
Sleep Code: **S**=Single, **D**=Double/Twin, **T**=Triple, **Q**=Quad, **b**=bathroom, **t**=toilet only, **s**=shower only, **CC**=Credit Card (Visa, MasterCard, Amex), **SE**=Speaks English, **NSE**=No English. Breakfast and the 7 percent IVA tax aren't included unless noted.

Madrid day-trippers darken the sunlit cobbles, but few stay to see Toledo's medieval moonrise. Spend the night. Classier places adjust rates according to the season: mid-July through mid-September is high, November through February is low. There are no private rooms for rent.

Hotel Maravilla is wonderfully central, quiet (unless you get a room on the street), and convenient. Despite its narrow halls and simple rooms, it offers a decent middle-range value in the old center (Sb-4,500 ptas, Db-7,000 ptas, Tb-9,300 ptas, Qb-11,300 ptas, includes breakfast and 7 percent IVA tax, elevator, CC:VM, just behind Plaza Zocódover, at Plaza de Barrio Rey 7, 45001 Toledo, tel. 925/22-83-17, fax 925/22-81-55, Ana and Gemma speak some English). Avoid their restaurant.

Hotel Carlos V is ideally located overlooking the cathedral, between the Alcázar and the Zocódover. It suffers from the obligatory stuffiness of a correct hotel, but has bright, pleasant rooms and elegant bathrooms (Sb-8,800 ptas, Db-12,800 ptas, Tb-16,300 ptas, breakfast-900 ptas, air-con, elevator, CC:VMA, Plaça Horno Magdalena 3, 45001 Toledo, tel. 925/22-21-00, fax 925/22-21-05, SE). Ask for a view room overlooking the cathedral.

Around the corner, the quiet, modern **Hostal Nuevo Labrador** is just as nice for about half the price (Sb-3,200 ptas, Db-6,400 ptas, Tb-8,500 ptas, Qb-10,700 ptas, Juan Labrador 10, 45001 Toledo, tel. 925/22-26-20, fax 925/22-93-99, NSE, worth learning to speak Spanish for). Down the same street, the smaller, family-run **Pensión Lumbreras** has a tranquil court-yard and 12 simple but newly renovated rooms, some with views (such as room #6), some with theme posters (one S-2,000 ptas, D-3,200 ptas, T-4,400 ptas, Q-5,400 ptas, breakfast-250 ptas, Juan Labrador 9, 45001 Toledo, tel. 925/22-15-71, NSE). View rooms don't cost any extra. Ask for "*con vista*."

Hotel Santa Isabel, in a 15th-century building just 2 blocks from the cathedral, has clean, comfortable rooms. Avoid only the few "*atico*" rooms that have only a skylight (Sb-4,300 ptas, Db-6,500 ptas, Tb-7,800 ptas, breakfast-450 ptas, 7 percent IVA tax included, parking-810 ptas, air-con, elevator, CC:VMA, Calle Santa Isabel 24, 45002 Toledo, tel. 925/25-31-20, fax 925/25-31-36).

Pensión Segovia is cheap, quiet, clean, and very central. It's also old, rickety, and dingy, with firm beds and memorable balconies. Duck your head; the ancient ceilings are low (D-2,700 ptas, T-3,600 ptas, shower-200 ptas; from Plaza Zocódover go down Calle de la Sillería and take the second right to a tiny square, Calle de Recoletos 2, 45001 Toledo, tel. 925/21-11-24).

Across from the Alcázar is **Hotel Alfonso VI**, a big, touristy establishment with large, airy rooms, tour groups, and souvenirs for sale all over the lobby. I hate to steer anyone there, but in central Toledo you take what you can get (Sb-9,200 ptas, Db-14,200 ptas, Tb-16,400 ptas, breakfast-910 ptas, includes 7 percent IVA tax, attached restaurant and bar, CC:VMA, General Moscardo 2, 45001 Toledo, tel. 925/22-26-00, fax 925/21-44-58, SE). Ask for a view room.

The best splurge in town is the **Hostal de Cardenal**. This 17th-century cardinal's palace built into Toledo's wall is quiet and elegant, with a cool garden and a fine restaurant. The only drawback to this poor-man's *parador* is its location, at the noisy, dusty old gate of Toledo (Sb-7,000 ptas, Db-11,500 ptas, Tb-15,000 ptas, CC:VMA, near Puerta Bisagra, Paseo de Recaredo 24, 45004 Toledo, tel. 925/22-49-00, fax 925/22-29-91, stuffy staff SE).

For those who want it all and will leave the town center and pay anything to get it, Toledo's **Parador Nacional Conde de Orgaz** is one of Spain's most famous, enjoying the same Toledo view El Greco made famous from across the Tejo Canyon (Db-19,500 ptas with a view, CC:VMA, a windy mile from town at Cerro del Emperador s/n, 45002 Toledo, tel. 925/22-18-50, fax 925/22-51-66; SE—if you've got money).

Sleeping Outside of Town on the Road to Madrid

Hostal Gavilánes II is bright and modern, with 15 very comfortable rooms and easy parking (1,000 ptas/day), a 15-minute walk from Plaza Zocódover (Sb-5,200 ptas, Db-6,700 ptas, Tb-9,000 ptas, Qb-10,600 ptas, includes breakfast, air-con, CC:VM, Marqués de Mendigorría 14, 45003 Toledo, tel. 925/21-16-28, NSE). Check out their sweet suite (9,000 ptas). There are several hotels in Toledo with the name of Gavilánes; this one is directly across from the bullring, Plaza de Toros.

Cheaper, though not as good a value for the money, is the neighboring **Hostal Madrid**, with clean, simple rooms (Sb-3,200 ptas, Db-4,300 ptas, Tb-5,800 ptas, CC:VM, Calle Marqués de Mendigorría 7, 45003 Toledo, tel. 925/22-11-14, NSE). This *hostal* spreads its rooms throughout two buildings on either side of the street; the reception area is in the building on the same side of the street as the bullring.

Hostal Santa Barbara is 3 blocks from the train station, with easy parking (Db-4,200 ptas, Avenida Santa Barbara 8, 45006 Toledo, tel. 925/22-02-98, NSE). The youth hostel **Residencia Juvenil San Servando** is lavish but cheap, with small rooms, swimming pool, views, and good management (975 ptas per bed; San Servando castle near the train station, over the Puente Viejo outside town, tel. 925/22-45-54, NSE). They can direct you to nearby budget beds when the hostel is full.

Eating in Toledo

A day full of El Greco and the romance of Toledo after dark puts me in the mood for suckling pigs—roasted. For a splurge, the palatial **Hostal de Cardenal Restaurante** serves wonderfully prepared local specialties, including pigs and *perdiz* (partridge); call 925/22-08-62 to reserve (lunch starts at 13:00, dinner at 20:30). **Restaurante-Meson Palacios** on Alfonso X, near Plaza de San Vicente, is another good bet (lunch at 13:00, dinner at 19:30, closed Sunday night). There are three **Casa Aurelio** restaurants in town; each has reasonably priced, if salty, food and a classy atmosphere (2,500-pta menu, closed Sunday and Tuesday, CC:VA, at Plaza Ayuntamiento 8 near the cathedral, tel. 925/22-77-16, other branches at Sinagoga 1 and at Sinagoga 6). Cheaper but still classy alternatives are **Rincón de Eloy** at Juan Labrador 16 (1,500-pta menu) and **Restaurante El Cobertizo**.

You'll find several budget restaurants behind the
Zocódover. **Bar La Parrilla** is an easy place to munch a few
tapas (bar on ground floor with posted menu clearly listing
tapas prices; decent restaurant upstairs; Plaza de Barrio Rey,
take the alley from Plaza Zocódover past Café Casa Telesforo
to a small square). If Angel's working, give him a high five and
ask for a free shrimp.

For breakfast, **Cafetería Croissanterie Repostería**
serves fresh croissants and *churros* (between Plaza Zocódover
and the cathedral at Comércio 38). These *churros* are as good
as any—and they still rival *lutefisk* as the leading European
national dish of penitence. For heartier appetites, they serve a
huge tortilla McMuffin. And I can't walk past the place without picking up one of their *napolitana de chocolates* (freshest in
the morning).

For a sweet and romantic evening moment, get one of
these chocolate pastries, or whatever suits your sweet tooth, and
head down to the cathedral. Sit on the Plaza del Ayuntamiento
(there's a comfortable perch 10 yards down the lane from the
huge granite bowling ball) with the fountain on your right,
Spain's best-looking city hall behind you, and her top cathedral,
built back when Toledo was Spain's capital, shining brightly
against the black night sky before you.

For Toledo's famous almond-fruity-sweet *mazapan*, try
Casa Telesforo at Plaza Zocódover 17 (daily 9:00–24:00). The
bars and cafés on the plaza are reasonable. Sit outside and
enjoy the people-watching.

Picnics are best assembled at the Mercado Municipal on
Plaza Mayor (on the Alcázar side of the cathedral, open until
14:00, closed Sunday). This is a fun market to prowl, even if you
don't need food. If you feel like munching a giant communion
wafer, one of the stalls sells crispy bags of *obleas* (a great gift for
your favorite pastor).

Transportation Connections—Toledo

To Madrid by train (9/day, 75 min, Madrid's Atocha station),
by bus (2/hr, 75 min, Madrid's Estación sur Autobuses, Metro:
Menendez-Alvaro). Toledo bus info tel. 925/21-58-50, train
info tel. 925/22-30-99 or 925/22-12-72.

Those relying on public transportation should use Madrid
as a hub and visit Toledo as a side trip from Madrid. By car,
Madrid is a 40-mile, one-hour drive.

Car Rental: Avis is within Toledo's city walls at Galeria Comercial 107, Paseo del Miradero (tel. 925/21-45-35), and Hertz is across from the train station at Paseo Rosa 40 (tel. 925/25-38-90). Figure on about 9,000 ptas a day for the economy size.

LA MANCHA

(Visit only if you're driving between Toledo and Granada.) Nowhere else is Spain so vast, flat, and radically monotonous. La Mancha, Arabic for "parched earth," makes you feel small—lost in rough seas of olive-green polka dots. Random buildings look like houses and hotels that were thrown off some heavenly Monopoly board. It's a rough land where roadkill is left to rot, where bugs seem to ricochet off the windshield and keep on flying, and where hitchhikers wear red dresses and aim to take you for the ride. This is the setting of Cervantes' *Don Quixote*, published in the 17th century, after England sank the Armada and the Spanish Empire began its decline. Cervantes' star character fought doggedly for good, for justice, and against the fall of Spain. Ignoring reality, Don Quixote was a hero fighting a hopeless battle. Stark La Mancha was the perfect stage.

The epitome of Don Quixote country, the town of **Consuegra** must be the La Mancha Cervantes had in mind. Drive up to the ruined 12th-century castle and joust with a windmill. It's hot and buggy here, but the powerful view overlooking the village, with its sun-bleached, light-red roofs, modern concrete reality, and harsh, windy silence makes for a profound picnic (a one-hour drive south of Toledo). The castle belonged to the Knights of St. John (12th and 13th centuries) and is associated with their trip to Jerusalem during the Crusades. Originally built from the ruins of a nearby Roman circus, it has been newly restored. Sorry, the windmills are post-Cervantes, only 200 to 300 years old.

If you've seen windmills, the next castle north (above Almonacid, 12 kilometers from Toledo) is more interesting than the Consuegra castle, and free. Follow the ruined lane past the ruined church up to the ruined castle. The jovial locals hike up with kids and kites.

Route Tips for Drivers

Granada to Toledo (250 miles, 5 hrs): The Granada–Toledo drive is long, hot, and boring (see La Mancha, above). Start early to minimize the heat and make the best time you can. Follow signs for Madrid/Jaen/N323 into what some call the Spanish Nebraska—La Mancha. After Puerto Lapice, you'll see the Toledo exit.

View the city from many angles along the Circunvalación road across the Tejo Gorge. Drive to the Parador Conde de Orgaz just south of town for about the same view (from the balcony) as El Greco's famous portrait of Toledo.

Enter Toledo by the north gate and park in the open-air guarded lot (cheap but not safe overnight) or in one of two garages. The garage just past the Alcázar is easy and as central as you need (1,000 ptas/24 hrs). You can usually park free in the lot just down the street from the garage or in the huge dirt lot below and behind the Santa Cruz Museum.

Toledo to Madrid (40 miles, 1 hr): It's a speedy *autovía* north, past one last bullboard, to Madrid. The highways converge into M30, which circles Madrid. Follow it to the left ("Nor y Oeste") and take the Plaza de España exit to get back to the Gran Vía. If you're airport-bound, keep heading into Madrid until you see the airplane symbol (N-II). I drove from Toledo's Alcázar to Madrid's airport in just under an hour (but then, I'm a travel writer).

GRANADA

Granada is a fascinating city with a beautiful, often snowcapped, Sierra Nevada backdrop. This is our Moorish pilgrimage. The last stronghold of the Moorish kingdom in Spain, Granada has the monuments to prove it. Its exotically tangled Moorish quarter bustles throughout the day, and its lush Alhambra fortress glows red in the evening. Let your senses off their leash. Bite into a pomegranate—the city's namesake and symbol—and experience Granada.

There is an old saying: "Give him a coin, woman, for there is nothing worse in this life than to be blind in Granada." This city has much to see, yet it reveals itself when it chooses. Glimpse the town in jigsaw-puzzle pieces through the intricate lattice of a Moorish window. Hear water burbling, sight unseen, among the labyrinthine hedges of the Generalife garden. Listen to a flute trilling deep in the swirl of alleys around the cathedral. For a time, we are all blind in Granada.

Planning Your Time
Granada is worth one day and two nights. If you're traveling by train, the overnight connection to or from Madrid (or Barcelona) is so good that I'd give the city a night and a day. The Costa del Sol's best beach town, Nerja, is just two quick hours away (by bus), postcard-perfect white hill towns like Ronda are three hours (bus or train), and Sevilla is an easy four-hour train ride.

Stroll the pedestrian-zone shopping scene in the morning and tour the royal chapel and cathedral (both closed 13:00–16:00), then do the Alhambra after lunch (open all day). Have dinner in the Albaicín (Moorish quarter) and be at the Albaicín viewpoint for sunset.

Orientation (tel. code: 958)

Granada is big (200,000 people), but the sights are all within a 20-minute walk of Plaza Nueva, where dogs wave their tails to the rhythm of the street musicians. This center of the historic city is in the Darro River Valley, which separates two hills: one with the great Moorish palace, the Alhambra, and the other with the best-preserved Moorish quarter in Spain, the Albaicín. To the southeast are the cathedral, royal chapel, and Alcaicería (Moorish market), where the city's two main drags, Gran Vía de Colón and Calle Reyes Católicos, come together.

Tourist Information: There are two Turismos. One is at Corral del Carbon (Monday–Saturday 9:00–19:00, Sunday 10:00–14:00; from Plaza de Isabel Católica, take Reyes Católicos in opposite direction from Alhambra, take first left, walk through keyhole arch, tel. 958/22-59-90). The other TI is on Plaza de Mariana Pineda (Monday–Friday 9:30–19:00, Saturday 10:00–14:00, both TIs have shorter hours off-season, tel. 958/22-66-88). Get the 100-pta Granada map and verify your Alhambra plans. Check the posted bus and train schedules.

Arrival in Granada

By Train: The RENFE train station is connected to the center by frequent buses or a 20-minute walk down Avenida Constitución and Gran Vía de Colón. Taxis are cheap (500 ptas to the center).

Exiting the train station, walk straight ahead down the tree-lined road. At the first major intersection (Avenida de la Constitución), you'll see the bus stop at your right. Take buses #4, #9, or #11 and ask, "*¿Plaza Isabel Católica?*" Buy your ticket (115 ptas) from the driver. Get off when you see the fountain of Plaza Isabel Católica in front of you (and the bus) at the stop near the cathedral; cross the busy Gran Via and walk 2 blocks to Plaza Nueva.

The train station has lockers for day-trippers and lots of schedules. You can pick up schedules at the station and buy

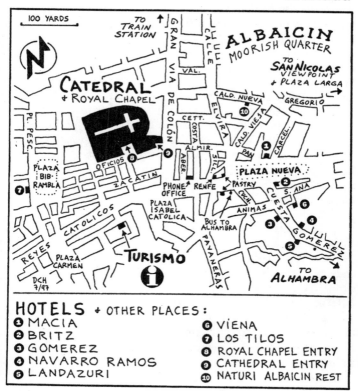

HOTELS + OTHER PLACES:

❶ MACIA
❷ BRITZ
❸ GOMEREZ
❹ NAVARRO RAMOS
❺ LANDAZURI

❻ VIENA
❼ LOS TILOS
❽ ROYAL CHAPEL ENTRY
❾ CATHEDRAL ENTRY
❿ NATURI ALBAICIN REST

tickets later at a travel agency or the downtown RENFE office (Monday–Friday 9:00–13:30 and 17:00–19:30, Calle Reyes Católicos 63, 1 block down from Plaza Nueva, tel. 958/27-12-72). This office might move or relocate in '98.

By Bus: Granada's main bus station (where all long-distance buses stop, tel. 958/18-50-10) is a bus or taxi ride from the center. Take bus #3 (115 ptas) to the city center and get off just after turning left through the Plaza Isabel Católica (with the fountain) at the stop opposite the cathedral. Plaza Nueva is 2 blocks east.

Getting Around Granada

Pick up a city bus map from a bus driver or the TI. Tickets cost 115 ptas; buy from the driver. A strip of ten tickets, called a *bonobus*, costs about 700 ptas at newsstands and tobacco shops, and can be shared by more than one person. (A tourist would most likely use a bus to/from the train/bus station, the Alhambra, and maybe the monastery.)

Helpful Hints

When you see women wanting to give you flowers, avoid them like the plague. A small phone office is at Plaza Nueva 2 (Monday–Friday 9:00–14:30 and 17:00–23:00, Saturday 10:00–14:30 and 18:00–23:00, closed Sunday). The post office is on Puerta Real (Monday–Friday 8:30–20:30, Saturday 9:30–14:00). To save yourself a trip to the train station or the bus station, get schedule information from the TI. Then buy train tickets at the RENFE office (see above), or you can buy bus or train tickets at either of two travel agencies near the TI (both open 9:30–13:00 and 17:00–20:00): Viajes Sacromonte (Angel Gavinet 6, tel. 958/22-55-99, SE) or 1 block away, Ecuador (Angel Gavinet 8, tel. 958/22-35-67, less English). You can also make *couchette* reservations for Granada–Madrid trains and Madrid–Paris trains (credit cards accepted).

Sights—Granada's Alhambra

▲▲▲Alhambra—The last and greatest Moorish palace is one of Europe's top sights, attracting up to 8,000 visitors a day. Nowhere else does the splendor of Moorish civilization shine so brightly.

There are three ways to get to the Alhambra:

(1) Walk 30 uphill minutes up Cuesta de Gomerez from Plaza Nueva. Keep going straight, with the Alhambra high on your left, and follow the street to the new entrance near the car parking.

(2) Catch the red minibus marked "Alhambra-Neptuno" from Plaza Nueva (115 ptas, every 15 min).

(3) Take a taxi (400 ptas, taxi stand on Plaza Nueva).

Don't drive. If you do, you'll park on the far, far side of the Alhambra; and when you leave, one-way streets will send you into the traffic-clogged center of Granada.

The Alhambra, with all due respect, is really a symbol of retreat. Granada was a regional capital for centuries before the Christian *Reconquista* (Reconquest) gradually took Córdoba (1236) and Sevilla (1248), leaving Granada to reign until 1492 as the last Moorish stronghold in Europe. As you tour this grand

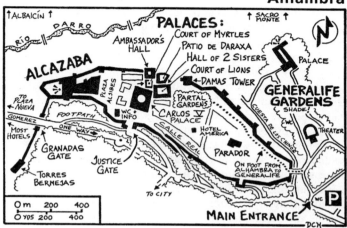

Alhambra

palace, remember that while Europe slumbered through the
Dark Ages, Moorish magnificence blossomed—busy stucco,
plaster stalactites, colors galore, scalloped windows framing
Granada views, exuberant gardens, and water, water everywhere.
Water, so rare and precious in most of the Islamic world, was
the purest symbol of life to the Moors. The Alhambra is decorated with water standing still, cascading, masking secret
conversations, and drip-dropping playfully.

The Alhambra consists of four sights: Charles V's Palace;
the Alcazaba (old fort); the Palacios Nazaries (Moorish palace);
and the Generalife garden. Charles V's Palace is free, and the
other sights require a combined ticket (725 ptas, free on Sunday, though you still must get a ticket; Monday–Saturday
9:00–20:00, Sunday 9:00–18:00; also on Tuesday, Thursday,
and Saturday open 22:00–24:00). During the day, buy your
Alhambra tickets at the main ticket office at the Generalife
entrance near the parking lot. Tickets for late evening visits are
purchased in the Alhambra TI office across from Charles V's
Palace. The main ticket office closes 60 minutes early and your
ticket is good only for the date stamped on it. Clean WCs are
downstairs from the ticket office and in the Alhambra TI
office, across from Charles V's Palace.

Buy the helpful guidebook *The Alhambra and the Generalife*
at the souvenir shops across from Charles V's Palace (600 ptas,

great layout plan included), or buy it in town and read it the night before. It's easy to get disoriented. Take time to understand the layout and history of this remarkable sight before entering. The Alhambra TI sells a map of the Alhambra (290 ptas); skip it if you bought the guidebook, which includes a map.

Try to avoid arriving as it opens—when countless tour groups do. The afternoons and evenings seem less crowded. The new computerized ticketing system regulates the number of people in the Alhambra's highlight, the Palacios Nazaries, by issuing you a half-hour window of time (which, if it's not too crowded you can select, but speak up) during which you must enter. You may have up to a two- or three-hour wait before your "appointment" to enter the Palacios Nazaries, time easily consumed at the other sights that have no time-entry restriction (read below). There are snack stands and restaurants in the Alhambra complex. The key to a successful Palacios Nazaries visit is avoiding large tour groups. Hang out by the entrance ten minutes before your half-hour to be the first one in for your platooned time. By hustling ahead, you'll enjoy the rooms in relative peace. Note: Once inside the Palacios Nazaries you can linger as long as you like.

Charles V's Palace—It's impressive but sadly out of place. Remind yourself that it's only natural for a conquering king to build his own palace over his foe's palace. This is the most impressive Renaissance building you'll see in Spain, designed by Michelangelo's student Pedro Machuca. Stand in the circular courtyard and climb to the upstairs, then imagine being here for one of Charles' bullfights. Inside the palace you'll find the Museo de Bellas Artes (free and skipable, Tuesday–Saturday 10:00–14:00) and the Museo Hispano-Musulman, showing off some of the Alhambra's best Moorish art (250 ptas, Tuesday–Saturday 9:00–14:30).

Alcazaba—This is the oldest, most ruined part of the Alhambra. It's basically a tower that offers some exercise and a great city view. From the top find the Albaicín viewpoint and Plaza Nueva. Is anybody skiing today? Look to the south and think of that day in 1492 when the cross and flags of Aragon and Castile were raised on this tower, and the fleeing Moorish King Boabdil looked back and wept. His mom chewed him out, saying, "Don't weep like a woman for what you couldn't defend like a man." Much later, Napoleon stationed his troops here, contributing substantially to its ruin when he left. Follow the arrows down and around to the . . .

Palacios Nazaries—Be mindful of your window of time and step into the jewel of the Alhambra, the Moorish royal palace, Palacios Nazaries. This is our best possible look at the refined and elegant Moorish civilization of Al-Andalus. If you can imagine a few tapestries, carpets, and some ivory-studded wooden furniture, the place is much as it was for the Moorish kings. Remember the palace themes: water, no images, "stalactite" ceilings throughout—and no signs telling you where you are.

Just off the Court of Myrtles, with the long goldfish pond, study the wooden ceiling of the Hall of the Boat (and guess how it got its name). It was once a waiting room for those who had an audience with the king. The attached room is the beautifully decorated and perfectly square Hall of the Ambassadors, which held the king's throne opposite the entrance. The walls, once painted and gilded, are still glorious.

Then find your way into the much-photographed Court of the Lions. (Notice the unexpected similarity to a Catholic monastery's cloisters.) Six hundred years ago, the Moors could read the Koranic poetry that ornaments this court and could understand the symbolism of the enclosed garden (the realization of paradise or truth) and of the 12 lions (signs of the zodiac or months). Imagine—they enjoyed this part of the palace even more than we do today. Off the far end is the King's Hall. Notice the Western-style painted ceilings in the niches. The origins of these jousting and hunting scenes, a jarring contrast to the lack of images throughout the palace, have prompted much debate but no conclusions.

On your way out, you'll pass through the simple room (marked with a large plaque) where Washington Irving wrote *Tales of the Alhambra*. If you haven't read it, souvenir stands and bookshops in Granada are happy to sell it to you.

Upon leaving the Palacios Nazaries, you'll pass under three arched hedges; turn left to get to Generalife or turn right to exit.

Generalife—On the hillside to the east, the garden with carefully pruned hedges is the Generalife (pronounced henneraw-LEEF-ay). This most perfect Arabian garden in Andalucía was the summer home of the Moorish kings, the closest thing on earth to the Koran's description of heaven. Consider a picnic in the Generalife. If you have a long wait before your entry to the Palacios, tour these gardens first.

More Sights—Granada

▲▲**Albaicín**—This is the best old Moorish quarter in Spain, with countless colorful corners, flowery patios, and shady lanes to soothe the 20th-century-mangled visitor. Climb high to the San Nicolás church for the best view of the Alhambra, especially early in the morning or at sunset.

The easiest approach is to taxi to the St. Nicolás church and explore from there (see directions from St. Nicolás, below). For the quickest, most scenic walk up the hill, leave from the west end of the Plaza Nueva on Calle Elvira, then turn right on tiny Calderería Nueva. Follow this stepped street past *tapas* bars and *teterías* (see Eating in Granada, below) as it goes left around the church, slants, winds, and zigzags up the hill, heading basically straight. (Resist the temptation to turn left on Muladar Sancha.) Near the crest, turn right on Camino Nuevo de San Nicolás, walking several blocks to the street that curves up left, leading to steps up to the church's viewpoint (a must). From there, walk north (away from the Alhambra) to the small street that leads from the upper-left corner of the small square, past the Biblioteca Municipal and continue to where it ends, then drop down to the right through the old Moorish wall into the tiny neighborhood square called Plaza Larga. Stop here for something to eat or drink. To reach my recommended El Ladrillo restaurants from here, leave Plaza Larga down the street with the "Do Not Enter" sign: for El Ladrillo II (indoor dining), stay on this street for about 3 blocks, it will be on your left; for El Ladrillo (outdoors), take the first left (by the "Clinical Dental"), then right, left, right and there you are. This is the heart of the Albaicín. Poke into one of the old churches. They are plain by design, to go easy on the Muslim converts who weren't used to being surrounded by images as they worshiped.

▲**Royal Chapel (Capilla Real)**—Without a doubt Granada's top Christian sight, this lavish chapel holds the dreams—and bodies—of Queen Isabella and King Ferdinand. Besides the royal tombs (walk down the steps), you'll find some great Flemish art (Memling), paintings by Botticelli and Perugino, the royal jewels, Ferdinand's sword, and the most lavish interior money could buy 500 years ago. Because of its speedy completion, the chapel is an unusually harmonious piece of architecture (250 ptas, Monday–Saturday 10:30–13:00 and

16:00–19:00, Sunday 11:00–13:00 and 16:00–19:00;
October–March, mornings only; entrance on Calle Oficios).
Cathedral—The only Renaissance church in Spain, this
cathedral is a welcome break from the dark Gothic and
gilded-lily Baroque of so many Spanish churches. Spacious,
symmetrical, and lit by a stained-glass-filled rotunda, it's well
worth a visit. The Renaissance facade and paintings of the
Virgin in the rotunda are by Granada's own Alonso Cano
(1601–1661) and the coin-op lighting is worthwhile (250
ptas, Monday–Saturday 10:30–13:00 and 16:00–19:00, Sunday 16:00–19:00 only; October–March, mornings only and
closed Sunday; entrance off Gran Vía de Colón).
Alcaicería—The neighborhood around the cathedral is the
site of the still-busy Moorish market. Fiercely ignore the
obnoxious ladies with flowers who want to read your palms
and empty your pockets. Explore the mesh of tiny shopping
lanes between the cathedral and the Calle Reyes Católicos.
Go on a photo and sound safari: popcorn machines popping,
men selling balloons, leather goods spread out on streets,
kids playing soccer, the whirring grind of knife sharpeners in
shops, barking dogs, dogged shoeshine boys. The flower
stalls on Plaza Bib-Rambla (behind the cathedral) are open
every day, all day. The small Mercado Municipal is liveliest
on Saturday, spilling out into the nearby streets (off Plaza
Ramanilla, best in mornings until 14:00, closed Sunday).
Sacromonte—This neighborhood, formerly Europe's most
disgusting tourist trap, famous for its cave-dwelling, foot-
stomping, flamenco-dancing Gypsies, was dead for years but is
making a comeback. You can ask at the TI about flamenco
(and personal safety), but I'd save flamenco for Sevilla.
Carthusian Monastery (La Cartuja)—Another church with
an interior that looks as if it squirted out of a can of Reddi
Wip, La Cartuja is nicknamed the "Christian Alhambra" for its
elaborate white Baroque stucco work. In the rooms just off the
cloister, notice the gruesome paintings of martyrs placidly
meeting their grisly fate. It's located a mile out of town, on the
way to Madrid—go north on Gran Vía and follow the signs or
take bus #8 from Gran Vía (250 ptas, daily 10:00–13:00 and
16:00–20:00; October–March, mornings only).
International Festival of Music and Dance—From late-June
to mid-July, you can enjoy some of the world's best classical
music in the Alhambra at reasonable prices.

Sleeping in Granada
(140 ptas = about $1, tel. code: 958)
Sleep Code: **S**=Single, **D**=Double/Twin, **T**=Triple, **Q**=Quad,
b=bathroom, **t**=toilet only, **s**=shower only, **CC**=Credit Card
(**V**isa, **M**asterCard, **A**mex), **SE**=Speaks English, **NSE**=No
English. Breakfast, like the 7 percent IVA tax, is not included.

In Granada I sleep on the Plaza Nueva, on Cuesta de
Gomerez (the road leading off the square up to the Alhambra—
can be noisy at night), or on the quiet pedestrian street, Calle
Navas. In July and August, with the streets littered with sun-
stroke victims, rooms are plentiful. September, October, and
November are more crowded, and you'll want to arrive early or
call ahead. Upon arrival, drive, bus, walk, or taxi to the Plaza
Nueva. You'll find many small, reasonable hotels to choose from
within a few blocks up Cuesta de Gomerez.

Sleeping on or near the Plaza Nueva
(zip code: 18009)
Right on the colorful Plaza Nueva is **Hotel Residencia
Macia**. This classy, hotelesque place is clean and modern. Half
of the 44 rooms have air-con and all rooms have a TV and
phone. Choose between an on-the-square view or a quiet room
(Sb-5,000 ptas, Db-8,500 ptas, Tb-11,500 ptas, show this book
upon arrival to get a 10 percent discount, buffet breakfast-600
ptas, elevator, CC:VMA, Plaza Nueva 4, tel. 958/22-75-36, fax
958/22-75-33, SE). They can help with parking at a distant
garage (2,000 ptas/day).

Hostal Residencia Britz is a no-nonsense place, ideally
located right on the square, with an elevator and some fine view
rooms (S-2,300 ptas, Sb-4,000 ptas, D-3,500 ptas, Db-5,000
ptas, coin-op washing machine, CC:VM, Plaza Nueva y
Gomerez 1, tel. 958/22-36-52, NSE).

Hostal Landazuri, run by friendly, English-speaking
Matilda Landazuri and her son Manuelo, is plain and homey. It's
a bit faded, but has a great roof garden with an Alhambra view
and a helpful management (S-2,000 ptas, Sb-3,000 ptas, D-2,700
ptas, Db-3,800 ptas, T-4,800 ptas, Tb-5,300 ptas, breakfast-225
ptas, Cuesta de Gomerez 24, tel. & fax 958/22-14-06). The Lan-
dazuris also run a good cheap café; try Manuelo's tomato-
omelette sandwich for lunch. Matilda will store bags if you're
taking a night train. They have a few free parking places, or you
can pay 1,000 ptas/day for underground parking.

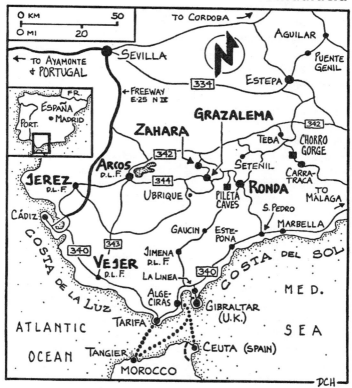

on your way in or out, spend a day hopping from town to town (Grazalema and Zahara, at a minimum) in the more remote interior, and enjoy Arcos early and late in the day.

Without a car and a lot of patience, you might keep things simple and focus only on Arcos and Jerez (both well-served by public buses). This is one area in which a rental car makes a lot of sense.

ARCOS DE LA FRONTERA

Arcos, smothering its hilltop and tumbling down all sides like an oversized blanket, is larger than the other Andalusian hill towns but equally atmospheric. The Old Center is a labyrinthine wonderland, a photographer's feast. Viewpoint-hop through town. Feel the wind funnel through the narrow streets as cars inch around tight corners. Join the kids' soccer game on the church-yard patio. The pleasant evening *paseo* and café scene are best at Plaza España and the adjacent Paseo Andalucía, the base of the hill where the new and old towns meet.

Though it tries, Arcos doesn't have much to offer other than its basic whitewashed self. The new English guidebook on Arcos, sold all over town, waxes poetic and at length about very little. Since the church is open until early evening and the town market is open in the morning, you can arrive late and leave early.

Orientation (tel. code: 956)

Tourist Information: The Turismo, on the main square across from the *parador*, is helpful and loaded with information, including bus schedules (weekdays 10:00–14:00 and 17:00–19:00, Saturday 10:00–14:00, sometimes open Sunday, Plaza del Cabildo, tel. 956/70-22-64). Ask about the TI's various one-hour walking tours of the Old Town, traditional patios, and Arcos by night (300 ptas, offered year-round by trilingual guides, depart from TI), and about the "Mississippi Paddle Boat" cruises around Lake Arcos (250 ptas, 2/day in summer, depart from Mesón de la Molinera). The TI will also arrange day tours (1,000 ptas per person) of surrounding towns and the countryside, if enough people are interested.

Arrival in Arcos: The bus station is on Calle Corregidores. As you leave the station, turn left on Corregidores, angle left uphill, cross the four-way intersection, angle right uphill and take Muñoz Vazquez up into town. Go up the stairs by the church to the main square and TI. It's a 15-minute walk, or catch a bus marked "Centro" (100 ptas), or take a taxi (400 ptas).

Helpful Hints: Arcos, Jerez, Vejer, and Tarifa all share the same telephone area code; if you're phoning between any of these cities, just dial the local number. Arcos' little post office is a few doors away from Hotel Los Olivos (Monday–Friday 8:30–14:30, Saturday 9:30–13:00, Paseo Boliches 26). Parking is available in Arcos' main square (100 ptas/hr).

Sights—Arcos

Church of Santa Maria—Arcos' spectacular location, on a pinnacle overlooking a vast Andalusian plain, is best appreciated from the top of the Church of Santa Maria bell tower (open at the caretaker's whim; entrance to the right of church entrance, no sign, just climb stairs and say "*Hola*"). As you

Arcos de la Frontera

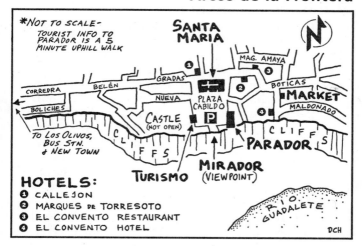

climb you'll pass through the tower-keeper's home. For a tip (about 200 ptas), she'll give you a key and direct you skyward. Climb to the bells and then on to the very top for the windy view. The bell loggia is impressive. Brace your ears. The church interior is also worth a look (175 ptas, Monday–Friday 10:00–13:00 and 16:00–18:30, Saturday 10:00–14:00, closed Sunday, on main square).

Markets and Fairs—Recinto Ferial, a park in the lower new town (near the bus station), is the site of a clothing market every Friday morning, open-air *tapas* bars every summer evening (from 21:00 on, mid-June–September), and Arcos' annual festival (five days centered around September 29, in celebration of the town's patron saint, St. Michael).

In the Old Town, the colorful produce market is perfect for picnickers and photographers (Monday–Saturday 9:00–14:00, closed Sunday, across from Hotel El Convento). Near the market is the Convento de Monjas Mercedarias and a chance to sample the nuns' locally renowned cookies. Go inside the atrium, ring the bell, and a nun will trade you a bag of cookies for a few hundred *pesetas*.

Flamenco—On Plaza Cananeo in the Old Town, amateur flamenco sizzles on Thursday evening (free, from 22:00, July–September).

Sleeping in Arcos
(tel. code: 956, zip code: 11630)

Sleep Code: **S**=Single, **D**=Double/Twin, **T**=Triple, **Q**=Quad, **b**=bathroom, **t**=toilet only, **s**=shower only, **CC**=Credit Card (Visa, MasterCard, Amex), **SE**=Speaks English, **NSE**=No English. A price range reflects off-season to peak-season prices. Breakfast isn't included, nor is the 7 percent IVA tax.

Hotel Restaurant El Convento, deep in the Old Town just beyond the *parador*, is the best value in town. Run by a hard-working family, this cozy, newly renovated ten-room hotel offers a few rooms with incredible view balconies (Sb-5,000–5,500 ptas, Db-7,500 ptas, third person-2,000 ptas, CC:VMA, Maldonado 2, tel. & fax 956/70-23-33, SE). See restaurant listing below.

Parador de Arcos de la Frontera is royally located, recently refurbished, and for all its elegance, reasonably priced. If you're going to experience a *parador* (and you can't get into the convent), this might be the one (Sb-12,000 ptas, Db-16,500 ptas, 1,000 ptas more with a terrace, CC:VMA, elevator, air-con, minibars, free parking, etc.; Plaza del Cabildo, tel. 956/70-05-00, fax 956/70-11-16, SE).

Hotel Los Olivos is a bright, cool, and airy new place with a fine courtyard, roof garden, bar, view, friendly English-speaking folks, and easy parking. This is a poor-man's *parador* (Sb-4,000–5,000 ptas, Db-7,000–9,000 ptas, third person-2,000 ptas, CC:VMA, San Miguel 2, tel. 956/70-08-11, fax 956/70-20-18). Their big American breakfast costs 600 ptas.

Hostal Callejon de las Monjas offers the closest thing to budget beds in the Old Town. The simple rooms are decent and clean, though frayed. The *hostal* is on a noisy street next to Santa Maria Church—ask for a *tranquilo* room in the back (Sb-3,000 ptas, D-3,500 ptas, Db-4,500 ptas, CC:V, Dean Espinosa 4, tel. 956/70-23-02, NSE). The friendly owner runs a tiny barber shop in the foyer.

Hotel Marques de Torresoto is a restored 17th-century palace with classy rooms (but few views), a peaceful courtyard, and a view terrace (Sb-6,600–7,000 ptas, Db-8,800–9,000 ptas, Db with salon-10,800 ptas, air-con, CC:VMA, across the street from Restaurante El Convento, Marques de Torresoto 4, tel. 956/70-07-17, fax 956/70-42-05, SE).

Hostal Málaga is surprisingly nice, with clean, attractive rooms, though inconveniently located about 2 kilometers from

the old city center (Sb-2,500–3,000 ptas, Db-4,5
air-con, TV, parking-500 ptas/day, two-level roof
CC:VMA, Ponce de Leon 5, tel. & fax 956/70-20-10
The similar **Hostal Voy-Voy** is next door (Sb-2,000–2
ptas, Db-2,500–5000 ptas, attached restaurant, CC:VMA
Ponce de Leon 9, tel. 956/70-14-12, NSE).

Eating in Arcos

The *parador* is very expensive, though a costly drink on its
million-dollar-view terrace can be rationalized. **Restaurante El
Convento** has a wonderful atmosphere and is graciously run by
Señora María Moreno and her husband, Señor Roldan (daily
13:00–16:00 and 19:00–22:30, near the *parador* at Marques
Torresoto 7, tel. 956/70-32-22). Their daughter, Raquel, speaks
English. The food is well worth the splurge. The hearty 2,500-
pta menu of the day includes a fine red house wine and circular
bread sticks *(picos de Arcos)*, a local specialty.

    Café Bar El Faro, located on the main street at the base
of the Old Town, is also good (closed Tuesday, Debajo
del Corral 16). The sign *"Hay caracoles"* means snails are available, and *"para llevar"* means "to go." Taste the great *tapas* at
the *típico* **Alcaravan**, in a cave 2 blocks off Plaza Cabildo in the
direction of the new town (closed Monday, Calle Nueva 1).
The entertaining **Mambo Bar** on the main square serves great
gazpacho. Drivers can enjoy what may be the best cheap eating
in Spain at the **roadside diner with the green dinosaur** in
Venta de los Rios, 15 minutes from Arcos toward Vejer.

Transportation Connections—Arcos

By bus to: Jerez (hrly, 30 min), **Ronda** (4/day, 2 hrs), **Cadiz**
(9/day, 2 hrs), **Sevilla** (2/day, 2.5 hrs). From **Jerez** there are
hourly connections to **Sevilla**.

MORE ANDALUSIAN HILL TOWNS: THE ROUTE OF THE PUEBLOS BLANCOS

There are plenty of undiscovered and interesting hill towns
to explore. About half the towns I visited were memorable.
Unfortunately, public transportation is frustrating; I'd do
these towns only by car. Good information on the area is
rare. Fortunately, a good map, the tourist brochure (pick it
up in Sevilla), and a spirit of adventure work fine. Here are
two of my favorite finds:

with a tingly setting under a
mb) has a spectacular view.
for those who want to hear
and elderly footsteps
rques de Zahara, with com-
ood value (Sb-3,500 ptas,
ptas, CC:VM, San Juan 3,
and fax 956/12-30-61, SE). **Vento**
(at the .2-km marker as you enter town) serves
great dinners.

▲**Grazalema**—Another postcard-pretty hill town, Grazalema
offers a royal balcony for a memorable picnic, a square where
you can watch local old-timers playing cards, and plenty of
quiet, whitewashed streets to explore. If you decide to stay the
night, **Fonda Garcia** is good (S-1,500 ptas, Sb-3,600 ptas,
D-3,000 ptas, Db-4,800 ptas, T-4,000 ptas, Tb-5,800 ptas,
breakfast-250 ptas, Calle Las Piedras 32, 11610 Grazalema,
tel. 956/13-20-14, NSE).

JEREZ
Jerez, with nearly 200,000 people, is your typical big-city mix
of industry, garbage, car bandits, and dusty concrete suburbs,
but it has two claims to touristic fame: horses and sherry.

Jerez is ideal for a noontime (or midday) visit on a weekday. See the famous horses, sip some sherry, wander through
the old quarter, and swagger out.

Orientation (tel. code: 956)
Tourist Information: The helpful Turismo gives out free
maps and info on the sights and walking tours (Monday–Friday
9:00–14:00 and 17:00–19:00, Saturday 10:00–14:00, closed
Sunday, Largo 39, tel. 956/33-11-50).

Arrival in Jerez: The bus station (at Calle Cartuja and
Madre de Dios) has a simple baggage checkroom at the
"Oficina Municipal" window (if it looks closed, knock on the
window). *Consigna* is the Spanish word for "baggage check."
The train station, a block away, has lockers (400 ptas).

Exit the bus station farthest from the WCs and turn left.
The center of town and the TI are a ten-minute walk away. At
the five-way intersection, angle right on Honda; then, at the
fountain, make a sharp left on the pedestrian street, Largo, to
reach the TI.

If you're arriving by train, angle right as you leave the station. Cross the intersection. The bus station is on your left. Continue straight, following directions from the bus station (above). Taxis into town cost about 400 ptas.

Sights—Jerez

▲▲**Sherry *bodega* tours**—Spain produces more than 10 million gallons per year of this fortified wine, ranging in taste from *fine* (dry) to *amontillado* (medium) to *dulce* (sweet). The name "sherry" comes from English attempts to pronounce Jerez. Your tourist map of Jerez is speckled with wineglasses. Each of these glasses is a sherry *bodega* that offers tours and tasting.

Tours offered by **Wisdom & Warter** are cleverly timed to allow you to see the horses, then take a tour at their shop a block away (300 ptas, 45-minute English tours at 13:15 on Monday, Tuesday, Wednesday, and Friday, 11:00 and 14:00 on Thursday; Calle Pizarro 7, reservations not necessary, open year-round, tel. 956/18-43-06 or 908/59-94-45. Note: 908 area code indicates mobile phone.).

Other bodegas do tours but are less convenient: **Bodega John Harvey** offers English tours weekdays at 10:30 and 12:00 (300 ptas, closed August, Calle de Arcos 53, reservations recommended, tel. 956/48-34-00). **Williams & Humbert** has weekday tours at 13:30 (300 ptas, closed most of August, Nuño de Canas 1, reservations required—confirm the tour is in English, tel. 956/34-65-39). **Gonzalez Byas** is the only *bodega* that offers daily tours (375 ptas on weekdays, tours offered 9:30–13:00, last tour at 13:00; 475 ptas on weekends, from 9:00–11:00, open year-round, Manuel Maria Gonzalez, must reserve, tel. 956/34-00-00).

▲▲**The Royal Andalusian School of Equestrian Art**— If you're into horses, this is a must. Even if you're not, this is horse art like you've never seen. The school does its Horse Symphony show each Thursday at noon (1,500–2,400 ptas, cash only, no CC, reservations tel. 956/31-11-11, fax 956/18-07-57). In addition to the Thursday show, extra performances are scheduled in summer (Saturday at noon in June, July, and September; Friday 22:30 in August; call for current schedule).

This is an equestrian ballet with choreography from classical dressage movements, purely Spanish music, and costumes from the 19th century. The stern horsemen and their talented

Jerez

and obedient steeds prance, jump, and do-si-do in time to the music, to the delight of an arena filled with mostly local horse aficionados.

Training sessions are open to the public on Monday, Tuesday, Wednesday, and Friday, 11:00–13:00, offering a 500-pta sneak preview. You can sip sherry in the arena's bar to complete the Jerez experience. If you're driving, follow signs from the center of Jerez to Real Escuela Andaluza de Arte Ecuestre (guarded parking lot). Otherwise, it's a 25-minute walk from the train station and a ten-minute walk from the TI.

Transportation Connections—Jerez

Jerez's bus station is shared by four bus companies, each with its own schedules, some specializing in certain destinations, others sharing popular destinations such as Sevilla and Algeciras. Shop around for the best departure time. By car it's a zippy 30 minutes from Jerez to Arcos.

By bus to: **Tarifa** (2/day, 2 hrs), **Algeciras** (8/day, 2.5 hrs), **Cadiz** (hourly, 50 min), **Arcos** (hrly, 30 min), **Ronda** (4/day, 2.5 hrs), **Sevilla** (14/day, 1.5 hrs), **Málaga** (1/day, 5 hrs), **Córdoba** (1/day, 3.5 hrs), **Madrid** (6/day, 8 hrs).

By train to: **Cadiz** (hrly, 50 min), **Sevilla** (12/day, 1 hr), **Madrid** (2/day, 4 hrs), **Barcelona** (4/day, 14 hrs).

MEDINA SIDONIA

(For drivers between Tarifa and Arcos)

This place has no Turismo (read "no tourists"). It is white as can be surrounding its church and castle-ruin-topped hill. Give it a quick look. Signs to Vejer route you through the middle to Plaza de España—great for a coffee stop. You can drive from here up to the church (Plazuela de la Yglesia Mayor) where, for a tip, the man will show you around. Even without a tip you can climb yet another belfry for yet another vast Andalusian view. The castle ruins just aren't worth the trouble.

VEJER DE LA FRONTERA

(For drivers between Tarifa and Arcos)

OK, one more whitewashed hill town. Vejer, south of Jerez and just 20 miles north of Tarifa, will lure all but the very jaded off the highway. Vejer's strong Moorish roots give it a distinct Moroccan (or Greek island) flavor—you know, black-clad women whitewashing their homes, and lanes that can't decide if they're roads or stairways. Only a few years ago women wore veils. The town has no real sights (other than its women's faces), no Turismo, and very little tourism, but makes for a pleasant stop.

The coast near Vejer is lonely, with fine but windswept beaches. It's popular with windsurfers and sand flies. The Battle of Trafalgar was fought just off Cabo de Trafalgar (a nondescript lighthouse today). I drove the circle so that you who buy this book need not.

A newcomer on Andalucía's tourist map, the Old Town of Vejer has only two hotels. The **Convento de San Francisco** is a poor-man's *parador* in a classy, refurbished convent (Sb-6,300 ptas, Db-8,500 ptas, but bargainable in off-season, CC:VMA, tel. 956/45-10-01, fax 956/45-04-25, SE). They have the rare but unnecessary Vejer town map. A much better value is the clean and charming **Hostal La Posada** (Sb-2,200 ptas, Db-4,300 ptas, cheaper off-season, Los Rededios 21, tel. 956/45-02-58, NSE). Both are at the entrance to the Old Town, at the top of the switchbacks past the town's lone traffic cop.

RONDA

With 40,000 people, Ronda is one of the largest white towns; and with its gorge-straddling setting, it's one of the most spectacular. While it can be crowded with Costa del Sol day-trippers, nights are peaceful. And since it's served by train and bus, Ronda makes a relaxing break for nondrivers traveling between Granada, Sevilla, or Córdoba.

Ronda's main attractions are its gorge-spanning bridges, the oldest bullring in Spain, and an interesting old town. The breathtaking ravine divides the town's labyrinthine (Old Town) Moorish quarter and its new, noisier, and more sprawling Mercadillo quarter. A graceful 18th-century bridge connects these two areas. Most things of touristic importance (tourist office, post office, hotels, and the bullring) are clustered within a few blocks of this bridge. The *paseo* scene happens in the new town, on Ronda's major pedestrian street, Carrera Espinel.

Orientation

Tourist Information: The TI is on the main square, Plaza España, opposite the bridge (Monday–Friday 10:00–14:00 and 16:00–19:30; Saturday 10:00–15:00 and 16:30–18:30; open Sunday only in high season, 10:30–15:30, tel. 95/287-1272). Buy the 100-pta map, and get local or regional information you need.

Arrival in Ronda: The train station is a 15-minute walk from the center. Turn right out of the station on Avenida Andalucía, turn left at the roundabout (bus station is on your right), then walk 4 blocks and you'll cross Calle Almendra (and several of my hotels). Keep going and you'll reach the pedestrian street in a few blocks. Turn right on the pedestrian street (Carrera Espinel) to reach the TI. From the bus station, cross the roundabout and follow directions above.

Car and Bike Rental: Velasco charges about 6,000 ptas per day for their smallest car (includes insurance, but not taxes; CC:V, Borrego 11, tel. 95/287-2782 or 95/216-5388). Autos Ronda is cheaper (CC:V, Calle Villanueva 3, across from Don Miguel hotel, tel. 95/287-9097). The best place to park is the underground lot at Plaza del Socorro (1 block from the bullring). Call to confirm that Jesus Rosado's bike shop still rents bikes before taking the long hike to Plaza del Ahorro 1, tel. 95/287-0221 (2 blocks from the train station).

Sights—Ronda

▲▲▲**Bridges**—Ronda's main bridge, called the Ponte Nuevo ("new bridge"), mightily spans the steep gorge. It was built in the 18th century to replace an earlier, less sturdy bridge. You can see the foundations of the original bridge (and a great view of the new bridge) from the park named "Vista Panoramica Jardines Ciudad de Cuenca"—from Plaza España walk down Calle Villanueva and turn right on Calle Los Remedios.

Ronda has two other bridges. The 17th-century Ponte Viejo ("old bridge") was built on the foundations of an Arabic bridge. The smaller, misnamed Roman bridge was actually built in the 14th century, long after the Romans' candle burned out.

Bullfighting Ring—The empty 18th-century ring looks overly tidy, but its small museum gives a truer picture of the gore and lore of bullfighting, displaying stuffed heads (of bulls), photos, artwork, posters, and costumes (250 ptas, daily 10:00–19:00, on Calle Virgen de la Paz, near the TI). Bull-fights are scheduled the first two weeks of September and occur occasionally in the spring. *Sol* means "sun" (cheap seats) and *sombra* means "shade."

▲▲**Mondragon Palace (Palacio de Mondragon)**—This beautiful Moorish building (built in the 14th century, lovingly restored in the 16th) houses an enjoyable prehistory museum with exhibits on Neolithic toolmaking and early metallurgy, with many captions in English. Even if you have no interest in your ancestors, this is worth it for the architecture alone (200 ptas, Monday–Friday 10:00–19:00, weekends 10:00–15:00, on Plaza Mondragon in the Old Town). Linger in the two small view gardens, especially the shady one. Wander out to the nearby Plaza de Maria Auxiliadora for more views.

Santa Maria la Mayor Cathedral—This 15th-century church was built on and around the remains of a mosque (that was itself built on the site of a temple to Julius Caesar). Partially destroyed by an earthquake, the reconstruction of the church resulted in the Moorish/Gothic/Renaissance/Baroque fusion (or confusion) you see today. Enjoy the bright frescoes and elaborately carved choir and altar. The treasury

Ronda

LODGING:

1. Royal
2. Ronda Sol
3. Biarritz
4. Atienza
5. El Tajo

6. La Española
7. Virgen del Rocio
8. Don Miguel
9. Reina Victoria

displays vestments that look curiously like matadors' bro-
caded outfits (150 ptas, daily 10:00–1800, in the Old Town).
Parador National de Ronda—Walk around and through this
newest of Spain's fabled *paradores*. The views from the walkway
just below the outdoor terrace are magnificent. Anyone is welcome at the cafés but you have to be a guest to use the pool.

Sleeping in Ronda
(140 ptas = $1, tel. code: 95, zip code: 29400)
Ronda is full of reasonably priced, good-value accommodations. It's most crowded from mid-March through May, and
August through September (though I've never had a problem
getting a room). June and July are not bad. Off-season is from
November through mid-March. Most of my recommendations
are a few minutes to the left of the main square if you're facing
the bridge. Beware—streets tend to change names with frustrating regularity. In the cheaper places, ask for a room with a
ventana (window) to avoid the few interior rooms. Breakfast
and the 7 percent IVA tax are usually not included.

Hotel Royal has clean, comfy, well-maintained rooms,
though some are on a busy street. Ask for a *tranquilo* room in
the back (Sb-3,600 ptas, Db-5,500 ptas, air-con, CC:VMA, 42
Virgen de la Paz, 3 blocks off Plaza España, tel. 95/287-1141,
fax 95/287-8132, some English spoken). Across the street, the
Alameda del Tajo park is a great people place.

The friendly **Hostal Ronda Sol**, less central but quieter, has a
homey atmosphere, pleasant rooms, and a plant-filled courtyard—a
fine value (S-1,500 ptas, D-2,500 ptas, Almendra 11, tel. 95/287-
4497, NSE). Run by the same owner, the next-door **Hostal Biarritz** offers clean rooms and a good value, though the Sol feels a bit
cheerier and brighter (S-1,500 ptas, D-2,500 ptas, Db-3,200 ptas,
Almendra 7, tel. 95/287-2910, NSE).

The 100-room **Hotel El Tajo** has pleasant, quiet rooms
once you get past the tacky Moorish decoration in the foyer
(Sb-4,000 ptas, Db-7,000 ptas, parking-1,000 ptas/day, CC:VM,
Calle Cruz Verde 7, a half-block off the pedestrian street, tel.
95/287-4040, fax 95/287-5099, some English spoken).

Huéspedes La Española has a perfect location just off Plaza
España around the corner from the tourist office. Its balcony and
view make it very popular. This inexpensive hotel was closed for
renovation in '97; call ahead for new prices (José Aparicio 3,
tel. 95/287-1052, NSE).

Hostal Virgin del Rocio, spotless and central, won't overwhelm you with friendliness (Db-3,000–4,000 ptas, breakfast-250 ptas, Calle Nueva 18, near Plaza España, tel. 95/287-7425).

Hostal San Francisco offers a fine value in a great location, just off the Plaza C. Abela, 1 block from the main pedestrian street (Db-3,000–3,500 ptas, Maria Cabrera 18, tel. 95/287-3299).

Ronda offers three tempting splurges. The gorge-facing **Don Miguel** is just left of the bridge. Many of its red-tiled and comfortable rooms have gorgeous views and view balconies—at no extra cost (Sb-6,000 ptas, Db-9,500 ptas, cheaper off-season, breakfast on terrace-400 ptas, parking-750 ptas/day, air-con, elevator, CC:VMA, Calle Villanueva 8, tel. 95/287-7722, fax 95/287-8377, SE).

You can't miss the striking **Parador de Ronda** on the Plaza España—it's an impressive integration of stone, glass, and marble. All rooms have hardwood floors and fantastic views (ask about their family-friendly duplexes), and are surprisingly reasonable, complete with a pool overlooking the bridge (Sb-12,000–15,000 ptas, Db-15,000–20,000 ptas, breakfast-1,200 ptas, garage-1,500 ptas, CC:VMA, Plaza España, tel. 95/287-7500, fax 95/287-8188, SE). Consider at least a drink on the terrace.

The royal **Reina Victoria**, hanging over the gorge at the edge of town, has a great view—Hemingway loved it—but you'll pay for it (Sb-10,000 ptas, Db-17,000 ptas, air-con, elevator, CC:VMA, Jerez 25, tel. 95/287-1240, fax 95/287-1075, SE).

Eating in Ronda

When choosing a place to eat, dodge the tourist traps. They say the best meal in Ronda is at the *parador* (*muy* elegant, figure 3,500 ptas). Plaza del Socorro, 1 block across the main street from the bullring, has plenty of cheap *tapas* bars and restaurants, and Pedro Romero, the little alley that runs between the square and the ring, offers several good possibilities. You'll get good *gazpacho* and cheap daily specials at **El Porton** (CC:VM, Pedro Romero 7, closed Sunday) and similar fare along with good *tapas* at **Hermanos Macias** next door. Menus are clearly posted, and each restaurant offers indoor and outdoor seating. Check out the food on customers' plates (without asking for a taste) and choose your restaurant.

The **Restaurant Pedro Romero** gets good reviews

(across from the bullring at Calle Virgen de la Paz 18). For a local *tapas* treat, duck into **Patatiu-Patutuu** for a board of potatoes and sausage with sauces; this place stays lively later (Calle Alemandra 5). The best view-drinks in town are sipped on the terraces of the Don Miguel Hotel or the Parador.

Transportation Connections—Ronda

By bus to: Arcos (4/day, 2 hrs), **Benoajan** (2/day, 30 min), **Jerez** (4/day, 3 hrs), **Grazalema** (2/day, 1 hr), **Zahara** (2/day, 1 hr), **La Línea** (1/day, 3 hrs), **Sevilla** (5/day, 2.5 hrs; see trains below), **Málaga** (9/day, 2 hrs; access other Costa del Sol points from Málaga, though Marbella and Fuengirola have a few direct trips—ask), **Nerja** (3.5 hrs, transfer in Málaga; can take train or bus from Ronda–Málaga).

By train to: Algeciras (4/day, 2 hrs) **Bobadilla** (4/day, 1 hr), **Málaga** (4/day, 2.5 hrs, transfer in Bobadilla), **Sevilla** (3/day, 3.5 hrs, transfer in Bobadilla), **Granada** (3/day, 3.5 hrs, transfer in Bobadilla), **Córdoba** (4/day, 3.5 hrs, transfer in Bobadilla). Transfers are a snap and time-coordinated in Bobadilla. With four trains arriving and departing simultaneously, double-check that you've jumped on the right one.

Near Ronda: Pileta Caves

The Pileta Caves (Cuevas de la Pileta) are about the best look a tourist can get at prehistoric cave-painting these days. The caves, complete with stalagmites, bones, and 25,000-year-old paintings, are 22 kilometers from Ronda, past the town of Benoajan, at the end of the road.

The farmer who lives down the hill from the caves leads groups through for one-hour tours (800 ptas, daily 10:00–13:00 and 16:00–17:00, closing times indicate last entrance). His grandfather discovered the caves. He is a master at hurdling the language barrier, and as you walk the cool kilometer, he'll spend over an hour pointing out lots of black and red drawings (five times as old as the Egyptian pyramids) and some weirdly recognizable natural formations such as the Michelin man and a Christmas tree. The famous caves at Altamira are closed, so if you want to see neolithic paintings in Spain, this is it.

While possible without wheels (taking the Ronda–Benoajan bus or train and a two-hour uphill hike), I wouldn't bother. (See Ronda car rental information.) By car, it's easy: Leave Ronda north on C339, exit toward Benoajan, then follow the signs, bearing right just before Benoajan, up to the dramatic dead-end. Leave nothing of value in your car.

Route Tips For Drivers—Andalucía

Sevilla to Arcos: The remote hill towns of Andalucía are a joy to tour by car with Michelin map #446 or any other good map. Drivers can zip south on N-IV from Sevilla along the river, following signs to Cádiz. Take the fast toll freeway (blue signs, E5, A4, 30 minutes, 830 ptas).The toll-free N-IV is curvy, lit, and dangerous. About halfway to Jerez, at Las Cabezas, take C343 to Villamartin. From there, circle scenically (and clockwise) through the thick of the Pueblos Blancos—Zahara and Grazalema—to Arcos.

It's about two hours from Sevilla to Zahara. You'll find decent but very winding roads and sparse traffic. You'll wonder why they cut the road so long on the way into Zahara. And then it gets worse if you take the tortuous series of switchbacks over the 4,500-foot summit of Puerto de Las Palomas on the direct but difficult road from Zahara to Grazalema. Remember to refer to your *Ruta de Pueblos Blancos* pamphlet.

Traffic flows through old Arcos only from west to east (coming from the east, circle south under town). The Turismo, my recommended hotels, and parking (Paseo Andalucía) are all in the west. Driving in Arcos is like threading needles. But if your car is small and the town seems quiet enough, follow signs to the *parador*, where you'll find the only old-town car park.

Arcos to Tarifa (80 miles): Drive from Arcos to Jerez in 30 minutes. Follow signs south to Medina Sidonia, then to Vejer and Tarifa. A great (but expensive) freeway connects Sevilla and Jerez de la Frontera. The toll-free highway next to it is nearly as fast.

COSTA DEL SOL: SPAIN'S SOUTH COAST

It's so bad, it's interesting. To northern Europeans, the sun is a drug and this is their needle. Anything resembling a quaint fishing village has been bikini-strangled and Nivea-creamed. Oblivious to the concrete, pollution, ridiculous prices, and traffic jams, tourists lie on the beach like game hens on skewers—cooking, rolling, and sweating under the sun.

Where Europe's most popular beach isn't crowded by high-rise hotels, most of it's in a freeway choke-hold. Wonderfully undeveloped beaches between Tarifa and Cádiz and east of Alveria are ignored, while lemmings make the scene where the coastal waters are so polluted that hotels are required to provide swimming pools. It's a fascinating study in human nature.

Laugh with Ronald McDonald at the car-jammed resorts, but if you want a place to stay and play in the sun, unroll your beach towel at Nerja.

You're surprisingly close to jolly olde England. The land of tea and scones, fish and chips, pubs and bobbies awaits you—in Gibraltar. And beyond "The Rock," the whitewashed port of Tarifa, the least-developed piece of Spain's generally overdeveloped south coast, provides an enjoyable springboard for a quick trip into Morocco (next chapter).

Planning Your Time

My opinions on the "Costa del Turismo" are valid for peak season. If you're there during a quieter time, and you like the

Costa del Sol

ambience of a beach resort, it can be an enjoyable stop. Off-season it can be neutron-bomb quiet.

The whole 150-mile-long coastline takes four hours to drive or six hours by bus. For the cynic, spend a day driving or busing across from Tarifa to Nerja or Granada. If you want to party on the beach, it can take as much time as Mazatlán.

NERJA

Somehow Nerja, while cashing in on the fun-in-the-sun culture, has actually kept much of its quiet, Old World charm. It has good beaches, a fun evening *paseo* that culminates in the proud Balcony of Europe terrace, enough pastry shops and nightlife, and locals who get more excited about their many festivals than the tourists do. For a taste of the British expatriate scene, drop into the TI or W.H. Smiffs' bookstore at 10 Almirante (a.k.a. Calle Cristo), or tune in to Coastline Radio at 97.7. The little open-air market, on San Miguel near the Nerja bus stop, is open mornings except Sunday, but the weekly market is more colorful, lively, and fun (Tuesday 9:30–14:00, along Herrera Oria and Ruperto Anduez).

Orientation (tel. code: 95)

Tourist Information: The helpful, English-speaking TI has town maps, bus schedules, and tips on beaches and side trips (Monday–Friday 10:00–14:00 and 17:30–20:00, Saturday 10:00–13:00, closed Sunday, Puerta del Mar 2, just off the

Nerja

Not to scale—
Bus info kiosk to
Balcon de Europa
is a 10 minute walk

To Caves,
Salobreña
& Granada

N-340   Av. de Pescia

To Malaga

To N-340

To Hell
(Torremolinos)

LODGING:
❶ DON PEQUE
❷ ATEMBENI
❸ MENA
❹ PLAZA CAVANA
❺ BALCÓN DE EUROPA
❻ CALA-BELLA
❼ HABITACIONES EL PATIO

MEDITERRANEAN SEA

BALCON DE EUROPA

DCH

Balcony of Europe, tel. 95/252-1531). Ask for the TI's free
Walks Around Nerja brochure, though gung-ho hikers will
prefer the more detailed *Twelve Walks Around Nerja* booklet
(550 ptas at Smiffs' bookstore).

Car Rental: Nerja has many car rental agencies. Autos Europa charges about 7,500 ptas per day for smaller models (Almirante 7, across from Smiffs' bookstore, tel. 95/252-1317).

Sights—Nerja

▲▲**Balcony of Europe (Balcón de Europa)**—This promenade on a bluff over the beach is the center of the town's *paseo*. It overlooks miles of coastline as well as a few little coves and caves below.

Beaches—Nerja has several good beaches. The sandiest (and most crowded) is down the walkway to the right of the Restaurante Marissal, just off the Balcony of Europe. The pebblier beach, full of fun pathways, crags, and crannies (head down through the arch to the right of the Turismo office), has a trail leading east to a bigger beach, Playa de Burriana.

▲**Caves of Nerja (Cuevas de Nerja)**—These caves, 4 km east of Nerja, have the most impressive piles of stalactites and stalagmites I've seen anywhere in Europe, with huge cathedrals and domed stadiums of caverns filled with expertly backlit formations and appropriate music. Well worth the time and money unless you've seen similar in the States (650 ptas, daily 10:30–14:00 and 15:30–18:00, shorter hours off-season, tel. 95/252-9520). To get to the caves, catch a bus from the Nerja bus stop on San Miguel (95 ptas, 12/day, 15 min).

Frigiliani—This picture-perfect whitewashed village, only 6 kilometers from Nerja, is easy by bus or car. It's a nice detour from the beach, particularly if you don't have time for the Pueblos Blancos hill towns.

Sleeping in Nerja
(140 ptas = about $1, tel. code: 95, zip code: 29780)
Sleep Code: **S**=Single, **D**=Double/Twin, **T**=Triple, **Q**=Quad, **b**=bathroom, **t**=toilet only, **s**=shower only, **CC**=Credit Card (Visa, MasterCard, Amex), **SE**=Speaks English, **NSE**=No English spoken.

The entire Costa del Sol is crowded during peak season. While August is most difficult, mid-July through mid-September is the prime time for Spanish workers to hit the beaches. In high season reserve ahead, arrive early, let the tourist office help you, or try a local home (*casa particular*). Any other time of year, you'll find Nerja has plenty of comfy, low-rise, easygoing, resort-type hotels and rooms. I've listed

rates from low season (winter) to high season (July–August).
At other times, you'll pay midrange.

Hotel Plaza Cavana overlooks a plaza lily-padded with
cafés. If you like marble floors, modern furnishings, an elevator, and a small rooftop swimming pool, dive in (Sb-6,500–
10,000 ptas, Db-9,000–15,000 ptas, extra bed-3,000 ptas, some
view rooms, air-con, parking-900 ptas/day, two-minute walk
from Balcón de Europa at Plaza Cavana 10, tel. 95/252-4000,
fax 95/252-4008, SE).

Within 3 blocks of the Balcony of Europe, you'll find the
boxy, hotelesque **Hostal Residencia Don Peque**. The reception room is smoky, but the rooms are pleasant (Sb-2,700–
4,800 ptas, Db-3,300–4,800 ptas, some rooms with air-con,
CC:VMA, Diputación 13, tel. 95/252-1318, NSE). **Hostal
Atembeni**, across the street, has a more small-town feel with
similarly comfortable rooms (Sb-2,200–3,500 ptas, Db-3,300–
4,700 ptas, ceiling fans, no air-con, CC:VMA, Diputación 12,
tel. 95/252-1341, NSE).

Hostal Residencia Mena is homey with lots of greenery,
but suffers from saggy beds. Some rooms have sea views and
balconies, and most are *tranquilo* (Sb-1,400–2,200 ptas,
Db-2,700–4,200 ptas, El Barrio 15, tel. 95/252-0541, NSE).

Hotel Cala-Bella looks like it was furnished at a garage
sale, but it's central, with some sea-view balconies (Sb-2,500 ptas,
Db-5,000–6,500 ptas, no air-con, tel. 95/252-0704, NSE).

Your most memorable splurge is the **Balcón de Europa,**
right on the water and on the square, with the prestigious
address Balcón de Europa 1 (Sb-7,000–10,500 ptas,
Db-11,000–16,000 ptas, add about 5,000 ptas for suite with
Jacuzzi, air-con, elevator, parking-900 ptas/day, CC:VMA, tel.
95/252-0800, fax 95/252-4490, SE).

Nerja's *parador*, housed in a new office-type building
rather than a castle, lacks character but has spacious, suite-
like, pricey rooms (Sb-11,500–15,500 ptas, Db-15,000–
19,500 ptas, add about 2,000 ptas for Jacuzzi, air-con,
free parking, swimming pool, 15-minute walk from town
center, CC:VMA, Almuñecar 8, tel. 95/252-0050, fax
95/252-1997, SE).

Habitaciónes El Patio is clean, friendly, and really local—
worth the communication struggles (Sb-2,200–3,200 ptas,
Db-3,200–4,700 ptas, Tb-4,750–6,200 ptas, Mendez Nuñez 12,
tel. 95/252-2930, NSE). It's in the residential section about a

two-minute walk from the Nerja bus stop, near the corner of
Calle America and Mendez Nuñez. The kids of the family
always seem to be dressed up and heading off to some festival,
dance, or concert. If no one answers, ask at the nearby fruit
shop.

Your cheapest and often most interesting bet is a **room in
a private home** (*casa particular*). Walk around the residential
streets within about 6 blocks of Calle La Parra with your rucksack. Ask around.

Eating in Nerja

You'll find plenty of lively eateries around the central
Balcony of Europe. Of course, the farther inland you go, the
cheaper and more local it gets, with sea views thumbtacked
onto the wall. Next to the Hotel Cala-Bella, **Cafeteria Anahi**
has good food and great views. Have dinner with the
Mediterranean as your tablecloth (daily 9:00–24:00, serves
meals all day). **Frituur Za Za** is a good place if you feel
like half a chicken (El Barrio 48). **Giovanni's** specializes in
good Italian ice cream, coffee, and conversation (2 Plaza
Cantarero, run by a friendly British couple). Check out the
eateries on Plaza Tutti Frutti.

Tapas: Three good places cluster around Herrera Oria
within 2 blocks of each other. **Los Cunaos** is most fun late in
the evening, when families munch *tapas*, men watch soccer
on TV, women chat, and kids wander around like it's home
(good seafood and prices, Herrera Oria 19, tel. 95/252-1107).
El Pulguilla specializes in seafood, with clams so fresh they
squirt (closed Monday, Bolivia 1, tel. 95/252-1384). **El Chispa**
is similarly big on seafood, with an informal restaurant terrace
in the back (San Pedro 12, tel. 95/252-3697). Remember that
tapas are snack-size portions. To turn *tapas* into a meal, ask for
a *ración*, a dinner-size portion.

Transportation Connections—Nerja

The Nerja bus station is actually just a bus stop on Avenida de
Pescia with an info booth (daily 8:00–14:00 and 15:00–20:00,
helpful schedules posted on booth, tel. 95/252-1504).

By bus to: Nerja Caves (12/day, 15 min), **Málaga**
(12/day, 1.5 hrs), **Granada** (2/day, more frequent with
Motril transfer, 2–3 hours), **Córdoba** (1/day, 4 hrs), **Sevilla**
(3/day, 4 hrs).

Transportation Connections—Málaga

The nearest train station to Nerja is in Málaga.

By train to: Ronda (3/day, 2–3 hrs, transfer in Bobadilla), **Madrid** (7/day, 4.5 hrs on Talgo train), **Córdoba** (6/day, 2 hrs on Talgo), **Granada** (3/day, 3–4 hrs, transfer in Bobadilla), **Sevilla** (2/day, 3 hrs), **Barcelona** (3/day, 14 hrs).

Buses: Málaga's bus station, just a block from the train station, has a helpful information office (located in the middle of the bus station) with an invaluable listing of all the schedules offered by the different bus companies (on Paseo de los Tilos, tel. 95/235-0061).

By bus to: Algeciras (17/day, 3 hrs), **Nerja** (13/day, 1.5 hrs), **Ronda** (4/day, 2.5 hrs), **La Línea** (5/day, 3 hrs), **Sevilla** (10/day, 3 hrs), **Granada** (14/day, 2 hrs), **Córdoba** (4/day, 3 hrs), **Madrid** (12/day, 7 hrs).

Sights—From Nerja to Gibraltar

These highlights are listed in east-west order from just east of Nerja to Gibraltar. Buses take about six hours to make this entire trip. They leave nearly hourly and stop at each town mentioned.

Almuñecar and Salobrena—Smaller and less touristy than Nerja, each has a fray of alleys in the Old Town and a salty, fishing-village atmosphere. These towns are east of the high-rise action and very enjoyable. In Salobrena, the **Hotel Salobrena**, with Mediterranean balconies, is a good value (Sb-4,500–6,000 ptas, 6,500–8,300 ptas, CC:VMA, CRTA Cádiz Barcelona 18680, tel. 95/861-0261, NSE).

Fuengirola/Torremolinos—The most built-up part of the region, where those most determined to be envied settle down, it's a bizarre world of Scandinavian package tours, flashing lights, pink flamenco, multilingual menus, and all-night happiness. Fuengirola is like a Spanish Mazatlán with a few less-pretentious, older, budget hotels between the main drag and the beach. The water here is clean and the nightlife fun and easy. James Michener's idyllic Torremolinos is long gone. If you've landed here and have a car, consider a side trip up to the small village of Mijas for fine Mediterranean views.

Marbella—This is the most polished and posh of the Costa del Sol's resorts. Look for the Turismo sign to the right as you enter the center of town. Cross the main street at the signal closest to the Turismo and walk up to the old city's pedestrian section, veering right. While the high-priced boutiques, immaculate streets, and beautifully landscaped squares are testimony to Marbella's arrival on the world-class-resort scene, cheap accommodations can still be found in old Marbella. Have a *café con leche* on the beautiful Plaza de Naranjas before wandering back down to new Marbella and the high-rise beachfront apartment buildings. Check out the beautiful beach scene before leaving. Marbella is an easy stop on the Algeciras–Málaga bus route (as you exit the bus station, take a left to reach the center of town).

San Pedro de Alcantara—This town's relatively undeveloped sandy beach is popular with young travelers. San Pedro's neighbor, **Puerto Banus**, is "where the world casts anchor." This luxurious jet-set port, complete with casino, is a strange mix of Rolls-Royces, yuppies, boutiques, rich Arabs, and budget browsers.

GIBRALTAR
One of the last bits of the empire that the sun used to never set on, Gibraltar is a fun mix of Anglican propriety, "God Save the Queen" tattoos, military memories, and tourist shops. The British soldiers you'll see are enjoying this cushy assignment in the Mediterranean sun as a reward for enduring and surviving an assignment in another remnant of the British Empire: Northern Ireland. While things are cheaper in pounds, your Spanish money works as well as your English words here. You'll need your passport to cross the border (and officials still seem happy to stamp it—ask or you'll get just a wave-through). Make Gibraltar a day trip; rooms are not cheap.

Orientation (tel. code: 350)
Tourist Information: You'll find TIs on Mackintosh Square (weekdays 10:00–18:00, Saturday 10:00–14:00, closed Sunday, tel. 350/74982) and in the Gibraltar Museum (same hours, tel. 350/74289). The unofficial TIs near customs and the city's gate are more commercial and less helpful.

   Arrival in Gibraltar: From La Línea, it's a five-minute walk to the border (flash your passport) and then a 20-minute walk into downtown Gibraltar (straight across the runway and up Winston Churchill Avenue, angling right at Shell station on Smith Dorrien Ave). Otherwise you can take double-decker bus #9 or #10 into the city (80 ptas, every 15 min, takes a roundabout route past a monolithic Safeway near the docks; get off at the Queensway stop, a block from the TI on Mackintosh Square).

You'll find plenty of aggressive cabbies at the border who'd love to give you a tour; for those with more money than time, this can be a fine value (as low as £10, or $15, per person if taxi is packed) for a ride up the Rock to the Apes' Den and St. Michael's Cave (1.5 hr). More people in a taxi means a lower cost per person—try to buddy up with other travelers. Organized tours (Blands, Exchange, Parodytour) have predictable set fees (around £10 per person) regardless of the number of people on the tour.

If you're day-tripping to Gibraltar, it's easy to store luggage in the lockers at the La Línea bus station or Alcegiras train station.

Drivers may encounter con artists dressed as traffic cops at the border, directing you here or there as if the law were on their side. You may be wise to pay the bribe to have your car watched. If you do drive, expect long delays both getting in and getting out. Drivers should park their car at the edge of Spain and walk into Gibraltar. Drive past the long line of cars waiting to cross the border and, ideally, find a parking meter just past the border station (good for all day if you have enough 100-pta coins).

Helpful Hints: A small Safeway is on Main Street, off Cathedral Square, next to Marks & Spencer (Monday–Saturday 8:00–20:00, Sunday 10:00–17:00). A little covered market bustles outside the Grand Casement Gate (north end of Main Street, 9:00–15:00 except Sunday).

Sights—Gibraltar

▲▲▲**The Rock**—The real highlight is the spectacular Rock itself. From the south end of Main Street, you can catch the cable car to the top (770 ptas one-way, 1,070 ptas round-trip; Monday–Saturday 9:30–17:15, closed Sunday and when it's windy; runs every ten minutes; includes admission to Apes' Den and St. Michael's Cave). The cable car drops you at a slick restaurant/view terrace at the very top of the Rock, from where you can explore old ramparts and drool at the 360-degree view of Morocco, the Strait of Gibraltar, Algeciras and its bay, and the twinkling Costa del Sol arcing eastward. Below you

Gibraltar

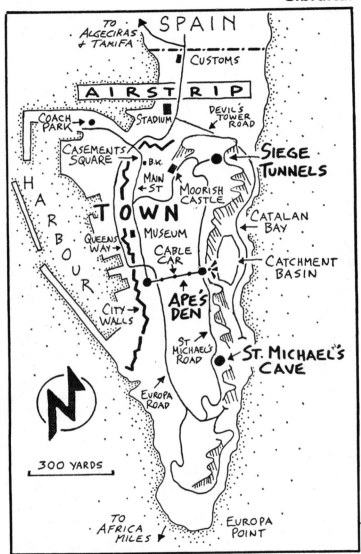

stretches the giant water "catchment system" that the British built to catch rainwater in the not-so-distant past, when Spain allowed neither water nor tourists to cross its disputed border.

The views are especially crisp on brisk off-season days. Buying a one-way ticket up saves a little money and gives you a chance to hike down to the various sites. Allow an hour to hike down, or up to 2.5 hours if you stop at each of the following five sights, all part of the Upper Rock Nature Reserve, which you'll see in order as you descend from the Top of the Rock.

With a round-trip ticket, your best strategy is to take the cable car up, hike downhill to St. Michael's Cave and the Apes' Den, then take the cable car down into town from the Apes' Den, skipping the other sights. Why hike at all, you ask? Because you'd miss St. Michael's Cave if you relied solely on the cable car.

All of the Upper Rock Nature Reserve sights have the same hours (daily 9:30–18:30). A pass for admission to all sites costs around 1,100 ptas (or 825 ptas if you show your cable-car ticket).

▲**St. Michael's Cave**—Studded with stalagmites and stalactites, eerily lit and echoing with classical music, this cave is dramatic, corny, and slippery when wet. Used since neolithic times, prepared (but never used) as a hospital in World War II, it's now a tourist site and auditorium for musical events. Notice the polished cross section of a stalagmite showing weirdly beautiful rings similar to a tree's (free with cable-car ticket).

Apes' Den—This small zoo without bars gives you a chance for a close encounter with some of the famous (and very jaded) apes of Gibraltar. Keep your distance from the apes and beware of their kleptomaniac tendencies. The man at the little booth posts a record of the names of all the apes. (Free with cable-car ticket. The cable car stops here.) If there's no ape action, wait for a banana-toting taxi tour to stop by and stir some up.

▲▲**Siege Tunnels**—Also called the Upper Galleries, these chilly tunnels were blasted out of the rock by the Brits during the Spanish and French siege of 1779 to 1783. Hokey but fun dioramas help recapture a time when Brits were known more for conquests than crumpets. The tunnels are at the northern end of the rock, about 2 km from the Apes' Den (at the fork in the road, follow the sign for "All Directions").

"Gibraltar, a City Under Siege" Exhibition—A spin-off of the siege tunnels, this excuse-for-a-museum gives you a look at life during the siege. It's worth a stop only if you already bought a combination ticket and it's "free" (just downhill from Siege Tunnels).

Moorish Castle—Actually more tower than castle, the building offers a tiny museum of Moorish remnants and carpets. The original castle was built by the Moorish Tarik-ibn-Zeyad in A.D. 711, but his name lasted longer than the castle. Gibel-Tarik (or Tarik's Hill) became Gibraltar. The view from the top is best appreciated by tall people. The tower marks the end of the nature reserve. Head downhill to reach the lower town and Main Street.

Gibraltar Museum—Built atop a Moorish bath, this museum in Gibraltar's lower town tells the story of a rock that has been fought over for centuries. Highlights are a 15-minute history film and the cavelike room that features prehistoric remains and artifacts (oddly hidden away in a room off the art gallery). The first Neanderthal skull was actually found in Gibraltar in 1848, though no one realized its significance until a similar skull found years later in Germany's Neanderthal Valley was correctly identified, stealing the name, claim, and fame from Gibraltar (440 ptas, Monday–Friday 10:00–18:00, Saturday 10:00–14:00, closed Sunday, on Bomb House Lane off Main Street, ignore misleading "closed" entrance).

Transportation Connections—Gibraltar

If you're leaving Gibraltar without a car, you must walk to La Línea, the nearest bus station (level 25-min walk). The region's main transportation hub is Algeciras, with lots of train, bus, and ferry connections. (For Algeciras connections, see Tarifa, below.)

La Línea by bus to: Algeciras (2/hr, 45 min), **Málaga** (4/day, 3 hrs), **Granada** (2/day, 4.5 hrs).

TARIFA

Europe's most southerly town is a pleasant alternative to gritty, noisy Algeciras. It's an Arabic-looking town with a lovely beach, an old castle, restaurants swimming in fresh seafood, inexpensive places to sleep, enough windsurfers to sink a ship, and best of all, hassle-free boats to Morocco.

As I stood on the town promenade under the castle, looking out at almost-touchable Morocco across the Strait of Gibraltar, I regretted only that I didn't have this book to steer me clear of wretched Algeciras on earlier trips. Tarifa, with daily one-hour trips to Tangier, is the best jumping-off point for a Moroccan side trip.

Tarifa has no blockbuster sights (and is pretty dead off-season). Its so-so castle, named after Guzmán El Bueno (a 13th-century Christian general who gained fame by proudly refusing to surrender the castle to the Moors as they killed his son), is surrounded by cool lanes and whitewashed houses. Don't miss the viewpoint patio near the castle. Tarifa's main harbor activity seems to be the daily coming and going of the boat to Tangier. A few minutes from downtown is a sheltered beach, Playa Chica, and on the western shore is a wild and desolate stretch of pristine coastline, the Playa de Lances.

Lately the town's character has changed (to many, suffered) as it has become famous as Europe's windsurfing paradise. With VW vans stacked high with windsurfing gear, lines of wind-blown beach huts, German menus, T-shirts, and thongs, Tarifa has become more of a busy resort.

Orientation (tel. code: 956)

Tourist Information: The TI is on Paseo Alameda (daily 9:30–14:30 and 18:00–20:00 July–August; off-season closed weekends September–June, tel. 956/68-09-93). Pick up a town map.

Ferry to Morocco: If you're going to Morocco, get your boat ticket as soon as possible—there's only one ferry a day and it does sell out. Prices are the same in the many travel agencies and hotels advertising trips to Morocco, so you might call ahead or stop by the first agency you see when you get to town. The going rate is 7,000 ptas for a round-trip all-day tour; 3,000 ptas for a one-way boat ride. (Tarifa travel agencies: Marruecotur, tel. 956/68-18-21, and Tour Africa at the boat dock, tel. 956/68-43-25.) See Morocco chapter for more information.

Arrival in Tarifa: The bus station (just a ticket office) is at 19 Batalla de Salado (Monday–Friday 7:15–11:15 and 16:00–20:00, weekends 15:00–19:45, tel. 956/68-40-38). When you get off the bus, orient yourself by facing the Old Town gate. The recommended hotels in the Old Town are through the gate; the hotels in the newer part of town are a couple of blocks behind you.

Sleeping in Tarifa
(140 ptas = about $1, tel. code: 956, zip code: 11380)

The first four listings (listed in the order you'll see them if you drive in from Sevilla) are right off the main drag, the Batalla del Salado, with easy parking, in the modern, plain part of town. Turn left out of the bus station ticket office and head away from the old city center. The last four are in or bordering the Old Town, very quiet and far from the windsurfing safari. Room rates vary with the season, sometimes doubling from low to high season. Prices are highest July through September. August is very crowded. October to December is mid-season, and January to May is low season. Particularly during high season, singles pay only a little less than the double-room price. Breakfast is extra, just like the 7 percent IVA tax.

Hotel La Mirada is shiny new with modern rooms, some with sea views (Sb-3,000–5,000 ptas, Db-5,000–7,500 ptas, extra bed-1,000 ptas, breakfast-350 ptas, elevator, great views from large terrace, attached restaurant, CC:VMA, Calle San Sebastián 48, tel. 956/68-44-27, fax 956/68-11-62, some English spoken). It's 2 blocks to the right of the main drag, and about 5 blocks away from the Old Town.

The motel-style **Hostal Tarik** is clean and pleasant but short on windows (Db-3,500–6,000 ptas, Tb-4,500–7,500 ptas, CC:VMA, Calle San Sebastián 32, tel. 956/68-06-48, NSE). Surrounded by warehouses, it's 1 block toward the town center from La Mirada.

Hostal Alborada is another squeaky-clean place with a pleasant courtyard. It's a couple of blocks closer to the Old Town on a plain street (Sb-2,000–4,800 ptas, Db-3,500–6,000 ptas, Tb-5,500–7,000 ptas, CC:VM, Calle San José 52, tel. 956/68-11-40, fax 956/68-19-35, Rafael Mesa Rodriguez and Juaquina, some English spoken).

The cheery, family-run **Hostal Avenida** has 11 tidy, comfy rooms and a pretty courtyard, but it's on a busy street leading into town. Ask for one of the four *tranquilo* rooms off the street (Sb-2,000–3,000 ptas, Db-3,500–6,000 ptas, Tb-4,500–7,000 ptas, CC:VM but cash preferred, Calle Pío XII, just off the main drag, tel. 956/68-48-18, NSE).

Hostal Villanueva is your best budget bet; friendly, though no English is spoken, and with a great terrace overlooking the Old Town. It's on a busy street, and the quiet rooms in the back come with the best views (Sb-2,000–2,500 ptas, Db-3,500–5,500 ptas, extra bed for 1,500 ptas, discounts for four-day stays, breakfast-300 ptas, attached restaurant, Avenida de Andalucía 11, just west of the Old Town gate, tel. 956/68-41-49).

Tarifa

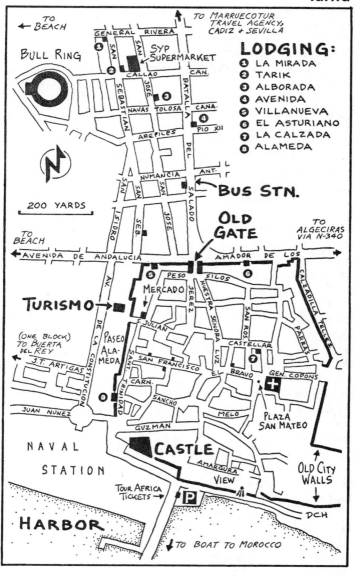

Hostal El Asturiano, nearly a mirror image of Villanueva, also has clean rooms and a restaurant but lacks a public rooftop terrace. Ask for a room *con vista*—with a view of Morocco (Db-3,500–6,500 ptas, T-5,000–7,000 ptas, Quint room #205-8,000–12,000 ptas, extra bed-1,500 ptas, breakfast-250 ptas, CC:VM, Amador de los Rios 8, tel. 956/68-06-19, NSE).

The following are inside the old city: **Hostal La Calzada** has eight well-appointed, quiet, and airy rooms right in the noisy-at-night, old-town thick of things (Db-4,500–6,000 ptas, Tb-5,000–7,000 ptas, closed October–March, CC:VMA, Calle Justino Pertinez 7, veer left and down from the Old Town gate, tel. 956/68-03-66 or 956/68-14-92, NSE).

Hostal Alameda glistens with pristine marble floors and happy pastels, overlooking a square where the local children play, on the edge of the Old Town near the port (Db-4,000–5,000 ptas, Tb-6,000–8,000 ptas, breakfast-450 ptas, CC:VM, Paseo Alameda 4, veer right upon entering the old gate and go all the way down, tel. 956/68-11-81, some English spoken). Its 11 bright rooms are above its restaurant (great *gazpacho*).

Eating in Tarifa

You'll find good *tapas* throughout the Old Town and good seafood in places around Plaza San Mateo. **Café Central** is the happening place nearly any time of day (all *tapas* are priced at 150 ptas, good salads, on the corner of El Bravo and Pedro Cortes, off Plaza San Mateo). Across the street is **Panadería la Francesa**, a tiny takeout French deli offering good, cheap sandwiches. The nearby **Melli Bar** is lively and serves a good *chorizo* dish. In the new town, **Meson El Agobio** has great seafood stew and prices (San Sebastian 4).

Calle San Francisco has some good restaurants. Try **Guzman El Bueno**, **Ricon de Juan**, or the cheap **Pizzeria La Capricciosa**.

The street Buerta del Rey, a family scene at night, is punctuated with snack bars. Stop by the *heladeria* for ice cream or **La Dulce Campesina** for tasty pastries and coffee.

Assemble a picnic lunch at any of the many groceries, the *mercado municipal* (Monday–Saturday 8:00–14:00, closed Sunday, in the Old Town), or the SYP supermarket (Monday–Saturday 9:30–14:00 and 17:00–21:30, closed Sunday, has simple cafeteria;

at the intersection of Callao and San Jose, near the hotels in the newer part of the town).

Transportation Connections—Tarifa

By bus to: Cadiz (8/day, 2 hrs), **Jerez** (1/day, 2 hrs), **Huelva** (1/day, 5 hrs), **Sevilla** (3/day, 3 hrs), **La Línea** and **Gibraltar** (7/day, 1 hr), **Málaga** (3/day, 4 hrs), **Algeciras** (10/day, 30 min).

Transportation Connections—Algeciras

Algeciras is only worth leaving. Use it as a transfer point, and then only if necessary. The train station is 4 blocks inland on the far side of the Hotel Octavio (up Juan de la Cierva). The Comes bus station, which offers frequent service to La Línea and Tarifa, is a half-block away (next door to the Hotel Octavio), and the TI is a couple of blocks down on the same street, Juan de la Cierva, as you head toward the sea (TI open Monday–Friday 9:00–14:00, tel. 956/57-26-36). The port is a couple of blocks beyond the TI. The string of travel agencies along the waterfront all sell ferry tickets and accept credit cards (for ferries to Morocco, see Morocco chapter). The Bus Málaga station is on the waterfront, kitty-corner from the port (offers 11 buses/day to Málaga, 3 hrs, Virgen Carmen 15).

By bus to: La Línea/Gibraltar (2/hr, 45 min), **Tarifa** (10/day, 30 min), **Jerez** (4/day, 2.5 hrs), **Sevilla** (4/day, 3 hrs), **Granada** (3/day, 5 hrs), **Málaga** (11/day, 3 hrs), **Madrid** (2/day, 12 hrs), **Lisbon** (3/week, 10 hrs). You can bus across the entire Costa del Sol and reach Nerja for dinner.

By train to: Ronda (4/day, 2 hrs), **Málaga** (3/day, 4 hrs, transfer in Bobadilla), **Granada** (3/day, 5 hrs, transfer in Bobadilla), **Sevilla** (3/day, 5 hrs, transfer in Bobadilla). All four rides are scenic and the trip to Málaga via Bobadilla is one of Spain's finest mountain train rides. There are also two trains each night to Madrid (12 hrs).

Route Tips for Drivers

Tarifa to Nerja via Gibraltar (150 miles): The short and scenic drive from peaceful Tarifa past Algeciras to La Línea (the Spanish town bordering Gibraltar) takes 45 minutes, passing an impressive forest of windmills. There's a scenic rest stop (with café) just outside Tarifa for great Rock-viewing. Upon arrival at the Gibraltar border, the resident con artist may tell you that you can't drive into Gibraltar. The local police say otherwise. There is often a long line of cars at the border, and parking in Spain and walking in is an option. The border is actually an airstrip, and when the light is green, look left, right, and up before crossing. From Gibraltar, the trip along the Costa del Sol is (barring traffic problems) smooth and easy by car. Just follow the coastal highway east. After Málaga, you'll follow signs to Almería and Motril.

Nerja to Granada (80 miles, 90 minutes, 100 views): Drive along the coast to Salobrena, catching E103 north for about 40 miles to Granada. While scenic side trips may beckon, don't arrive late in Granada without a firm reservation. In Granada, follow signs to the Alhambra and park (at least temporarily) on the Plaza Nueva or along Cuesta de Gomerez.

MOROCCO

MOROCCO

Go to Africa. As you step off the boat you realize that the hour-long crossing has taken you farther culturally than did the trip from the U.S.A. to Iberia. Morocco needs no museums; its sights are living in the streets. The one-day excursions (daily, year-round) from Tarifa are well-organized and reliable, and given the steep price of the boat passage alone, the tour package is a good value for those who can spare only a day for Morocco.

Morocco in a Day?

There are many ways to experience Morocco, and a day in Tangier is probably the worst. But all you need is a passport (no visa or shots required), and if all you have is a day, this is a real and worthwhile adventure. Tangier is the Tijuana of Morocco, and everyone there seems to be expecting you.

The tours organized in Tarifa charge 7,000 ptas and give you a round-trip crossing, a good guide to meet you at the harbor in Tangier and hustle you through the hustlers and onto your bus, and a bus tour. The latter includes a city tour, a trip to the desolate Atlantic Coast for some impressively rugged African scenery, the famous ride-a-camel stop, a walk through the *medina* (market) with a too-thorough look at a carpet shop, a chance to do battle with the sales-starved local merchants, and a big lunch in a palatial Moroccan setting with live music.

Sound cheesy? It is. But no amount of packaging can gloss over how exotic and different this culture really is. This kind

Morocco

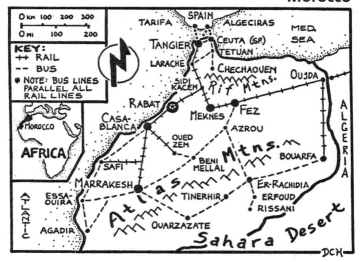

of cultural voyeurism is almost embarrassing, but it's nonstop action and more memorable than another day in Spain. The shopping is—Moroccan. Bargain hard!

The day trip is so tightly organized you'll have hardly any time alone in Tangier. For many people, that's just fine. Some, however, spend a night there and return the next day. Ask about the two-day, 12,500-pta tour at the tourist office in Tarifa. (See Ferry Connections, below, for travel agencies.) You can buy and sell dirhams at the Bank of Morocco branch in the Algeciras terminal. But for a short one- or two-day trip, there's no need to change money. Everyone you meet will be happy to take your *pesetas* or dollars.

Extended Tour of Morocco

Morocco gets much better as you go deeper into the interior. The country is incredibly rich in cultural thrills—but you'll pay a price in hassles and headaches. It's a package deal, and if danger's your business, it's a great option.

To get a fair look at Morocco, you must get past the hustlers and con artists of the north coast (Tangier, Tétouan). It takes a minimum of four or five days to make a worthwhile visit—ideally seven or eight. Plan at least two nights in either

Fès or Marrakech. A trip over the Atlas Mountains gives you an exciting look at Saharan Morocco. If you need a vacation from your vacation, check into one of the idyllic Atlantic beach resorts on the south coast. Above all, get past the northern day-trip-from-Spain, take-a-snapshot-on-a-camel fringe. Oops, that's us. Oh, well.

If you're relying on public transportation for your extended tour, sail to Tangier, blast your way through customs, listen to no hustler who tells you there's no way out until tomorrow, and walk from the boat dock over to the train station. From there, just set your sights on Rabat, a dignified, European-type town with fewer hustlers, and make it your get-acquainted stop in Morocco. Trains go farther south from Rabat.

If you're driving a car, sail from Algeciras to Ceuta, a Spanish possession. Crossing the border is a bit unnerving, since you'll be jumped through several bureaucratic hoops. You'll go through customs, buy Moroccan insurance for your car (cheap and easy), and feel at the mercy of a bristly bunch of shady-looking people you'd rather not be at the mercy of. Most cars are shepherded through by a guy who will expect a tip. Relax and let him grease those customs wheels. He's worth it. As soon as possible, hit the road and drive to Chefchaouen, the best first stop for those with their own wheels.

Orientation (Mental)

Thrills: Morocco *is* culture shock—both bad and good. It makes Spain and Portugal look meek and mild. You'll encounter oppressive friendliness, the Arabic language, squiggly writing, the Islamic faith, and ancient cities. It is a photographer's delight, very cheap, with plenty of hotels, surprisingly easy transportation, and a variety of terrain, from Swiss-like mountain resorts, to fairy-tale mud-brick oasis towns, to luxuriously natural beaches, to bustling desert markets.

Spills: Many travelers are overwhelmed by its intensity, poverty, aggressive beggars, brutal heat, and slick con men. Most of the English-speaking Moroccans that the tourist meets are hustlers. Most visitors have some intestinal problems. Most women are harassed on the streets by horny but generally harmless men. Things don't work smoothly. In fact, compared to Morocco, Spain resembles Sweden for efficiency. People don't see the world through the same filters we do, and some very good parents proudly name their sons Saddam. This is Islam.

Leave aggressive itineraries and split-second timing in Europe. Morocco must be taken on its own terms. In Morocco things go smoothly only *"Inshallah"*—if God so wills.

Helpful Hints

Friday: The Muslim day of rest, when most of the country (except Tangier) closes down.

Money: Change money only at banks, all of which have uniform rates. The black market is dangerous. Change only what you need and keep the bank receipt to reconvert if necessary. Don't leave the country with Moroccan money. (If you do, the Bank of Morocco branch in Algeciras may buy it back from you.)

Health: Morocco is much more hazardous to your health than Spain or Portugal. Eat in clean—not cheap—places. Peel fruit, eat only cooked vegetables, and drink reliably bottled water (Sidi Harazem or Sidi Ali). When you do get diarrhea, and you should plan on it, adjust your diet (small and bland meals, no milk or grease) or fast for a day, but make sure you replenish lost fluids. Relax; most diarrhea is not serious, just an adjustment that will run its course.

Information: For an extended trip, bring travel information from home or Spain. The green *Michelin Morocco* guidebook is good (if you read French). Also recommended are those published by Lonely Planet, the Rough Guides, and *Let's Go: Spain and Portugal* (which includes Morocco). Buy the best map you can find locally—names are always changing, and it's helpful to have towns, roads, and place names written in Arabic.

Language: The Arabic squiggle-script, its many difficult sounds, and the fact that French is Morocco's second language make communication tricky for English-speaking travelers. A little French goes a long way, but learn a few words in Arabic. Have your first local friend help you pronounce *min fadlik* (please; meen FAD-leek), *shókran* (thank you; SHOW-kron), *ismahli* (excuse me; ees-MAY-lee), *yeh* (yes; EE-yuh), *lah* (no; lah), and *maa salama* (goodbye; mah sah-LEM-ah). In markets, I sing "la la la la la" to my opponents. *Lah shókran* means "No, thank you." Listen carefully and write new words phonetically. Bring an Arabic phrase book. Make a point of learning the local number symbols; they are not like ours (which we call "Arabic").

Keeping your bearings: Navigate the labyrinthine *medinas* by altitude, gates, and famous mosques or buildings.

Write down what gate you came in so you can enjoy being lost—temporarily. *Souk* is Arabic for a particular *medina* "department" (such as leather, yarn, or metalwork).

Hustlers: While Moroccans are some of Africa's wealthiest people, you are still incredibly rich to them. This imbalance causes predictable problems. Wear your money belt. Assume con artists are more clever than you. Haggle when appropriate (prices skyrocket for tourists). You'll attract hustlers like flies at every famous tourist sight. They'll lie to you, get you lost, blackmail you, and pester the heck out of you. Never leave your car or baggage where you can't get back to it without your "guide." Anything you buy in their company gets them a 20 percent commission. Normally locals, shopkeepers, and police will come to your rescue when the hustler's heat becomes unbearable. I usually hire a youngster as a guide, since it's helpful to have a translator, and once you're "taken," the rest seem to leave you alone.

Marijuana: In Morocco marijuana *(kif)* is as illegal as it is popular, as many Westerners in local jails would love to remind you. Some dealers who sell it cheap make their profit after you get arrested. Cars and buses are stopped and checked by police routinely throughout Morocco—especially in the north and in the Chefchaouen region, which is Morocco's *kif* capital.

Getting around Morocco: Moroccan trains are quite good. Second class is cheap and comfortable. Buses connect all smaller towns quite well. By car, Morocco is impressively easy. Drive very defensively and never rely on the oncoming driver's skill. Night driving is dangerous. Pay a guard to watch your car overnight.

TANGIER

Tangier is split into two: the new, with the TI and fancy hotels; and the old, with the *medina*, the Kasbah (with its palace), cheap hotels, decrepit homes, and 2,000 wanna-be guides. The twisty, hilly streets of the Old Town are caged within a wall accessible by keyhole gates. A little square, Petit Socco, in the Old Town is lined with tea shops. The big square, Grand Socco, is the link between the old and new parts of town.

If you're on a tour, just follow your leader. Note that your leader meets you in Tangier after you get off the boat from Spain (not in Spain when you board).

If you're on your own, you'll be fighting off "guides." To minimize hustling, you can hire an official guide at the TI (3 hrs for 1500 ptas) or ask directions of people who can't leave what they're doing (such as the only clerk in a shop) or of women who aren't near men. Ask "Kasbah?" or wherever you want to go, and you'll get pointed in the right direction. Fewer hustlers are in the new (but less interesting) parts of town.

Planning Your Time

If you're a shopper, head straight for the market. Otherwise, head to the TI, get a map and advice, and walk to the Grand Socco and market. Ideally start with the highest point first (TI, Kasbah, palace, museums), then work your way downhill through the market.

Sleeping in Tangier
(8.2 dirhams = $1, tel. code: 9)

Sleep Code: **S**=Single, **D**=Double/Twin, **T**=Triple, **Q**=Quad, **b**=bathroom, **t**=toilet only, **s**=shower only, **CC**=Credit Card (Visa, MasterCard, Amex), **SE**=Speaks English, **NSE**=No English.

These hotels are centrally located near the TI and American Express (54 Boulevard Pasteur), walking distance from the market. The first two are four-star hotels. To reserve from Spain, dial 07 (Spain's international access code), 212 (Morocco's country code), 9 (Tangier's city code), then the local number.

Rembrandt Hotel, with a restaurant, bar, and (sometimes filled) swimming pool, has clean, comfortable rooms, some with views (Sb-500 dirhams, Db-600 dirhams, elevator, CC:VMA, tel. 93-78-70, fax 93-04-43, SE). Across the street the **Hotel Tanjah-Flandria** is more formal (less friendly), more expensive, and similarly furnished (Sb-600 dirhams, Db-700 dirhams, restaurant, elevator, rooftop terrace, CC:VMA, tel. 93-32-79, fax 93-43-47, SE).

Hotel Paris, across from the TI, is noisy, dingy, and friendly. Ask for a room in the back—and a mop. (Sb-200 dirhams, Db-275 dirhams, 42 Boulevard Pasteur, tel. 93-18-77, the helpful and informative manager SE.)

Ferry Connections from Spain

If possible, buy a round-trip ticket in Spain. (I've had departures from Morocco delayed by ticket-buying hassles there.) Boats run daily, year-round. Some hotels also sell the tours (same price as travel agencies). In summer Tangier is two hours earlier than Tarifa (one hour's difference in winter). Confirm the local time of departure. For each departure, you'll go through two different passport stamping lines (plan on spending one hour of your day in lines). Departing from Spain, passports are checked on the boat; arrive about 45 minutes before the departure time, or you'll spend the crossing standing in line on the boat.

Tarifa to Tangier: There's a daily one-hour crossing every morning around 9:30 (6,000 ptas round-trip, passengers only, free parking at Tarifa boat dock). Tour options are available (7,000 ptas for one day, 12,500 ptas for two days).

The major travel agencies in Tarifa are Marruecotur (Monday–Saturday 8:30–20:00, Sunday 8:30–13:00, shorter hours off-season, CC:VMA, Batalla de Salado 57, tel. 956/68-18-21, fax 956/68-02-56) and Tour Africa (daily 8:00–13:00 and 17:00–20:00, shorter hours at whim, at far end of the dock, GAT 143, CC:VMA, tel. 956/68-43-25, fax 956/68-48-35). Marruecotur also has another office at Tarifa: CN-340, km 82.5 (for drivers), which closes one hour earlier (tel. 956/68-40-75). Although it's smart to get tickets early, you rarely need to book more than a day in advance, even during peak season. Isnasa, the company that operates the boat line, also sells tickets (though not tours). Their office is on the Tarifa dock (daily 8:30–10:00 and 18:30–20:00, CC:VMA, buy tickets at dock or call office in Algeciras: tel. 956/65-28-00).

Algeciras to: Tangier (5 ferries/day; 6/day in summer; 2.5 hrs, 3,000 ptas each way, 9,300 ptas for a car; plus 1 hydrofoil/day, 1 hr, same cost), **Ceuta** (5 ferries/day, 1.5 hrs, 1,200 ptas each way, 8,200 ptas for a car; plus 6 hydrofoils/day, 30 min, 2,000 ptas each way). Ceuta, an uninteresting Spanish possession in North Africa, is the best car-entry point but is not for those relying on public transport. From Ceuta, drive into Morocco. For more info on ferry schedules, call the Algeciras TI (Monday–Friday 9:00–14:00, tel. 956/57-26-36).

Sights—Moroccan Towns

▲▲**Chefchaouen**—Just two hours by bus or car from Tétouan, this is the first pleasant town beyond the Tijuana-type north coast. Monday and Thursday are colorful market days. Stay in the classy old Hotel Chaouen on Plaza el-Makhzen. This former Spanish *parador* faces the Old Town and offers fine meals and a pleasant refuge from hustlers. Wander deep into the whitewashed Old Town from here.

▲▲**Rabat**—Morocco's capital and most European city, Rabat is the most comfortable and least stressful place to start your North African experience. You'll find a colorful market (in the old neighboring town of Salé), several great bits of Islamic architecture (mausoleum of Mohammed V), the king's palace, mellow hustlers, and comfortable hotels.

▲▲▲**Fès**—More than just a funny hat that tipsy Shriners wear, Fès is the religious and artistic center of Morocco. It bustles with craftsmen, pilgrims, shoppers, and shops. Like most large Moroccan cities, it has a distinct new town (*ville nouvelle*) from the French colonial period and a more exotic— and stressful—old Arabic town where you'll find the *medina*. The Fès marketplace is Morocco's best.

▲▲▲**Marrakech**—Morocco's gateway to the south, this market city is a constant folk festival bustling with *djellaba*-clad Berber tribespeople, a colorful center where the desert, mountain, and coastal regions merge. The new city has the train station, and the main boulevard (Mohammed V) is lined with banks, airline offices, a post office, a tourist office, and comfortable hotels. The old city features the mazelike *medina* and the huge Djemaa el-Fna, a square seething with people, usually resembling a 43-ring Moroccan circus. Near this square you'll find hordes of hustlers, plenty of eateries, and cheap hotels (to check for bugs, step into the dark hotel room, then flip on the lights and count 'em as they flee).

▲▲▲**Over the Atlas Mountains**—Extend your Moroccan trip three or four days with an excursion south over the Atlas Mountains. Take a bus from Marrakech to Ouarzazate (short stop), then to Tinerhir (great oasis town, comfy hotel, overnight stop). Next day, go to Er Rachidia (formerly Ksar es Souk) and take the overnight bus to Fès.

By car, drive from Fès south, staying in the small mountain town of Ifrane, and then continue deep into the desert country past Er Rachidia and on to Rissani (market days: Sunday, Tuesday, and Thursday). From there you can explore nearby mud-brick towns still living in the Middle Ages. Hire a guide to drive you past where the road stops, cross-country to an oasis village (Merzouga) where you can climb a sand dune to watch the sun rise over the vastness of Africa. Only a sea of sand separates you from Timbuktu.

Transportation Connections—Morocco

Trains from Tangier to: Rabat (4/day, 6 hrs), **Casablanca** (5/day, 6 hrs), **Marrakech** (5/day, 10 hrs), **Fès** (2/day, 6 hrs), **Ceuta** and **Tétouan** (hrly buses, 1 hr).

From Fès to: Casablanca (8/day, 5 hrs), **Marrakech** (4/day, 9 hrs), **Rabat** (7/day, 4 hrs), **Meknes** (10/day, 1 hr), **Tangier** (5/day, 5 hrs).

From Rabat to: Casablanca (12/day, 1.5 hrs), **Fès** (6 buses/day, 5.5 hrs), **Tétouan** (2 buses/day, 4 hrs).

From Casablanca to: Marrakech (6/day, 5 hrs).

From Marrakech to: Meknes (4/day, 10 hrs), **Ouarzazate** (4 buses/day, 4 hrs).

PORTUGAL

LISBON

Lisbon is a wonderful, ramshackle mix of now and then. Old wooden trolleys shiver up and down its hills, bird-stained statues mark grand squares, taxis rattle and screech through cobbled lanes, and well-worn people sip coffee in Art Nouveau cafés. Lisbon, like Portugal in general, is underrated. The country seems somewhere just beyond Europe. The pace of life is noticeably slower than in Spain. Roads are rutted. Prices are cheaper. The economy is based on fishing, cork, wine, and manufacturing. Be sure to balance your look at Iberia with enough Portugal.

While Lisbon's history goes back to the Romans and the Moors, the glory days were the 15th and 16th centuries, when explorers like Vasco da Gama opened new trade routes around Africa to India, making Lisbon one of Europe's richest cities. The economic boom fueled the flamboyant art boom called the Manueline period, named after Portugal's King Manuel I. Later, in the early 18th century, the gold and diamonds of Brazil, one of Portugal's colonies, made Lisbon even wealthier.

Then, on All Saints' Day in 1755, while most of the population was in church, the city was hit by a tremendous earthquake. Candles quivered as far away as Ireland. Lisbon was dead center. Two-thirds of the city was leveled. Fires started by the many church candles raged throughout the city, and a huge tidal wave blasted the waterfront. Forty thousand of Lisbon's 270,000 people were killed.

Under the energetic and eventually dictatorial leadership of Prime Minister Marquis Pombal, Lisbon was rebuilt in a progressive grid plan with broad boulevards and square squares. Bits of pre-earthquake Lisbon charm survive in Belém, the Alfama, and the Baírro Alto district.

Portugal's vast colonial empire is virtually gone. Many remaining bits disappeared with the 1974 revolution that delivered her from the right-wing Salazar dictatorship. Emigrants from former colonies such as Mozambique and Angola have added diversity and flavor to the city, making it more likely that you'll hear African music than Portuguese *fado* these days.

But Lisbon's heritage survives. The city seems better organized, cleaner, and more prosperous and people-friendly now than in the 1980s. Square and elegant outdoor cafés, exciting art, entertaining museums, a hill-capping castle, the saltiest sailors' quarter in Europe, and much more, all at bargain-basement prices, make Lisbon a world-class city.

Lisbon will host EXPO '98 "The Ocean and the Seas" from June to September 1998, celebrating the 500th anniversary of Vasco da Gama's voyage to India and focusing on the importance of healthy, clean waters in our environment. The fairgrounds are along the river, east of the Santa Apolonia train station. Expect crowds, higher prices, and lots of excitement. Reserve your hotel early. The dramatic new Vasco da Gama bridge will link the fairgrounds to the south side of the river.

Planning Your Time

With three weeks in Iberia, Lisbon is worth two days: one for the city and one for day trips.

Day 1: Start by touring the castle São Jorge and surveying the city from its viewpoint. After a coffee break at the café next to Alfama viewpoint, Miradour de Santa Luzia, descend into the Alfama. Explore. Back in the Baixa (bai-shah, lower city), have lunch in the Rossio area and walk to the funicular near Praça dos Restauradores. Start the described walk through the Baírro Alto with a ride up the funicular. This afternoon might be a good time to joyride on trolley #28. If it's not later than 15:00, art-lovers can take the Metro or a taxi to the Gulbenkian Museum. After a break at the hotel, have dinner at Cervejaría da Trinidade. Finish off with a *fado* show in the Baírro Alto.

Day 2: Trolley to Belém, tour the tower, monastery, and coach museum. Have lunch in Belém (picnics are ideal). You could catch the train or drive to Sintra to tour the Pena Palace and explore the ruined Moorish castle. If you have a car, drive out to Cabo da Roca. Spend the evening in the resorts of Estoril or Cascais, or back in Lisbon. If you're itchy for the beach, you could drive five hours from Sintra to the Algarve.

A third day could easily be spent at the Museum of Ancient Art and browsing through the Rossio, Baírro Alto, and Alfama.

The Gulbenkian museum and the side trip to Sintra/Cabo da Roca are time-consuming and rush Lisbon. If you'd appreciate more time to absorb the general ambience of the city, spend a full two days in Lisbon and do the museum (the Gulbenkian is mediocre by Paris or Madrid standards) and side trip only if you have a third day.

Orientation (tel. code: 01)

Lisbon's center is a series of parks, boulevards, and squares bunny-hopping between two hills down to the waterfront. The main boulevard, Avenida da Liberdade, goes from the high-rent district downhill, ending at the Praça dos Restauradores (TI, Rossio train station), where an obelisk celebrates the restoration of Portuguese independence from Spain. The monumental Rossio and Figueira squares (with plenty of buses, subways, cheap taxis, and pigeons leaving in all directions) are just beyond that. Between the Rossio and the harbor is the flat lower city, the Baixa, with its many cafés, bustling shops, elegant architecture, and checkerboard street plan (rebuilt after the earthquake on a grid plan with uniform five-story buildings). Several streets are pleasant pedestrian zones, making this area even more enjoyable. The mosaic-decorated Rua Augusta is every bit as delightful as Barcelona's Ramblas for strolling. Most of Lisbon's prime attractions are within walking distance of the Rossio.

The three characteristic neighborhoods that line the downtown harborfront are: Baixa (with its gridplan business district, in the middle), the Chiado/Baírro Alto (Lisbon's "Latin Quarter," on a hill to the west), and the tangled, medieval Alfama (topped by the castle on the hill to the east).

Avenida da Liberdade is the tree-lined Champs Elysées of Lisbon, connecting the Rossio with the newer upper town (airport, bullring, popular fairgrounds, Edward VII Park, and breezy botanical gardens).

Tourist Information

The main tourist information office gives out a map and free monthly magazines on events: *Lisboaem* and *What's on in Lisbon* (with more English) are both better than the *Cultural Agenda* (daily 9:00–20:00, free room-finding service, at the lower end of Avenida da Liberdade in the Palacio da Foz at Praça dos Restauradores, Metro: Restauradores, 3 blocks north of Rossio, tel. 01/346-6307). The TI's city map is nearly useless. The Falk Map, sold for 1,100$ at bookstores *(liveiros)*, is excellent.

Arrival in Lisbon

By Train: Lisbon has four train stations. Rossio station is the most centrally located (within walking distance of most of my hotel listings) and handles trains from Sintra (and Óbidos and Nazaré, with transfers at Cacém). There's a handy train information office on the ground floor of the station (Monday–Friday 9:00–18:00, weekends 10:00–19:00). Lisbon's Santa Apolonia station covers Coimbra, nearly all of Portugal (except the south), Madrid, and other international trains. It's just past the Alfama, with foreign-currency change machines and good bus connections to the town center (buses #9, #39, #46, and #90 go from the station through the center and up Avenida da Liberdade). A taxi from Santa Apolonia to any hotel I recommend should cost around 700$ (including the luggage supplement). If there's a long taxi-stand lineup, walk a block away and hail one off the street. The Barreiro train station, a 30-minute ferry ride across the Tagus River *(Rio Tajo)* from Praça do Comércio, is for trains to the Algarve and points south (the 160$ ferry ticket is generally sold to you with a train ticket). Caís do Sodre station handles the 30-minute rides to Cascais and Estoril. If you'll be leaving Lisbon by train, check to see if your train requires a reservation (boxed "R" in timetable, or ask at train station); if so, reserve early.

By Bus: Lisbon's Rodoviara bus station is at Avenida Casal Ribeiro 18 (Metro: Saldanha, tel. 01/354-5439). Take a taxi to get downtown, or if you have more time than money, turn right out of the bus station on to Avenida Casal Ribeiro and walk to its end at the grand Avenida Republica, turn right there and walk 4 more blocks to the Metro. Take the Metro

(70$, buy at machines) to the Rossio metro stop (transfer at Rotunda) and you've made it. The bus station is within walking distance of American Express (good place to cash traveler's checks; see Helpful Hints, below).

By Plane: Lisbon's easy-to-manage airport (tel. 01/840-2060), just 8 kilometers northeast of downtown, has a 24-hour bank, ATM and bill-changer machines, a tourist office, reasonable taxi service (1,500$–center), good city bus connections into town (#44 and #45, 150$), and an airport bus. The Aero-Bus runs between the airport and the Caís Sodre train station, with various stops including Restauradores, Rossio, and Praça do Comércio (430$, 3/hr, 30 min, operates 7:00–21:00, buy ticket on bus). Your ticket is actually a one-day Lisbon transit pass that covers bus, tram, and elevator rides. If you fly in on TAP airline, show your ticket at the TAP welcome desk on the arrivals level to get a free one-way voucher for the Aero-Bus (TAP tel. 01/841-6990). A Lisbon transit pass (sold in one-day and three-day versions) covers the Aero-Bus trip to the airport if you're flying out of Lisbon.

Getting Around Lisbon

By Metro: Lisbon's simple, fast, 70$-per-ride subway runs only north of Praça Rossio (Rossio Square) into the new town. You'll need it only for the Gulbenkian Museum, the fairgrounds, a bullfight, and the long-distance bus station. Bring change for the ticket machines, as many stations are un-staffed. Remember to validate your ticket. Metro stops are marked with a red "M." *Saida* means exit.

By Trolley, Funicular, and Elevator: For fun and practical public transport, use the trolley system, the funicular, and the Eiffelesque elevator (tickets at the door, going every few minutes) that connect the lower and upper towns. One ride on any of these costs 150$. The 430$ day pass and the 1,000$ three-day transit pass cover all public transportation (including the extensive city bus system) except for the Metro.

The Bilhete Unico de Coroa gives you two trips on the tram, bus, or elevator for only 150$ (half the cost of two one-way tickets). Buy these tickets at Carris booths (on Praça Figueira or at the base of the Santa Justa elevator—up a few stairs and behind the elevator). Since they're not advertised, you'll have to ask for them. Each ticket is good for only one ride and does not include transfers.

By Taxi: Lisbon taxis are abundant and use their meters. Rides start at 250$ and you can go anywhere in the center for under 500$. Especially if there are two of you, Lisbon cabs are a great, cheap timesaver.

Helpful Hints

Most museums are free on Sunday until 14:00 and closed all day Monday (a good day to explore Lisbon's neighborhoods or Sintra's Pena Palace and Moorish ruins). Bullfights are occasionally on Thursday and more frequently on Sunday. Tuesday and Saturday are flea-market days in the Alfama.

Pedestrian Warning: Sidewalks are narrow and drivers are daring; cross streets with care.

Language: Remember to try to start conversations in Portuguese (see Survival Phrases, near the back of this book). Fortunately, many people in the tourist trade speak some English. Otherwise, try Portuguese (ideal), Spanish, or French, in that order.

Time Zone Change: Portuguese time is usually one hour earlier than Spanish time.

LisboaCard: This card covers all public transportation (including the Metro), allowing free entrance to many museums and discounts on others. If you plan to museum-hop, the card is a good value, particularly for a day in Belém (covers your transportation and every worthwhile sight in Belém). Do not buy it to use on a Monday, when virtually all sights are closed throughout Lisbon and Belém, or on a Sunday, when many sights are free until 14:00 (24-hour card/1,500$; 48-hour card/2,500$, 72-hour card/3,250$; includes explanatory guidebook, buy at Rua Jardím do Regedor 50, off the southeast corner of Praça dos Restauradores, across the square from TI, tel. 01/343-3672, or at the Monastery of Jerónimos in Belém). You can buy the card in advance; just say what date and time you want it to "start."

Banking: Bring a Visa or MasterCard with a pin code to take advantage of the omnipresent Multibanco cash machines. Traveler's checks cost a small fortune to cash at banks; the fee ranges from 1,000$ to 2,500$ (bank hours are generally Monday–Friday 8:30–11:45 and 13:00–15:00). Shop around and try to cash in all your checks at once. American Express, in the Top Tours office at Avenida Duque de Loule 108, cashes any kind of traveler's check at a decent rate without a commission, but is not very central (Monday–Friday

Lisbon

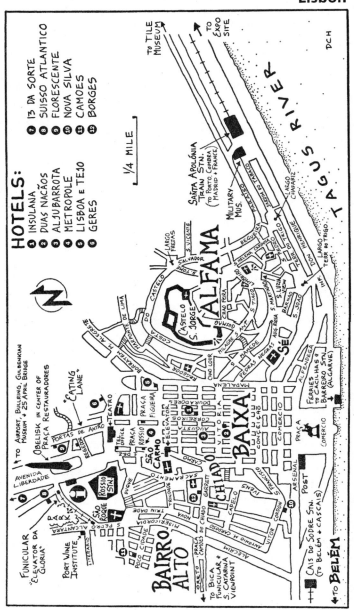

9:30–13:00 and 14:30–18:30, Metro: Rotunda, tel. 01/315-
5885). Automatic bill-changing machines are available and
seductive, offering fair rates but high fees.

Post Office and Telephones: The post office, at Praça
dos Restauradores 58, has easy-to-use metered phones
(Monday–Friday 8:00–22:00, weekends 9:00–18:00). The telephone center, on the northwest corner of Rossio Square, sells
phone cards and also has metered phone booths (daily 8:00–
23:00, accepts credit cards). Most of Lisbon's phone booths
require a different kind of phone card than is used in the rest
of Portugal. It's not worth buying one of Lisbon's "modern"
cards (inserted sideways into a small slot) just before you
leave Lisbon. The rest of Portugal uses the old-fashioned
cards (inserted lengthwise into a long slot). If you have only a
few calls to make in Lisbon, use a metered phone at the telephone office, post office, or bar.

Do-It-Yourself Walking Tours—Lisbon

▲▲**The Baírro Alto and Chiado Stroll**—This colorful upper-
city walk starts at the funicular and ends with the elevator (each
a funky 150$ experience in itself). Leave the lower town on the
funicular (called Elevator da Gloria), near the obelisk at Praça
dos Restauradores. Leaving the funicular on top, turn right to
enjoy the city view from the San Pedro Park belvedere.

If you're into port (the fortified wine that takes its name
from the city of Oporto), you'll find the world's greatest selection across the street from the lift at Solar do Vinho do Porto
(run by the Port Wine Institute, Rua São Pedro de Alcantara
45, 10:00–23:30, closed Sunday). In a stuffy '60s-decor living-
room atmosphere you can, for 150$ to 2,000$ per glass poured
by an English-speaking bartender, taste any of 300 different
ports, though you may want to try only 150 or so and save the
rest for the next night. Fans of port describe it as "a liquid
symphony playing on the palate."

Follow the main street (Rua São Pedro de Alcantara)
downhill a couple of blocks (it turns into the Rua Misericordia).
São Roque Church (open 8:00–17:00) is on your left at Largo
Trinidade Coelho. It looks like just another church, but wander
slowly under its flat, painted ceiling and notice the rich side
chapels. The highlight is the Chapel of St. John the Baptist (left
of altar, gold and blue), which looks like it came right out of
the Vatican. It did. Made at the Vatican out of the most precious

materials, it was the site of one papal mass; then it was taken down and shipped to Lisbon—probably the most costly chapel per square inch ever constructed. Notice the beautiful mosaic floor and the three paintings that are actually intricate mosaics, a Vatican specialty. The São Roque Museum has some impressive old paintings and church riches (150$, 10:00–17:00, closed Monday).

After a visit with the poor pigeon-drenched man in the church square, continue downhill along Rua da Misericordia into the Chiado (SHEE-ah-doo) district. Shoppers can duck into the chic Centro Comercial Espaço Chiado at Rua da Misericordia #14 (with chic public-enough toilets and classy bars; closed Sunday) en route to Praça Luis de Camões (named after Portugal's best-loved poet).

A left takes you to a small square (Largo Chiado, the torn-up site of a future Metro stop, which should be completed by the time you get here) past **A Brasileira** café and the classy Rua Garrett. Coffeehouse aficionados enjoy this grand old café, reeking with smoke and the 1930s (open daily). After 2 downhill blocks on Rua Garrett, take a left uphill along Calle Sacramento, which leads to another pleasant square, Largo dos Carmo, with the ruins of the Convento do Carmo (likely closed until some time in '98 due to the new Metro addition; if open, peek in to see the elegant, earthquake-ruined Gothic arches for free, or pay 300$ to get all the way in and see the museum, Monday–Saturday 10:00–17:30, closed Sunday). Follow the trolley tracks alongside the church to the Santa Justa elevator. Climb the spiral stairs one floor to the small observatory deck or to the top of this Eiffelian pimple for a great view café (daily, English spoken, reasonable coffee, expensive eats). The elevator takes you down into the Baixa.

▲▲▲**Alfama Stroll**—Europe's most colorful sailors' quarter goes back to Visigothic days. It was a rich district during the Arabic period and finally the home of Lisbon's fisherfolk (and of the poet Luis de Camões, who wrote, "our lips meet easily high across the narrow street"). One of the few areas to survive the 1755 earthquake, the Alfama is a cobbled playground of Old World color. A visit is best during the busy midmorning market time or in the late afternoon/early evening, when the streets teem with locals.

Start at the top and work your way down. Take trolley #28 to the Largo Santa Luzia; admire the view from the small terrace. Probably the most scenic cup of coffee in town is enjoyed from the nearby Cerca Moura bar/café terrace (Largo das Portas do Sol 4). Then follow the yellow signs (and tour groups) up to the Castelo São Jorge, the city castle, with a history going back to Roman days. It caps the highest hill above the Alfama and offers a pleasant garden and Lisbon's top viewpoint but nothing in the way of an interior. Orient yourself from this perch (daily until sunset, bus #37 from Praça Figueira).

Drop back down to Largo Santa Luzia and wander deep into the Alfama. Use the Beco Santa Helena stairway to connect the upper Alfama's Largo das Portas do Sol and the Santa Luzia viewpoint with the lower Alfama. (Descending from the viewpoint: behind the Santa Luzia church, take Rua Norberto de Araujo down a few stairs, go left under the arch, and you'll hook up with Beco Santa Helena.) This urban jungle's roads are squeezed into tangled and confusing alleys, bent houses comfort each other in their romantic shabbiness, and the air drips with laundry and the smell of clams and raw fish. Get lost. Poke aimlessly, sample ample grapes, peek through windows, buy a fish. Don't miss Rua de São Pedro, the liveliest street around. On Tuesday and Saturday mornings, the fun Feira da Ladra flea market rages on the Campo de Santa Clara (a good 20-minute walk, worth it only if it's flea market day).

Tours—Lisbon
▲▲**Ride a Trolley**—Lisbon's vintage trolleys, most from the 1920s, shake and shiver all over town, somehow safely weaving within inches of parked cars, climbing steep hills, and offering sightseers breezy wide-open-window views of the city. Line #28 is a Rice-A-Roni Lisbon joyride. Starting at the Estrela basilica and park, it runs through the Chiado, Baixa, and Alfama to Santa Clara church near the flea market. Stops from west to east include the top of Bica funicular, Chiado square, top of Rua Victor Cordon, in Baixa on Rua da Conceicão between Augusta and Prata, at the cathedral (*Sè*), at the Alfama viewpoint (Santa Luzia Belvedere), at Portas do Sol, and at the Santa Clara church. Just pay the conductor as you board, sit down, and catch the pensioners as they lurch at each stop.

City Bus Tours—Two tours give tired tourists a lazy two-hour overview of the city. Neither is great, but both are handy, daily, and inexpensive. **Tagus Tour** lets you hop on and off their topless double-decker buses (2,000$, hourly departures start at 11:00 May–September, covers the town and Belém, taped commentary in English, Portuguese, and French). On the **Hills Tour** you follow the rails on restored turn-of-the-century trams through the Alfama and Baírro Alto (2,800$; live, trilingual guide; up to five departures in summer, two afternoon-only departures during off-season, runs March–October). Both tours leave from the same info kiosk on Praça do Comércio (tel. 01/363-9343). It's a stress-free way to see the town (though subject to traffic jams).

Sights—Lisbon

▲▲**Gulbenkian Museum**—This is the best of Lisbon's 40 museums. Gulbenkian, an Armenian oil tycoon, gave his art collection (or "harem," as he called it) to Portugal in gratitude for the hospitable asylum granted him there during World War II. Now this great collection, spanning 2,000 years, is displayed in a classy and comfortable modern building. Ask for the excellent English text explaining the collection.

You'll stroll chronologically through the ages past the great Egyptian, Greek, and Middle Eastern sections. There are masterpieces by Rembrandt, Rubens, Renoir, Rodin, and artists whose names start with other letters (500$, free all day Sunday; from June–September open Tuesday, Thursday, Friday, and Sunday 10:00–17:00, Wednesday and Saturday 14:00–19:30; off-season open 10:00–17:00; always closed Monday; pleasant gardens; good, air-conditioned cafeteria; bus #46 from Rossio or Metro from Rossio to São Sebastião, Berna 45, tel. 01/793-5131).

▲▲**Museum of Ancient Art (Museu Nacional de Arte Antiga)**—This is the country's best for Portuguese paintings from her glory days, the 15th and 16th centuries. You'll also find the great European masters (such as Bosch, Jan van Eyck, and Raphael) and rich furniture, all in a grand palace (500$, Tuesday 14:00–18:00, Wednesday–Sunday 10:00–18:00, closed Monday, bus #40 or #60 from Praça Figueira, Rua das Janeles Verdes 9, tel. 01/397-6002).

▲**Museu Nacional do Azulejo**—This museum, filling the Convento da Madre de Deus, features piles of tiles which, as you've probably noticed, are an art form in Portugal (400$, Tuesday 14:00–18:00, Wednesday–Sunday 10:00–18:00, closed

Monday; ten minutes on bus #59 or #105 from Praça Figueira,
Rua da Madre de Deus 4, tel. 01/814-7747).

Sè (Cathedral)—Just a few blocks east of Praça do Comércio,
it's not much on the inside, but its fortresslike exterior is a
textbook example of a stark and powerful Romanesque fortress
of God. Started in 1150, after the Christians reconquered
Lisbon from the Islamic Moors, its crenelated towers made a
powerful statement: the Reconquista was here to stay.

▲The 25th of April Bridge—At a mile long, this is the third-
longest suspension bridge in the world. Built in 1966, it was
originally named for the dictator Salazar but renamed for the
date of Portugal's revolution and freedom.

Cristo Rei—A huge statue of Christ (à la Rio de Janeiro) overlooks Lisbon from across the Tagus River. While it's designed
to be seen from a distance, a lift takes visitors to the top for a
great view (250$, daily 10:00–18:00). Catch the ferry from
downtown Lisbon (leaves every ten minutes from Praça do
Comércio) to Cacilhas, then take a bus marked "Cristo Rei"
(leaves from the ferry dock every 15 minutes). Taxis to or from
the site are too expensive.

Sights—Lisbon's Belém District

Three miles from downtown Lisbon, the Belém District is a
sprawling pincushion of important sights from Portugal's
Golden Age, when Vasco da Gama and company made it
Europe's richest power. This is the best possible look at the
grandeur of pre-earthquake Lisbon. While the monastery is
great, its several museums are somewhere between good and
mediocre, depending upon your interests. The new Belém
Cultural Center, filled with exhibition halls (check out what's
showing), concert halls, and a snazzy good-value cafeteria with
a salad bar, puts this area on the contemporary culture map.
You can get to the sights of Belém by taxi or bus (#27, #28,
#29, #43, #49, and #51), but I'd ride the sleek new tram #15
(how about those window screens?) from Praça do Comércio
or Figueira (buy tickets from machine on-board, no change) to
the second stop in Belém (Mosterio dos Jerónimos). The best
picnic grounds are in the park near the Monument to the
Discoveries. You'll find several good restaurants along Rua de
Belém between the coach museum and the monastery. At
Pastel de Belém, a handy dessert shop, have a *café com leite*
with the house specialty, *pasties de Belém.*

Belém

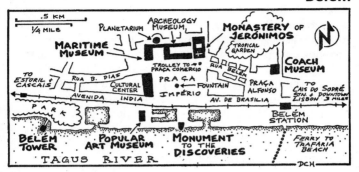

▲**Monument to the Discoveries**—This giant monument was built in 1960 to honor Prince Henry the Navigator on the 500th anniversary of his death. Huge statues of Henry and other of Portugal's leading explorers line the giant concrete prow. Note the marble map chronicling Portugal's empire-building, on the ground in front. Inside you can ride a lift to a fine view (320$, Tuesday–Sunday 9:30–18:00, closed Monday).

▲▲**Monastery of Jerónimos**—This is, for me, Portugal's most exciting building. The giant church and its cloisters were built as a thanks for the discoveries. Vasco da Gama is buried here (from back of church facing altar, his tomb is on the left). Notice how nicely the Manueline style combines Gothic and Renaissance features with motifs from the sea, the source of wealth that made this art possible. Don't miss the elegant cloisters (church free, 400$ for cloisters, get the 200$ English pamphlet, Tuesday–Sunday 10:00–17:00, closed Monday). Go upstairs for a better view (and the women's toilet; men's downstairs).

▲**Belém Tower**— The only purely Manueline building in Portugal (built in 1515), this tower protected Lisbon's harbor and today symbolizes the voyages that made it powerful. This was the last sight sailors saw as they left and the first when they returned loaded with gold, spices, and social diseases. Its collection of 15th- and 16th-century armaments is barely worth the admission and the 15-minute walk from the Monastery, but if you do go in, climb up for the view (400$, Tuesday–Sunday 10:00–17:00, closed Monday, tel. 01/362-0034).

▲**Coach Museum (Museu dos Coches)**—Claiming to be the most visited sight in Portugal, it's impressive, with more than

70 dazzling 18th-century carriages (450$, Tuesday–Sunday 10:00–17:00, closed Monday, tel. 01/363-8022).

Popular Art Museum (Museu de Arte Popular)—This museum takes you through Portugal's folk art one province at a time (300$, Tuesday–Sunday 10:00–12:30 and 14:00–17:00, closed Monday, Avenida Brasilia).

Maritime Museum (Museu de Marinha)—A cut above the average European maritime museum. Sailors love it (300$, free on Wednesday, Tuesday–Sunday 10:00–18:00, closed Monday, Praça do Império).

Evening Entertainment—Lisbon

From the Baixa, nighttime Lisbon seems dead. But head up into the Baírro Alto and you'll find plenty of action. The Jardím do São Pedro is normally festive and the Rua Diario de Noticias is lined with busy bars.

▲**Fado**—Mournfully beautiful, haunting ballads about lost sailors, broken hearts, and sad romance are one of Lisbon's favorite late-night tourist traps. Be careful, this is one of those cultural clichés that all too often becomes a rip-off. The Alfama has many touristy *fado* bars, but the Baírro Alto (plenty of joints around Rua Diario de Noticias, Rua das Gaveas, and Rua Norte) is your best bet. **Canto do Camões** is great, run by friendly Gabriel (Travessa da Espera 38, call ahead to reserve, tel. & fax 01/346-5464). At *fado* bars, things don't start until 21:30 and then take an hour or two to warm up. A *fado* performance isn't cheap (expect a 2,500–3,000$ cover), but a good one is a great experience. Many *fado* joints require dinner (5,000–6,000$). Get advice from your hotel or the TI.

▲▲▲**Portuguese Bullfight**—If you always felt sorry for the bull, this is Toro's Revenge—in a Portuguese bullfight, the matador is brutalized along with the bull. After an exciting equestrian prelude in which the horseman (*cavaleiro*) skillfully plants barbs in the bull's back while trying to avoid the padded horns, a colorfully clad, eight-man team (suicide squad) enters the ring and lines up single file facing the bull. The leader prompts the bull to charge, then braces himself for a collision that can be heard all the way up in the cheap seats. As he hangs onto the bull's head, his buddies then pile on, trying to wrestle the bull to a standstill. Finally, one guy hangs on to *el toro's* tail and "water-skis" behind him. Unlike at the Spanish *corrida*, the bull is not killed in front of the crowd at the Portuguese *tourada* (yet it *is* killed later).

You're most likely to see a bullfight in Lisbon, Estoril, or on the Algarve. The season lasts from Easter through October. Get schedules in the tourist office; fights start late in the evening. In Lisbon there are fights at Campo Pequeño on Thursday nights from mid-June through September at 22:00 (tickets from about 2,000$). Nearby arenas advertise fights on Sunday. Tickets are available at the door or at the green ABEP kiosk across the square from Lisbon's central tourist office.

▲**People's Fair (Feira Popular)**—Consider spending a low-brow evening at Lisbon's Feira Popular, which bustles with Portuguese families at play. Pay the entry fee, then enjoy rides, munchies, great people-watching, entertainment, music—basic Portuguese fun. Have dinner among the chattering families, with endless food and wine paraded frantically in every direction. Food stalls dispense wine from the udders of porcelain cows. Fried ducks drip, barbecues spit, and dogs squirt the legs of chairs while, somehow, local lovers ignore everything but each other's eyes. (200$, nightly, May 1–September 30, 19:00–midnight, Saturday and Sunday 15:00–midnight. Located on Avenida da República at the Entre-Campos Metro stop.)

Movies—Lisbon reels with theaters, and unlike in Spain, most films are in the original language with subtitles. Many of Lisbon's theaters are classy, complete with assigned seats and ushers, and the normally cheap tickets go for half price on Monday. Check the cinema listings in the monthly magazine *Lisboaem* (free at TI).

Shopping

Lisbon offers decaying but still elegant department stores, teeming flea markets, classy specialty shops, and one of Europe's largest modern shopping centers. The Mercado Ribeira open-air market, next to the Caís do Sodre train station, bustles every morning except Sunday—great for picnic stuff and local sweaters. And for the gleaming modern side of things, taxi to Amoreiras Shopping Center de Lisboa (open daily 10:00–24:00, Avenida da Duarte Pacheco, bus #11 from Rossio, you can see its pink and blue towers from a distance) for its more than 350 shops, theaters, and piles of eateries.

Sleeping in Lisbon
(170$ = about $1, tel. code: 01)

Sleep Code: **S**=Single, **D**=Double/Twin, **T**=Triple, **Q**=Quad, **b**=bathroom, **t**=toilet only, **s**=shower only, **CC**=Credit Card (Visa, MasterCard, Amex), **SE**=Speaks English, **NSE**=No English. Breakfast is usually included.

Lisbon has plenty of cheap and handy rooms, but this is EXPO '98 (June–September), so reserve as early as you can. Off-season, prices are soft.

Physically, Lisbon is a tired and well-worn city; rooms in the center feel the same way. To sleep in a well-located place with local character, you'll be climbing dark stairways into a world of cracked plaster, taped handwritten signs, dingy carpets, cramped and confusing floor plans, and ramshackle plumbing. If you're on a tight budget, arrive without a reservation and bargain. If you have a room reserved, taxi there from the station if you arrive at night. While old Lisbon seems a little sleazy at night, with normal discretion my listings are safe.

Singles cost nearly the same as doubles. Rooms with bathtubs often cost more than rooms with showers. Addresses like 26-3 stand for street #26, third floor (which is fourth floor in American terms). Never judge a place by its entryway.

Sleeping Downtown in Baixa
(zip code: 1100)

Central as can be, this area bustles with lots of shops, traffic, people, buskers, pedestrian areas, and urban intensity. I've listed places that are in relatively quiet areas or on pedestrian streets.

Albergaria Residencial Insulana, on a pedestrian street, is very professional with 32 quiet and comfortable, if a bit smoky, rooms (Sb-7,500$, Db-8,500$, Tb-11,000$, includes breakfast, elevator, all with air-conditioning, CC:VMA, Rua da Assuncão 52, tel. 01/342-3131, fax 01/342-3131, SE).

Residencial Duas Nacões is a hardworking old hotel in the heart of Rossio on a classy pedestrian street (S-3,500$, Sb-6,000$, D-4,500$, Db-7,500$, Tb-9,000$ with breakfast, elevator, CC:VMA, Rua Augusta e Rua da Vitoria 41, tel. 01/346-0710, fax 01/347-0206, SE). Some rooms smell musty, others are OK. Ask to see another if the first won't do.

Pensão Aljubarrota is just renovated and a fine value if you can handle the long climb up four floors and the bubbly black-vinyl flooring. Once on top you'll have spotless rooms and cute tiny balconies from which to survey the Rua Augusta scene (S-3,200$, D-5,200$, Ds-6,200$, T-6,900$, includes breakfast, Rua da Assuncão 53-4, tel. & fax 01/346-0112, SE).

Sleeping Downtown on Rossio and Praça da Figueira (zip code: 1100)

Hotel Metropole, on Rossio Square, has 1920s elegance and beautiful rooms, some overlooking the square. If you're in the mood for a splurge, this is the place (Sb-17,900$, Db-19,800$, extra bed-3,500$, includes breakfast, air-con, elevator, double-paned windows, CC:VMA, Rossio 30, tel. 01/346-9164, fax 01/46-9166, SE).

Lisboa e Tejo is another oasis, newly and tastefully refurbished, with comfortable rooms and a welcoming staff (Sb-10,000–12,000$, Db-12,000–15,000$, prices vary according to room size, includes breakfast, air-con, CC:VMA, Rua do Poço do Borratém, from southeast corner of Praça da Figueira, walk 1 block down Rua Dos Condes de Monsanto and turn left, tel. 01/886-6182, fax 01/886-5163, SE).

Pensão Residencial Gerês, your best budget bet downtown, has bright, basic, cozy rooms (S-5,500$, Sb-7,000$, D-7,000$, Db-8,500$, T-9,000$, Ts-10,000$, CC:VMA, Calçada do Garcia 6, located off the northeast corner of Rossio—at the entrance of pedestrian street Rua das Portas de St. Antão, look uphill to see the sign 1 block away, tel. 01/881-0497, fax 01/888-2006, some English spoken). Recently remodeled, it lacks the dingy smokiness that pervades Lisbon's cheaper hotels.

Sleeping Uptown along Avenida da Liberdade

Pensão Residencial 13 da Sorte, a simple, but cheery place, has full bathrooms in each of its 23 rooms and bright, small-town tiles throughout (Sb-6,000$, Db-6,000–7,500$, Tb-7,500$, no breakfast, elevator, CC:VMA, Rua do Salitre 13, 1200 Lisbon, tel. 01/353-9746, fax 01/353-1851, SE). Coming from the Rossio Station up Avenida da Liberdade, turn left on Rua do Salitre at the big "Cerveja Sagres" sign (ten-minute walk). Back rooms are quieter.

Hotel Suisso Atlantico is formal, hotelish, and stuffy, with tour groups and drab carpets throughout, but it has decent rooms and a TV lounge. If you want a functional hotel and practical location, it's a good value (Sb-7,500$, Db-9,500$, Tb-11,300$, includes breakfast, parking available, CC:VMA, Rua da Gloria 3-19, 1200 Lisbon, behind the funicular station, around the corner from the tourist office on a quiet street 1 block off Praça dos Restauradores, tel. 01/346-1713, fax 01/346-9013, SE).

Residencial Florescente is a slumber mill with 100 rooms on a thriving pedestrian street a block off Praça dos Restauradores. It's institutional, but rooms are clean and some even approach charm (Ss-5,000$, Ds-5,500–6,500$, Db-6,000–8,500$, no breakfast, CC:VMA, Rua Portas S. Antão 99, 1100 Lisbon, tel. 01/346-3517, fax 01/342-7733, SE).

Sleeping in Bairro Alto
(zip code: 1200)

Just west of downtown, this area is more colorful, with less traffic. It's a bit seedy but full of ambience, good bars, local *fado* clubs, music, and markets. The area may not feel comfortable for women alone at night, but the hotels themselves are safe.

Residencial Nova Silva feels a little dumpy and unloved. Still, it's a quiet, ramshackle place on the crest of the Baírro Alto overlooking the river. The five rooms with grand little river-view balconies give you bird noises rather than traffic noises (priority for longer stays). It's 3 blocks from the heart of Chiado on the scenic #28 tram line, with the easiest street parking of all my listings (S-4,500$, Ss-5,000$, Sb-6,000$, D-5,000$, Ds-5,500$, Db-6,000–7,000$, breakfast-400$, no elevator, Rua Victor Cordón 11, tel. 01/342-4371, fax 01/342-7770, SE).

Residencial Camões lies right in the seedy thick of the Baírro Alto but offers fine rooms with a friendly, safe atmosphere (S-2,500$, Sb-3,500$, D-4,500$, Db-5,500$, includes breakfast, Travessa Poco da Cidade 38, 1 block south of São Roque Church and to the right, you'll see the sign a couple of blocks up, tel. 01/346-7510, fax 01/346-4048, some English spoken).

Hotel Borges is a big, dark, tired, smoky, formerly regal place with one of the old town's best addresses (Sb-9,000$, Db-10,500$, includes breakfast, cheaper off-season, elevator, CC:VMA, Rua Garrett 108, on the shopping street next to A Brasiliera café, tel. 01/346-1951, fax 01/342-6617, SE). A Metro stop is scheduled to be at their doorstep in 1998.

Eating in Lisbon

Eating in the Alfama

This gritty chunk of pre-earthquake Lisbon is full of interesting eateries, especially along the Rua San Pedro (the lower main drag) and on Largo de São Miguel. For a seafood feast (2,600$ menu) after your Alfama exploration, consider dining high in the Alfama at the **Farol de Santa Luzia** restaurant (Largo Santa Luzia 5, across from the Santa Luzia patio viewpoint overlooking the Alfama, no sign but many window decals, closed Sunday, tel. 01/886-3884). For cheap and colorful dinners, walk past Portas do Sol (dip into a dark bar for a damp appetizer) and follow the trolley tracks along Rua da São Tome to a square called Largo Rodrigues Freitas, where **Nossa Churrasqueira** is busy feeding happy locals on rickety tables and meager budgets (closed Monday). If that's too touristy, walk from there down the steepest lane, Rua do Salvador, to the little eatery a few doors down at #81 (Restaurante Gema de Ova). This road continues downhill into the less touristed fringe of the Alfama. While in the Alfama, brighten a few dark bars. Have an aperitif, taste the *branco seco* (local dry white wine). Make a friend, pet a chicken, read the graffiti, pick at the humanity ground between the cobbles.

Eating in Baírro Alto

Lisbon's "high town" is full of small, fun, and cheap places. Fishermen's bars abound. Just off São Roque's Square you'll find two fine eateries: the very simple and cheap **Casa Trans-Montana** (closed Sunday) down the steps of Calcada do Duque at #43; and the **Cervejaría da Trinidade** (1 block down from Sao Roque at Rua Nova da Trinidade 20C), a Portuguese-style beer hall covered with historic tiles and full of fish and locals (daily 12:00–24:00, CC:VMA, tel. 01/342-3506). You'll find many lesstouched restaurants deeper into the Baírro Alto on the other (west) side of Rua Misericordia.

Eating in Rossio, Baixa, and Beyond

The "eating lane" is a galloping gourmet's heaven, a galaxy of eateries with small zoos hanging from their windows for you to choose from (opposite the Rossio station, just off Praça dos Restauradores down Rua do Jardím do Regedor and Rua das Portas de St. Antão). The seafood is some of Lisbon's best. For cod and vegetables prepared faster than a Big Mac and served with more energy than a soccer team, stand or sit at the **Restaurant/Cervejaría Beira-Gare** (a greasy spoon in front of the Rossio station at the end of Rua 1 de Dezembro, 6:00–24:00, closed Sunday). To get a simple fish sandwich, ask for a *filete pescada no pão*.

Farther down the same street is **Celerio**, a handy supermarket that's bigger than it looks (8:30–20:00, until 19:00 Saturday, closed Sunday, Rua 1 de Dezembro 67-68). On the next block, same street, same hours, Celerio runs a health-food store at #65.

Stand with the locals at **Pastelaria Tentacão**, on the east side of Praça Figueria, and munch one of their *prato do dia* (daily specials, all under 1,000$). The house specialty to try (or avoid) is *leitão*, a suckling pig sandwich.

The Rossio area is lined with local eateries (like **Restaurant X** at Rua dos Correeiros #116, look for the red X). The **Os Unidos** snack bar at Rua dos Fanqueiros 161 is fun and friendly (closed Sunday).

Just off the Avenida da Liberdade on the Rua do Salitre (near the Pensión Residencial da Sorte 13) are two locally popular and slightly upscale restaurants: **Cerevejaria Ribadouro**, at the corner of Avenida da Liberdade and Rua do Salitre, and **Forno Velho**, at Rua do Salitre 42.

And don't miss a chance to go purely local with hundreds of Portuguese families having salad, fries, chicken, and wine at the **Feira Popular** (nightly from 19:00, May–September, on Avenida da República, Metro: Entre-Campos).

Transportation Connections—Lisbon

Remember to reserve ahead if your train requires a reservation.

By train to: Madrid (2/day, 10–12 hrs, ideal overnight), **Faro** (4/day, 5 hrs), **Paris** (1/day, 26 hrs), **Porto** (12/day, 3.5 hrs), **Évora** (5/day, 3 hrs), **Lagos** (5/day, 5 hrs, overnight possible, likely transfer in Tunes), **Coimbra** (17/day, 2.5 hrs), **Nazaré Valado** (4/day, 2.5 hrs), **Sintra** and **Cascais** (4/hr, 45 min). Train information: tel. 01/888-4025 or 01/888-5092.

To Salema: Both bus and train take about five hours from Lisbon to Lagos. Trains from Lisbon to the **south coast** leave from the Barreiro station across the Tagus from downtown. Boats shuttle train travelers from Praça do Comércio to the Barreiro train station with several departures each hour (160$, 30-min ride, note that schedule times listed are often when the boat sails, not when train departs). The 23:00–6:45 night train, while no fun, allows you to enjoy the entire day on the Algarve.

By bus to: Coimbra (12/day, 2.5 hrs), **Nazaré** (8/day, 2.25 hrs), **Fatima** (9/day, 2.5 hrs), **Alcobaça** (5/day, 2 hrs), **Óbidos** (5/day, 2 hrs, transfer in Caldas de Rainha), **Évora** (12/day, 2.5 hrs), **Lagos** (10/day, 5 hrs, easier than the train, must book ahead, get details at tourist office). Buses leave from Lisbon's Rodoviara bus station at Avenida Casal Ribeiro 18 (Metro: Saldanha, tel. 01/354-5439).

Driving in Lisbon

Driving in Lisbon is big-city crazy. Entering from the north, a series of boulevards takes you into the center. Navigate by following signs to Centro, Avenida da República, Praça dos Marques de Pombal, Avenida da Liberdade, Praça dos Restauradores, Rossio, and Praça do Comércio. Consider hiring a taxi (cheap) to lead you to your hotel.

There are many safe underground pay lots (follow the blue "P" signs), but they get more expensive by the hour, up to 4,000$ per day. The one under Praça dos Restauradores (under the obelisk, next to the Turismo) is within a five-minute walk of most of my hotel listings. Choose a hotel with parking in mind. Consider the airport's guarded lot (1,800$ for one day, 3,100$ for two days, 3,900$ for three days). Downtown, tourists' cars are not safe overnight.

(For ideas on the drive south to the Algarve, see the Algarve chapter.)

NEAR LISBON: SINTRA, CABO DA ROCA, CASCAIS, ESTORIL, AND ÉVORA

The natural Lisbon escape is nearby Sintra—where you can climb through the Versailles of Portugal, the Pena Palace; romp along the ruined ramparts of a deserted Moorish castle on a neighboring hilltop; and explore the rugged and picturesque westernmost tip of Portugal at Cabo da Roca. You can also mix and mingle with the jet set (or at least press your nose against their windows) at the resort towns of Cascais or Estoril.

If you're heading south, you might venture inland to historic Évora, exploring dusty droves of olive groves and scruffy seas of peeled cork trees along the way.

Planning Your Time

While Évora is a stop on the way to Portugal's south coast, the other sights combine to make a fine day trip from Lisbon. Remember that there are two bullrings out here, and it's more likely that your schedule will hit a fight here than in Lisbon. If this is the case, plan accordingly.

Without a car, I'd skip Cabo da Roca and do Sintra, Cascais, and Belém as individual side trips from Lisbon.

By car, the 70-mile circular excursion (Lisbon–Belém– Sintra–Cabo da Roca–Cascais–Lisbon) makes for a good day. Traffic congestion around Sintra can mess up your schedule. Follow the coast from Praça do Comércio west, under the bridge to Belém. Continue west to just before Cascais, where Sintra (11 km) is signposted. Sintra itself is far easier by train than by car from Lisbon.

Drivers who are eager for beach time can leave Lisbon, do the Sintra circle, and drive directly to the Algarve that evening (5 hrs).

SINTRA

Just 12 miles north of Lisbon, Sintra was the summer escape of Portugal's kings. Byron called it a "glorious Eden," and today it's mobbed with tourists. Still, you could easily spend a day in this lush playground of castles, palaces, sweeping coastal views, and exotic gardens. The helpful tourist office on the town's main square can provide a map and directions to the castles and can arrange *quartos* (rooms in private homes) for budget overnighters (daily 9:00–19:00, less off- season, tel. 01/923-1157).

Sights—Sintra

National Palace (Palacio Nacional)—This strange but lavishly tiled palace takes less than an hour to tour (400$, 10:00–13:00 and 14:00–17:00, last entry a half-hour before closing, closed Wednesday, ten-minute walk from train station).

▲▲**Castelo dos Mouros**—These 1,000-year-old Moorish castle ruins, lost in an enchanted forest and alive with winds of the past, are a castle-lover's dream come true and a great place for a picnic with a panoramic Atlantic view. To get from Sintra to the ruins, take a 2-mile walk, a taxi, or a bus—possibly, maybe three buses per day in July only (300$ round-trip). Ruins are free and open 10:00 to 18:00 daily (close at 17:00 off-season).

Lisbon Area

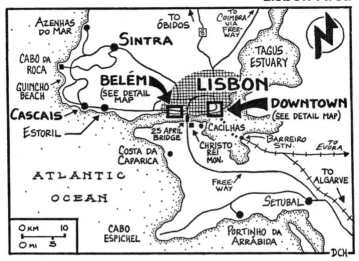

▲▲Pena Palace (Palacio de Pena)—This magical hilltop palace sits high above Sintra, a short steep 15-minute walk from the ruined Moorish castle. Portugal's German-born Prince Ferdinand hired a German architect to build him a fantasy castle, mixing elements of German and Portuguese style. He got a crazy fortified casserole of Gothic, Arabic, Moorish, Walt Disney, Renaissance, and Manueline architectural bits and decorative pieces. Built in the 1840s, the palace is preserved just as it was when the royal family fled Portugal in 1910 (during a popular revolt that led to the replacement of the royalty by a modern republic). Signs direct you to the palace (400$, 10:00–18:30, closed Monday; closes at 16:30 off-season). For a spectacular view of Lisbon and the Tagus, hike for 15 minutes from the palace to the Chapel of Santa Eufemia.

Monserrate—Just outside of Sintra is the wonderful garden of Monserrate. If you like tropical plants and exotic landscaping, this is definitely for you (300$, daily 10:00–17:00).

Sleeping in Sintra

A great splurge is the beautifully-restored **Casa Miradouro**, a 19th-century mansion with six comfortable rooms and views of

the sea and mountains (Sb-10,000–15,000$, Db-13,000–
18,500$, Rua Sotto Major 55, down the hill from the National
Palace, tel. 01/923-5900, fax 01/924-1836).

Transportation Connections—Sintra

Sintra is an easy day trip from Lisbon (4 trains/hr, 45 min one-
way from Lisbon's Rossio station). Buses connecting Sintra and
Cascais (one-hour trip, bus stop is across the street from the
Sintra train station) stop a ten-minute walk from Cabo da Roca.

CABO DA ROCA

Wind-beaten, tourist-infested Cabo da Roca is the westernmost point in Europe. It has a fun little shop, a café, and a tiny
Turismo that sells a "proof of being here" diploma (closes at
18:00). Nearby, on the road to Cascais, you'll pass a good
beach for wind, waves, sand, and the chance to be the last person in Europe to see the sun set.

CASCAIS AND ESTORIL

Before the rise of the Algarve, these towns were the haunt
of Portugal's rich and beautiful. Today they are quietly
elegant, with noble old buildings, beachfront promenades, a
bullring, a casino, and more fame than they deserve. Cascais
is the more enjoyable of the two, not as rich and stuffy,
with a cozy touch of fishing village, great seafood, and a
younger, less pretentious atmosphere. Both are an easy day
trip from Lisbon (4 trains/hr, 40 min from Lisbon's Caís do
Sodre station).

For a Swim

The water at Cascais isn't very clean, and the Lisbon city
beach at Costa da Caparica is good but crowded. For the best
swimming around, drive (public transportation is difficult) 30
miles south to the golden beaches, shell-shaped bay, restaurants, and warm, clean water at Port Portinho da Arrabida. Or
better yet, head south to the Algarve.

ÉVORA

Deep in the heart of Portugal, in the barren, arid plains of the
southern province of Alentejo, Évora has been a cultural oasis
for 2,000 years. With a beautifully untouched provincial
atmosphere, fascinating whitewashed Old Quarter, plenty of

museums, a cathedral, and even a Roman temple, Évora stands proudly amid groves of cork and olive trees.

The major sights (Roman temple of Diana, early Gothic cathedral, archbishop's palace, and a luxurious *pousada* in a former monastery) crowd close together at the town's highest point. Osteophiles eat up the macabre "House of Bones"chapel at the Church of St. Francis, lined with the bones of 5,000 monks. A subtler but still-powerful charm is contained within the town's medieval wall. Find it by losing yourself in the quiet lanes of Évora's far corners.

The **Turismo** is at the central square, Praça do Giraldo 73 (Monday–Friday 9:00–17:00, Saturday 9:00–12:30 and 14:00–17:00, tel. 066/22671). Note: All of Evora's phone numbers will change in spring of 1998.

For budget sleeping and eating, look around the square. For a splurge, sleep in one of Portugal's most luxurious *pousadas*, the **Convento dos Loios** (Db-28,000$, CC:VM, across from the Roman temple, tel. 066/24051, fax 066/27248, SE). I ate well for a moderate price at **O Fialho** (closed Monday, Travessa Mascarhenas 14). For very local atmosphere, eat at the **"Restaurant"** just off the Praça at Rua Romano Romalha 11. On the same street, **Picanha** offers typical Portuguese and Brazilian food.

Three trains and three buses connect Évora daily with Lisbon (3 hrs). One daily bus connects Évora and Lagos/Algarve (5 hrs).

THE ALGARVE

The Algarve, Portugal's southern coast, has long been known as Europe's last undiscovered tourist frontier. That "jumbo shrimp" statement contradicts itself. The Algarve is well-discovered, and if you go to the places featured in tour brochures, you'll find it much like Spain's Costa del Sol—paved, packed, and pretty stressful. But there are a few great beach towns left, mostly on the western tip, and this part of the Algarve is the south coast of any sun-worshipper's dreams.

For some rigorous rest and intensive relaxation in a village where the tourists and the fishermen sport the same stubble, make sunny Salema your Algarve hideaway. It's just you, a beach full of garishly painted boats, your wrinkled landlady, and a few other globetrotting experts-in-lethargy. Nearby sights include Cape Sagres, Europe's "Land's End" and home of Henry the Navigator's famous navigation school, and the jet-setty resort of Lagos. Or you could just work on a tan and see how slow you can get your pulse in sleepy Salema. If not now, when? If not you, who?

Planning Your Time

The Algarve is your vacation from your vacation. How much time it deserves depends upon how much time you have and how much time is necessary to recharge your solar batteries. On a three-week Iberian blitz, I'd give it three nights and two days. After a full day sightseeing in Lisbon, I'd push it by driving five hours around dinner time to gain an entirely free

The Algarve

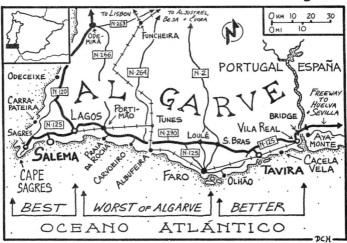

beach day. With two days, I'd spend one enjoying side trips to Cape Sagres and Lagos and another just lingering in Salema. Plan on an entire day to get from Salema to Sevilla (with a break in Tavira). With more time, I'd probably spend it in Salema. Eat all dinners in Salema unless you're fighting bulls in Lagos. The only other Algarve stop to consider is Tavira.

Getting Around the Algarve

Train and bus service between the main towns along the south coast is good. Trains run nearly hourly between Lagos and the Spanish border and buses take you west from Lagos, where trains don't go. (See end of chapter for Transportation Connections.) Bus and train service gets skimpy on weekends.

SALEMA

One bit of old Algarve magic still glitters quietly in the sun— Salema. You'll find it at the end of a small road just off the main drag between the big city of Lagos and the rugged southwest tip of Europe, Cape Sagres. This simple fishing village, quietly discovered by British and German tourists, has a few hotels, time-share condos up the road, some hippies' bars with rock music, English and German menus, a classic beach, and endless sun.

Salema's flatbed truck market rolls in each morning—one truck for fish, one for fruit, one for vegetables, and a five-and-dime truck for clothing and other odds and ends.

A highlight of any Salema day is watching the fishing boats come and go (a tractor drags them in). Fishermen unload pottery jars inhabited by octopi who made their final mistake.

In summer, local boats offer scenic trips along the coast. For a two-hour fishing-boat trip from Salema along the coast and back, catch a ride with Sebastian (2,500$ per person, June–September, one or two tours daily, morning is best for bird-watching, two to six passengers, tel. 082/69-54-58 or ask for Sebastian at the beachside fishermen's hut or at Pensión Mare).

Horizonte, an industrious travel agency, changes money at the best rate in town; posts bus schedules and sells long-distance bus tickets (e.g., to Lisbon and Sevilla); rents cars, mopeds, and mountain bikes; books flights and hotels; offers apartment rentals in Salema; and runs all-day jeep tours to the nature park on the southwest coast (daily 9:30–20:00, July–September; off-season Monday–Saturday 9:30–20:00; weekends 9:30–13:00, CC:VM, Salema Beach Club, five-minute walk from Hotel Residencial Salema, cross bridge and head uphill away from beach, turn right at phone booth, tel. and fax 082/69-59-20).

Sleeping in Salema
(140$ = about $1, tel. code: 082, zip code: 8650)
Sleep Code: **S**=Single, **D**=Double/Twin, **T**=Triple, **Q**=Quad, **b**=bathroom, **t**=toilet only, **s**=shower only, **CC**=Credit Card (Visa, MasterCard, Amex), **SE**=Speaks English, **NSE**=No English. When a price range is given, the lowest is the winter rate, the highest is the peak-season summer rate.

Salema is crowded in July, August, and September. The town has three streets, five restaurants, several bars, a lane full of fisherfolk who happily rent out rooms to foreign guests, and an ever-growing circle of modern condo-type hotels, apartments, and villas up the hillside.

For maximum comfort, there's no need to look beyond John's Pensión Mare. For economy and experience, go for the *quartos* (rooms rented out of private homes; see below).

Pensiónes and Hotels
Pensión Mare, a blue-and-white building looking over the village above the main road into town, is the best good, normal

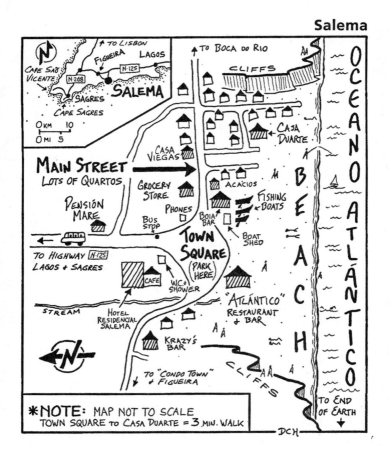

hotel value in Salema (Sb-5,000–5,500$, Db-6,500–9,000$, Tb-8,000–10,000$, the biggest breakfast in town, CC:VM, Praia de Salema, Vila do Bispo 8650, Algarve, tel. 082/69-51-65, fax 082/69-58-46, web site: www.algarve.co.uk.). An easygoing Englishman, John, runs this place, offering five comfortable rooms and a tidy paradise. He speaks English better than I do and will hold rooms until 18:00 with a phone call.

Hotel Residencial Salema is the big (many say too big) hotel in town. Its red-tiled rooms with white bedspreads are sharp and modern (Sb-6,000–11,000$, Db-6,500–12,000$, extra bed 30 percent more, includes breakfast, all rooms have balconies and partial views; changes money, rents cars and mopeds, closed November–March, CC:VMA, tel. 082/69-53-28, fax 082/69-53-29, SE).

Estalagem Infante do Mar is a four-star hotel on top of the cliff. Its rooms are plain but all have balconies and the views are spectacular—ask for an upstairs room to get a full sea view (Sb-5,400–10,300$, Db-6,000–12,000$, extra bed 30 percent more, includes breakfast, pool, bar, restaurant, parking, changes money, has no address except its name, CC:VMA, tel. 082/69-01-00, fax 082/69-01-09, SE). It's a stiff ten-minute walk uphill from the Hotel Residencial Salema, cross bridge, then head uphill.

Casa Saudade, a miniature *parador*, is a tastefully remodeled apartment with a kitchen, two bedrooms, and two terraces (14,000$ per day, three-night minimum stay required, Rua Beco de 1 Maio #9; head up "*quartos* street," turn left after Viegas' brown-tiled building, go to end of quiet alley; to reserve, call John of Pensión Mare at tel. 082/69-51-65 or Wilfried at tel. & fax 082/69-50-20).

Quartos and Camping

Quartos abound along the residential street (running left from the village center as you face the beach). At the waterfront ask one of the locals, or ask at the Boia Bar or the Mini Market. Prices vary with the season (3,000–6,000$ doubles), breakfast is not included, and credit cards are useless. Many places offer beachfront views. It's worth paying extra for *com vista* rooms, since the backside places tend to be dark and musty. Few *quartos*' landladies speak English, but they're used to dealing with visitors. Many will clean your laundry for a few *escudos*. If you're settling in for a while or are on a tight budget, park your bags and partner at a beachside bar and survey several places. Outside of July and August, prices can be soft.

Señor and Señora Boto rent two clean, comfortable rooms (D-2,500–3,000$, no views) and a spacious apartment with two bedrooms, bath, kitchenette and fridge, terrace, and balcony with a view (Db-6,000–7,000$, great value for up to four people). It's at the top of "*quartos* street" at #4 Rua dos Pescadores (on the left), a five-minute uphill walk from the town square (tel. 082/69-52-65, NSE).

The only sizable place on "*quartos* street" is the brown-tiled building, #64, where **Ercilia Viegas** rents seven doubles. Only one has a view and none have sinks, but there are three bathrooms and a communal kitchenette on the pleasant sun terrace (D-2,500–3,000$, Db with private kitchenette, terrace, and view-5,000$, tel. 082/69-51-28, NSE, but her daughter Selinha, who lives in Lisbon, tel. 01/25-33-75, speaks English and can arrange a room for you).

At the friendly **Acacios**, the two adjoining upstairs rooms are best, with kitchenette, balcony, and great ocean view (S-2,500–3,000$, Db-5,000–6,000$, on "*quartos* street" at #91, tel. 082/69-54-73, NSE).

Casa Duarte has five pleasant rooms (four with views), a communal kitchenette, and two terraces (D-3,000–5,500$, tel. 082/69-51-81 or 082/69-53-07; daughter, Cristina, who works at the Mini-Market, speaks English). It's farther up and on a side alley closer to the water at #7. From "*quartos* street," turn right at the Clube Recreativo, then left on the paved path, then angle right on the dirt path to the freestanding building.

Campers (who don't underestimate the high tides) sleep free and easy on the beach (public showers available in the town center) or at a fine new **campground** half a mile inland, back toward the main road.

Eating in Salema

Fresh seafood, eternally. Salema has six or eight places to eat. Happily, those that face the beach are the most fun with the best service, food, and atmosphere. The **Atlantico** is popular, right on the beach, and especially atmospheric when the electricity goes out and faces flicker around candles. The **Boia Bar**, at the base of the residential street, has a few tables within splashing distance of the surf, good tunes, huge portions, good dinners, and a hearty loss-leader breakfast, giving you bacon, eggs, toast, coffee, and fresh-squeezed orange juice for the cost of two glasses of o.j. anywhere else in town. Those with a car and a few extra bucks enjoy seafood dinners at the tiny **Rio Negros** (reservations recommended, 2 km east of Salema in the untouristy town of Vale de Boi, Largo do Poco 4, tel. 082/69-53-30).

FIGUEIRA

You missed the untouristed Salema by about six years. For a less glamorous and less touristy option, stay in the town of Figueira, a mile from Salema and the water, where dogs hog the shade, and old men still whittle.

Merryl and Rev Revill, British expatriates, run **Casa Meranka,** a charming guest house with two rooms, a 20-minute walk from your own private beach. The Revills are converting their guest rooms to small apartments, and hoping to attract tourists wanting longer stays. They still take short-term guests, but call as far in advance as possible. Don't expect many vacancies in high season. The Revills can arrange jeep safaris to the remote interior and are a wealth of local information (Db-5,000–8,000$, Rua do Rossio, Figueira 8650 Vila do Bispo, tel. and fax 082/69-53-03). Breakfast (optional) is served in the garden (except on Sunday and bank holidays). The **Restaurant Ninas,** across the street, is the place for a fine meal in Figueira.

CAPE SAGRES

This is the rugged and historic southwestern tip of Portugal, the spot closest to the edge of our flat earth in the days before Columbus. Prince Henry the Navigator, determined to broaden Europe's horizons, sent sailors ever farther into the unknown. He lived here at his navigators' school, carefully debriefing shipwrecked and frustrated explorers as they washed ashore.

Today fishermen cast from its towering crags, local merchants sell seaworthy sweaters ($20), and the windswept landscape harbors sleepy beaches, a salty village, and the lavish **Pousada do Infante.** For a touch of local elegance, pop by the *pousada* for breakfast. For 1,300$ you can sip coffee and nibble on a still-warm croissant while gazing out to where, in the old days, the world dropped right off the table. The *pousada,* a reasonable splurge offering a classy hotel in a magnificent setting (Db-25,000$, 8650 Sagres, tel. 082/64-42-22, fax 082/64-42-25), offers a warm welcome to anyone ready to pay so much for a continental breakfast.

Sagres is a popular gathering place for the backpacking bunch, with plenty of private rooms available right in town. The beach and bar scene are great for the *Let's Go* crowd. From Salema, Sagres is a short drive, hitch, or half-hour bus trip (nearly hourly trips from Salema, check return times).

The best secluded beach in the region is Praia do Castelo, just north of Cape Sagres (from the town of Vila do Bispo, drive inland and follow the signs for 15 minutes). If you have a car and didn't grow up in Fiji, this really is worth the drive.

Overlooking the deserted beach, **Castelejo Restaurante**
specializes in seafood *cataplanas*, a hearty stew that feeds two
to three people (12 km from Salema at Praia do Castelo, tel.
082/66777).

LAGOS

The major town and high-rise resort on the west end of the
Algarve is actually a pleasant place. The Old Town that
surrounds the Praça Infante D. Henrique and the fort is a
whitewashed jumble of pedestrian streets, bars, funky craft
shops, outdoor restaurants, and sunburned tourists. The
church of San Antonio and the adjoining regional museum are
worth a look. The beaches with the exotic rock formations (of
postcard fame) are near the fort. On most Saturdays at 18:30
from June through mid-September, Lagos has a small for-
tourists bullfight in its dinky ring. Seats are a steep 3,000$, but
the show is a thriller. Signs all along this touristy coastline
advertise this "Stierkampf." Lagos is understandably famous
(and crowded) for its beautiful beaches and rugged cliffs.

The Turismo, on Largo Marques de Pombal, is loaded with
information and posts bus and train schedules (Monday–Friday
9:30–12:30 and 14:00–19:00, and weekends until 17:30, tel.
082/76-30-31). To reach the TI from the bus station, take the
busy Avenida dos Descobrimentos toward the coast to Praça Gil
Eanes. Take Lima Leitão (at the far end of the square) to the TI.

If you're hauling luggage, Lagos isn't the place for a day
trip; neither the bus nor train stations offer luggage storage.
And if you're continuing on to Sevilla by bus or train, read
ahead and don't leave Lagos without schedules.

Sleeping and Eating in Lagos
(170$ = about $1, tel. code: 082, zip code: 8600)
When a price range is given, the lowest is the winter rate, the
highest is the peak-season summer rate.

Casa de São Goncalo de Lagos, a beautifully decorated
18th-century home with a garden, lovely tilework, parquet
floors, and elegant furnishings, is an excellent splurge. The
downstairs rooms are plain in comparison; head upstairs or
head elsewhere (Sb-7,000–10,000$, Db-8,500–14,000$,
includes breakfast, closed November–mid-March, CC:VMA,
Rua Candido dos Reis 73, on a pedestrian street 2 blocks from
the Turismo, tel. 082/76-21-71, fax 082/76-39-27, SE).

If you missed the last bus to Salema (leaves Lagos around 20:00), these listings are within 1 or 2 blocks of the bus station: **Pensão Residencial Solar**, a good budget bet, has simple, clean rooms (Sb-4,000–9,000$, Db-6,500–11,000$, includes breakfast, elevator, CC:VMA, from the parking lot facing the bus station, look up to see the yellow sign to your left, Rua Antonio Crisogono dos Santos 60, tel. 082/76-24-77, fax 082/76-17-84, SE). They have smaller, cheaper rooms in the center of town. The sternly run **Albergeria Marino Rio**, on the busy main street, has modern rooms with street noise and views in front; quieter, viewless rooms in back (Db-8000–15,500$, extra bed 1,700–5,500$, swimming pool, elevator, CC:VMA, Avenida dos Descobrimentos-Apartado 388, next to bus parking lot, tel. 082/76-98-59, fax 082/76-99-60, SE). Most hotels will store luggage for you after you check out, but the Rio won't.

The Club-Med-like **youth hostel** is a lively, social and very cushy experience (1,900$ per bed in quads with breakfast and kitchen facilities, some doubles available for 4,800$, hostel card required, Rua Lancarote de Freitas 50, tel. 082/76-19-70).

Lagos' pedestrian streets are lined with cafés. Near the main square, **Casa do Zé** specializes in *ameijoas a bolhão pato*, or clams with garlic sauce (daily 06:00–24:00, Rua Portas de Portugal 65). The *mercado* (public market), next door, awaits picnic shoppers every morning except Sunday.

Transportation Connections—Lagos and Salema

Lagos to: Lisbon (8 trains/day, 5 hrs, possible transfer in Tunes; 4 buses/day, 5 hrs), **Évora** (1 bus/day, 5 hrs), **Vila Real St. Antonio** (3 trains/day, more frequent with transfer in Tunes, 4 hrs), **Tavira** (7 trains/day, 3.5 hrs, 2 daily express trains do it in 2 hrs).

Lagos and Salema: Lagos is your Algarve transportation hub and the closest train station to Salema (15 km). Buses go almost hourly between Lagos and Sagres (1-hr ride, last bus departs Lagos around 20:00), about half of them going right into the village of Salema—the others drop you at the top of its dead-end road, a 20-minute walk downhill into the village. From Lagos' train station (ignore the "*quartos* women" who tell you Salema's 50 km away), walk straight out, go left around the big building, cross the bridge and then the main boulevard, and walk straight into the bright yellow EVA bus station.

Before heading to Salema, pick up return bus schedules and train schedules for your next destination. For your venture into Lagos, if any, Sagres buses also stop on the waterfront. Allow 2.500$ for a taxi from Lagos to Salema.

Lagos and Sevilla: The direct bus between Lagos and Sevilla is worth every *escudo* (about 3,000$, 5 hrs, 1/day except Monday from June–September, 1/day Thursday–Sunday April and May). The bus departs from the Lagos bus station and arrives at Sevilla's Plaza de Armas bus station, with stops at Algarve towns such as Tavira. The only drawback is that there are no official bathroom stops. Gut it out, bring a catheter, or be prepared to ask the driver for a minute's wait at a stop.

Other than the direct bus, getting to Sevilla is a very long day by bus, or bus and train. From Salema, take an early bus to Lagos (I walked up to the main road to catch the Sagres–Lagos express bus). From Lagos you have two options: (1) take a bus or train to Faro (about 2 hrs either way) and catch the Faro–Sevilla bus (2 buses/day, 5 hrs) or; (2) take the train until the last stop in Vila Real de San Antonio (several good morning departures, allow 4.5 hours with a possible transfer in Tunes or Faro), which connects directly to a river-crossing ferry (200$, 17 boats/day) to the pleasant Spanish border town of Ayamonte. From the Ayamonte dock, walk through the town (angling slightly to the right) and find the bus stop next to the main square (shops take *escudos*, banks change coins). From Ayamonte to Sevilla, either catch a direct bus to Sevilla (4/day, 2.5 hrs) or transfer at Huelva (frequent buses, easy transfer).

Huelva note: From Huelva, buses run at least hourly to Sevilla (1 hr) and the new Huelva bus station is heavenly: English information, ATMs, and a bank that changes Portuguese coins and sells phone cards. You could take one of 4 daily trains to Sevilla from Huelva (2 hrs, but I wouldn't)— bus and train stations are connected by a 15-minute walk along Avenida Italia. Sunday schedules are limited and more frustrating. (See the end of Sevilla chapter for more specifics.)

TAVIRA

Straddling a river, with a lively park, chatty locals, and boats sharing its waterfront center, Tavira is a low-rise, easygoing alternative to the other, more aggressive Algarve resorts. It's your best east Algarve stop. With good train service and handy bus connections to Sevilla (and other destinations), many travelers find Tavira more accessible than Salema.

Tavira is on the Lagos/Vila Real de San Antonio trans-Algarve train line, with hourly departures both east and west. The train station is a ten-minute walk from the town center: leave the station following the yellow "Turismo" sign and follow this road downhill to the river and the Praça da República. The Turismo is up the cobbled steps on your left as you enter the Praça da República from the Avenida da Liberdade (daily 9:30–19:00 June–September; off-season 9:30–12:30 and 14:00–17:30, Rua Galeria 9, tel. 081/32-25-11). Arriving by bus is a snap: leave the snazzy new station with the river on your left and you'll be at the Praça da Republica in a few minutes.

For a short stop in Tavira, get to the river and enjoy the park at Praça da República, then climb to the beautiful gardens and views inside the old Moorish castle walls, above the Turismo. Tavira may tempt you to stay longer (it did me) with its great beach island, Ilha da Tavira. Catch the bus from the central bus station (or rent a bike and ride) to Quatro Aguas, then take the five-minute ferry to Ilha da Tavira (runs from about April–September). A new summer-only boat will take bathers painlesssly right from Tavira to the island. Either way, get details at the Turismo. Another fine beach, the Barril Beach resort, is just 4 km from Tavira: walk, rent a bike, or take a city bus to Pedras del Rei, then catch the little train (runs May–September), or walk ten minutes any time of the year from Pedras del Rei to the resort. Ask at the Turismo.

Sleeping and Eating in Tavira
(170$ = about $1, tel. code 81, zip code: 8800)

Hotels are reasonable in Tavira. My favorite is the **Residencial Lagaos**. It's spotless, homey, and a block off the river. Friendly, English-speaking Maria offers a communal refrigerator, a rooftop patio with a view made for wine and candles, and laundry washboard privileges (S-2,500$, D-4,500$, Db-5,500$, Tb-6,000$, less off-season, Rua Almirante Candido dos Reis 24, tel. 081/32-22-52). Cross the Roman footbridge from Praça da República, follow the middle fork on the other side, and turn right where it ends.

The modern, hotelesque **Residencia Princesa do Gilão** offers bright, modern, riverfront rooms, some with balconies and a view (Sb-6000$, Db-7,000$, Rua Borda de Agua de Aguiar 10;

cross the Roman bridge and turn right along the river; tel. and
fax 081/32-51-71, SE).

For a modest splurge consider the **Hotel Mare's** red-tiled
and smartly appointed rooms, firm beds, sauna, and roof-top
terrace. Some rooms on the second floor have fine balconies
overlooking the river—ask (Db-5,500–8,000$, Rua Jose Pires
Padinha, on the Turismo side of the river just beyond the market hall, tel. 081/32 58 15, fax 081/32-58-19).

Pensão Castelo is friendly and sleepable, with several
new family-apartments almost completed (Sb-3,000–4,000$,
Db-4,000–5,000$, about 10,000$ for the apartments, very near
the Turismo at Rua da Liberdade 4, tel. 081/32-39-42, SE).

Tavira is filled with fine reasonable restaurants. For
seafood, I liked the inexpensive and relaxed **Restaurant Bica**,
below the Residencial Lagaos (see first hotel listing, above).
For Italian cuisine, cross the Roman bridge from Praça da
República and take the middle fork: on your left will be
Patrick's Place (great lasagne), to the right look for signs to
Aquasul (pasta, pizza, and more). Many mini-supermarkets
make picnicking a breeze in Tavira.

Transportation Connections—Tavira
To: Lisbon (8 trains/day, 5 hrs; 5 buses/day, 5 hrs), **Lagos** (12
trains/day, 2–3.5 hrs), **Sevilla by bus** (2/day, 3.5 hrs, easy
transfer in Huelva; 1 direct bus, 3 hrs, May–October, Thursday–
Sunday), **Sevilla by train, ferry, and bus** (4/day, 5–6 hrs, see
Lagos–Sevilla Transportation Connections, above).

CACELA VELHA
Just a few miles east of Tavira (1 km off the main road), this
tiny village sits happily ignored on a hill with its fort, church,
one restaurant, a few *quartos*, and a beach with the open sea
just over the sandbar, a short row across its lagoon. The
restaurant serves a fried-at-your-table sausage-and-cheese
specialty. If you're driving, swing by, if only to enjoy the
coastal view and imagine how nice the Algarve would be if
people like you and me never discovered it.

Route Tips for Drivers in the Algarve
Lisbon to Salema (150 miles, 5 hrs): Following the blue "Sul
Ponte" signs, drive south over Lisbon's 25th of April Bridge. A
short detour just over the bridge takes you to the giant concrete

Christ in Majesty statue. Continue south past Setubal following N262 (and signs to Setubal, Alcacer, Algarve, Faro, Grandola, Sines, Cercal, Odemira, Vila do Bispo, Sagres, Lagos, Salema) to the south coast.

You'll pass the likable riverside town of Alcacer do Sal and grove after grove of cork trees with their telltale peeled trunks. After Grandola you could take a side trip to Praia de Melides, an ugly shantytown with lots of private rooms for rent and a beautiful sandy beach. Just south of Melides and right on the road, you can take a walk along some coastal sand dunes and have a snack at Costa de Santo Andre. Just east of Vila do Bispo, you'll hit Figueira and the tiny road to the beach village of Salema. Decent roads, less traffic, and the glory of waking up on the Algarve make doing this drive at night a reasonable option. The Algarve has good roads and lots of traffic.

Algarve to Sevilla (150 miles): Drive east along the Algarve. In Lagos, park along the waterfront by the fort (and Mobil gas station). To avoid traffic, take the inland route from Lagos, following signs to Faro, then Loule, to Tavira. It's a two-hour drive from Salema to Tavira. Leaving Tavira, follow signs to Vía Real, then España. You'll cross into Spain (where it is one hour later) over the new bridge and effortlessly (90 minutes by freeway) into Sevilla. At Sevilla, follow the signs to Centro Ciudad (city center), drive along the river, and park (at least to get set up) near the cathedral and tower.

CENTRAL PORTUGAL: COIMBRA AND NAZARÉ

While the far north of Portugal has considerable charm, those with limited time enjoy maximum travel thrills on or near the coast of central Portugal. This is an ideal stop if you're coming in from Salamanca or Madrid, or interested in a small-town side trip north from Lisbon.

The college town of Coimbra (three hours north of Lisbon by train, bus, or car) is Portugal's Oxford and its easiest-to-enjoy city. Browse through the historic university, the hilltopping cathedral, and the lively Old Quarter of what was once Portugal's leading city.

Nazaré, an Atlantic coast fishing town–turned–resort, is black-shawl traditional and beach-friendly. You'll be greeted by the energetic applause of the forever surf and big plates of smiling steamed shrimp. Have fun in the Portuguese sun in a land of cork groves, eucalyptus trees, ladies who wear seven petticoats, and men who stow cigarettes and fishhooks in their stocking caps.

Several other worthy sights are within easy day-trip distance of Nazaré: You can drop by the patriotic pride and architectural joy of Portugal, the Batalha monastery. If the spirit moves you, the pilgrimage site at Fatima is nearby. Alcobaça has Portugal's largest church (and saddest romance). And Portugal's almost edibly cute walled town of Óbidos is just down the road.

Planning Your Time

Few Americans give Portugal much time. Most do Lisbon and the south coast. On a three-week trip through Spain and Portugal, Coimbra (KWEEM-bra), and Nazaré each merit a day. There's another day's worth of sightseeing in Batalha, Alcobaça, and Fatima. If you're connecting Salamanca or Madrid with Lisbon via this region, I'd do it this way (for specifics on Transportation Connections, see end of chapter):

By Car
Day 1: Leave Salamanca early, breakfast in Ciudad Rodrigo, early afternoon arrive in Coimbra, tour university and old cathedral.
Day 2: Shop and browse the Old Quarter, picnic lunch at Batalha, tour church, visit Fatima, evening in Nazaré.
Day 3: A 30-mile, triangular side trip from Nazaré visiting Alcobaça (town, monastery, wine museum) and São Martinho do Porto. Afternoon back in Nazaré with a look at Sitio and beach time. Seafood dinner.
Day 4: Visit Óbidos on your way to Lisbon. Arrive in Lisbon by noon.

By Train
Day 1: The only alternative to the miserable 4:55–10:45 Salamanca–Coimbra train connection is spending half of yesterday on a bus. Spend the day seeing Coimbra.
Day 2: Catch morning bus (or train) from Coimbra to Nazaré. Set up and relax in Nazaré, Sitio, and beach. Seafood dinner.
Day 3: Do the triangular loop (Nazaré–Batalha–Alcobaça–Nazaré) by bus.
Day 4: Train into Lisbon.

COIMBRA
Don't be fooled by Coimbra's drab suburbs. Portugal's most important city for 200 years, Coimbra remains second only to Lisbon culturally and historically. It was the center of Portugal while the Moors still controlled Lisbon. Only as Portugal's maritime fortunes rose was landlocked Coimbra surpassed by the ports of Lisbon and Porto. Today Coimbra is Portugal's third-largest city (pop. 100,000), with its oldest and most prestigious university (founded 1307). When school is in session, Coimbra bustles. During school holidays, it's sleepier. Coimbra's got a great Arab-flavored Old Quarter—a maze of people, narrow streets, and tiny *tascas* (restaurants with just four or five tables).

Coimbra

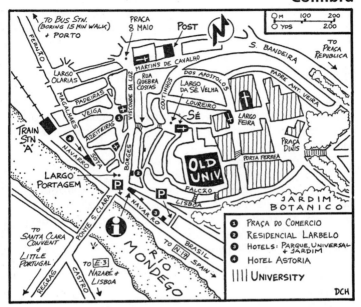

Orientation (tel. code: 039)

Coimbra is a mini-Lisbon—everything good about urban Portugal without the intensity of a big city. I couldn't design a more enjoyable city for a visit. There's a small-town feeling in the winding streets set on the side of the hill. The high point is the old university. From there, little lanes meander down like a Moroccan *medina* to Rua de Ferreira Borges (which turns into Visconde da Luiz), the main business and shopping street, and the Mondego River. The crowded, intense Old Quarter of town is the triangle between the river and the Rua de Ferreira Borges.

From the Largo da Portagem (main square), everything is within an easy walk. The Old Quarter spreads out like an amphitheater: timeworn houses, shops, and stairways, all leading up to the university. The best views are looking up from the south end of Santa Clara Bridge, and looking down from the observation deck of the university or the arcade in the Machado de Castro Museum. The TI and plenty of good budget rooms are along the river, within 4 blocks of the train station.

Tourist Information: Pick up a map at the TI at Largo da Portagem (entrance on Navarro, Monday–Friday 9:00–19:00, weekends 9:00–13:00 and 14:30–17:30, closes earlier off-season, tel. 039/23886, new number in spring—039/82-38-86). Here you can get all bus schedules and information on sights in central Portugal. Other TIs, with similar hours, are on Praça Dinis and Praça da República (near the university).

Helpful Hints: Most of Coimbra's phone numbers will change in the spring of 1998—call the TI's new number (039/82-38-86) for help if you have trouble reaching a hotel. The travel agency Abreu sells bus tickets to Salamanca and beyond, and accepts credit cards (Rua da Sota 2, near train station A and across from recommended Pensão Vitoria, tel. 039/27011). Banks and ATM machines are easy to find along Avenida Navarro and the Rua de Ferreira Borges. Avis has an office in train station A (tel. 039/34786, fax 039/280-4595) and Hertz is at Rua Joao de Ruao 1 (tel. 039/37491, fax 039/22027).

Arrival in Coimbra

By Train: There are two Coimbra train stations, A and B. Major trains (e.g., trains from Lisbon and Salamanca) stop only at B (big). From there, it's easy to catch a three-minute shuttle train to the very central A station (take the A train). Local trains (e.g., to/from Nazare) stop at both stations. Station A has a helpful English-speaking information office (*informações*) tucked away in a waiting room, with all the train schedules you'd need (daily 9:00–13:00 and 14:00–18:00, tel. 039/34998).

By Bus: The bus station, on Avenida Fernão de Magalhaes (tel. 039/27083), is a boring 15-minute walk from the center. If you leave the bus station without getting the schedules you'll need for your onward journey, you can get them at the TI. Exit the bus station to the right and follow the busy street into town or take a taxi (400$). Local buses are expensive (200$), and by the time the bus comes along (#5 or #14), you could already have walked downtown.

Sights—Coimbra

Old Cathedral (*Sè Velha*)—This dinky 13th-century Romanesque church is built like a compact fortress, complete with crenelations. The altarpiece is flamboyant Gothic, and the walls are lined with 16th-century tiles from Sevilla. The peaceful cloister (entrance near back of church) is the oldest Gothic cloister in Portugal. Its decaying walls, neglected courtyard, and overgrown roses offer a fine framed view of the cathedral's grassy dome (church is free, cloisters cost 100$, daily 10:00–12:00 and 14:00–19:30, may be closed off-season, but you're always welcome to drop by during the 19:00 evening mass).

To get to the cathedral and the university from Largo da Portagem (and the TI), follow the pedestrian street Rua de Ferreira Borges into the city center, then turn right under a 12th-century arch (the marketplace is down the stairs back to your left), and go up the steep alley called Rua de Quebra Costas—"Street of Broken Ribs." Two little squares and 150 uphill steps later, you'll hit the old cathedral. Beyond that is the university.

▲**Old University**—Coimbra's 700-year-old university was modeled after the Bologna university (Europe's first, A.D. 1139). It's a stately, three-winged former royal palace (from when Coimbra was the capital), beautifully situated overlooking the city. At first, law, medicine, grammar, and logic were taught. Then, with Portugal's seafaring orientation, astronomy and geometry were added.

Three sections are worthwhile: the Grand Hall, St. Michael's Chapel, and King John's Library.

The Grand Hall (Sala dos Capelos, two doors down from the ticket office), decorated with gloomy portraits of Portuguese kings and an elaborately painted ceiling, is still the site of the university's major academic ceremonies. Check out the narrow observation deck overlooking the city.

St. Michael's Chapel, from the 16th century, sports a colorful ceiling, gleaming tilework, and an unusual "stepped" altarpiece. Its exuberant Baroque organ bristles with pipes and cherubs (chapel is free; just push open the door). The Museum of Sacred Art is one door away (toward the bookshop); John the Baptist points the way to art that nuns and priests would find fascinating.

King John's Library holds 300,000 books in an 18th-century setting. The zealous doorkeeper locks the door at every opportunity. Buzz to get in. The inlaid rosewood reading tables and precious wood shelves are a reminder that Portugal's wealth was great—and imported. Enjoy the literary view and imagine being a student in Coimbra 500 years ago.

To reach the old university, turn right just past Se Velha
Cathedral, and walk up a steep street to steeper steps, finally
entering (to your right) a wrought-iron gate to the courtyard.
The university seems to be designed as a tourist IQ test. Few
sites are marked prominently. With your back to the gate, the
ticket office hides upstairs to your right, near the bell tower.
Straight ahead, across the courtyard, is the hallway leading to
St. Michael's Chapel, the Museum of Sacred Art, WCs, a
bookshop, and a downstairs snack bar. King John's Library is
the columned building to the far left of this hallway. Tickets
are 250$ apiece for the Grand Hall, Museum of Sacred Art,
and King John's Library (or 500$ for the works, daily
9:30–12:00 and 14:00–17:00). Study the necessary map in the
English brochure.

Machado de Castro Museum—This grab-bag museum,
containing chunks of Roman Coimbra, a carriage, ceramics,
religious sculpture, a chapel, and an eerie Roman crypt (down
the stairs), is notable for its striking arcaded viewpoint overlooking the city's red-tiled roofs. Go upstairs for the best
view (250$, Tuesday–Sunday 9:30–12:00 and 14:00–17:30,
closed Monday, snack bar inside, on Dr. José Rodrigues
Largo). Visit this before or after the old university, since both
are roughly at the same altitude.

▲▲**Old Quarter**—If you can't make it to Morocco, this dense
jungle of shops and markets may be your next-best bet. For a
break from this intense shopping and sightseeing experience,
surface on the either spacious Praça do Comércio or the Praça
8 Maio for coffee or a beer (*cerveja*).

Portugal dos Pequeñitos (Little Portugal)—This is a children's (or tourist's) look at the great buildings and monuments
of Portugal in miniature, scattered through a park a couple of
blocks south of town, across the Santa Clara bridge (600$,
daily 10:00–19:00, until 17:30 off-season).

Sights—Near Coimbra

Conimbriga Roman Ruins—Not much of this Roman city has
survived the ravages of time and barbarians. Still, there are
some good floor mosaics and a museum (350$ covers both sites,
daily 9:00–13:00 and 14:00–20:00, museum opens one hour
later and closes two hours earlier and all day Monday; ruins
close at 18:00 off-season). The ruins are about 15 km south of
Coimbra on the Lisbon road; drivers turn left at Condeixa. On

weekdays, two buses leave for the ruins each morning from the stop across the street from Coimbra's Hotel Astoria and return late afternoon (255$). Buses run to Condeixa from the Coimbra bus station, leaving about a mile walk. Check bus schedules at the Coimbra TI.

Kayaks and Boats—O Pioneiro will take you from Coimbra to Penacova (25 kilometers away) by minibus and give you a kayak and instructions. It's a three- to four-hour paddle downstream on the Rio Mondego to Coimbra (3,000$, daily April–September, one- and two-person kayaks available, tel. 039/47-83-85 to reserve, best time to phone is from 13:00–15:00 and 20:00–22:00, SE). Most people stop to swim or picnic on the way back, so it often turns into an all-day journey. For the first 20 km you'll go with the flow, but you'll get your exercise paddling the last flat 5 kilometers.

If you'd rather let someone else do the work, O Basofia boats cruise up and down the river daily in summer (1,200$, 3/day, fewer off-season, 1.5 hrs; depart from dock across from TI, tel. 039/40-41-35).

Sleeping in Coimbra
(170$ = about $1, tel. code: 039, zip code: 3000)
Sleep Code: **S**=Single, **D**=Double/Twin, **T**=Triple, **Q**=Quad, **b**=bathroom, **t**=toilet only, **s**=shower only, **CC**=Credit Card (Visa, MasterCard, Amex), **SE**=Speaks English, **NSE**=No English. Almost no one speaks English. Try broken Spanish, French, or sign language. Breakfast isn't included unless noted. *Warning: Most phone numbers will change in spring—call the TI's new number (039/82-38-86) for help if you have trouble reaching a hotel.*

The listings are an easy walk from the central Coimbra A station. The driver's easiest bet is to choose one of the places that line the riverside Avenida E. Navarro at the base of town, within 2 blocks of Santa Clara Bridge (the road from Spain). They have noisy front rooms, so choose the rear or try a listing off the river, in the city center.

Hotel Astoria gives you the thrill of staying in the city's finest old hotel for a painless price (Sb-10,000–12,000$, Db-12,000–15,000$, extra bed-3,200$, includes breakfast, CC:VMA, central as can be at Avenida Navarro 21, tel. 039/22055, fax 039/22057, SE). Rooms with river views cost no extra.

Pensão Vitoria is basically a restaurant with 20 tidy rooms tucked away upstairs. Many rooms have just been remodeled, with air-conditioning added. If you're on a budget, this is a fine value (S-2,500$, Ss-4,000$, D-3,000$, Ds-5,000$, CC:V, Rua da Sota 3; cross the street straight out of the train station and turn left, then turn right; tel. 039/24049, NSE).

Hotel Braganca, on a busy intersection next door to the A train station, is less than a minute's walk from the interesting Old Quarter. The ugly lobby disguises clean, comfortable, and well-maintained rooms, with modern bathrooms (Sb with shower-$5,000, Sb with tub-7,000$, Db with shower-8,000$, Db with tub-9,500$; to save money, ask for a room with a shower—*chuveiro*; includes breakfast, air-con, elevator, CC:VMA, Largo das Ameias 10, tel. 039/22171, fax 039/36135, SE).

On Largo da Portagem, in front of the bridge, **Residencial Larbelo** mixes frumpiness and elegance beautifully (Sb-4,000$, Ds-4,000–5,000$, Db-5,000–6,000$, Largo da Portagem 33, tel. 039/29092, fax 039/29094, NSE). Despite the vinyl, the old-fashioned staircase makes you almost glad there's no elevator . . . almost.

Rivoli Pensão offers the best location, 3 blocks off the river on the lovable Praça do Comércio (S-2,000$, D-4,500$, Ds-5,000$, Ts-5,800$, no rooms have toilets, Praça do Comércio 27, tel. 039/25550, NSE). It's a bit eccentric and plain but friendly and a fine value.

Hospedaria Simões is buried in the exotic heart of the cobbled hillside, just below the old cathedral. Run by the friendly Simões family, it offers 18 clean rooms but only six have windows; ask for a *quarto com janela* (Sb-2,500$, Db-3,500$, Tb-4,500$, Qb-5,600$, from Rua Borges Ferriera, go uphill through old gate toward the university and cathedral, take first right, Rua Fernandes Tomas 69, tel. 039/34638).

Pensão Residencial Jardím is elegantly faded, family-run for 25 years, and bursting with thoughtful touches that have been around since the turn of the century. It has giant rooms and a TV lounge (S-4,000$, Sb-4,000–5,000$, D-4,000$, Db-6,000$, Tb-7,000$, Avenida Navarro 65, tel. 039/25204, NSE).

The youth hostel, **Pousada de Juventude**, on the other

side of town in the student area past the Praça da República, is
friendly, clean, well-run, and recently remodeled but is no
cheaper than a simple *pensão* (1,500$ beds in four-bed rooms,
closed 12:00–18:00, Rua Antonio Henriques Seco 14, tel. & fax
039/22955, SE).

Eating in Coimbra

This is a town filled with fun and cheap eateries. Wander the
Old Town between the river and the Praça do Comércio and
browse the posted menus. These three places are within a minute's walk of the train station and each other, either on or just
off Rua da Sota in the Old Quarter. The quirkiest and smallest
(four to five tables) is **Zé Manel** (12:00–15:00, 19:00–02:00,
closed Saturday evening and all Sunday, Beco do Forno 12,
directly behind Hotel Astoria). The walls are hung with hats,
money, an alligator skin, and much more. Larger and classier are
O Serenata (9:00–23:00, closed Monday, Largo da Sota 6-7,
CC:VMA) and **Calado & Calado** (9:00–22:00, closed Sunday,
Rua da Sota 14).

Adega Paço do Conde is super for grilled food. After
you choose your seafood or meat selection from the display
case, it's popped on the grill for you. Lots of locals, including
families, like this place and so do I (daily 10:00–20:00, Rua
Paço do Conde 1, CC:VMA, take the last left off Praça do
Comércio, opposite the church on Adelino Veiga, and go 1
block).

For an acceptable meal on a great square, eat at **Restaurant
Praça Velha** (daily 8:00–01:00, Praça do Comércio 72). There
are a few local-style cafés near the old cathedral, such as the
classy **Restaurant Trovador** (12:00–15:00 and 19:30–22:30,
closed Sunday, CC:VM, next to the cathedral). The owner gives
you a rebate on your admission ticket to the old cathedral—
bring it along. He also offers *fado* daily in summer at 21:00
(Friday and Saturday only in off-season). **Restaurant Barca
Serrana**, across from the Praça 8 Maio at Rua Direita 32 serves
a great homemade stewed beef dish called *chafara*. The café
Santa Cruz (next to the Santa Cruz church) is Old World elegant and offers great people-watching over the Praça 8 Maio
from its outdoor tables.

Picnickers can forage at the municipal *mercado* behind
the Santa Cruz church (8:00–14:00, closed Sunday, near the
gardens called Jardím de Manga) or shop at the supermarket

Minipreço behind train station A. The well-maintained gardens along the river across from the TI are picnic pleasant.

Transportation Connections—Coimbra

By bus to: Alcobaça (2/day, 1.5 hrs), **Batalha** (3/day, 1.25 hrs), **Fatima** (9/day, 1 hr), **Nazaré** (6/day, 1.75 hrs), **Lisbon** (17/day, 2.5 hrs), Évora (8/day, 8.25 hrs), **Lagos** (7/day, 10 hrs).

By train to: **Nazaré/Valado** (6/day, 3.5 hours, transfer in Figueira de la Foz—bus is far better). Train information: tel. 039/34998.

To Salamanca: One train a day drops you in Salamanca at 2:00 in the morning (6-hr trip). The better option is the direct bus (1/day Tuesday–Saturday, 6 hrs, worth the 2,600$ even if you have a railpass; can buy ticket at bus station or at travel agency Abreu, at Rua da Sota 2, near train station, tel. 039/27011).

NAZARÉ

In the summer it seems that most of this famous town's 10,000 inhabitants are in the tourist trade. While the fishing action has been moved to a new harbor a 30-minute walk south of town, the place still feels salty. The beach promenade is a congested tangle of oily sunbathers, hustlers, plastic souvenirs, dogs engaged in public displays of affection, and overpriced restaurants.

Off-season Nazaré is almost empty of tourists—inexpensive, colorful, and relaxed—with enough salty fishing-village atmosphere to make you pucker.

Any time of year, even with its crowds, almost even in August, Nazaré is a fun stop offering a surprisingly good look at old Portugal. Somehow the traditions survive, and the locals are able to go about their black-shawl ways, ignoring the tourists. Wander the back streets for a fine look at Portuguese family-in-the-street life. Women grill fish over tiny home-made hibachis on the curb, as laundry flaps in the wind and kids play soccer.

Nazaré doesn't have any blockbuster sights. The beach, the funicular ride up to Sitio for shopping, and a great coastal view (along with the "sightseeing" my taste buds did) are the bright lights of my lazy Nazaré memories.

Plan some beach time here. Sharing a bottle of *vinho verde*, a new-wine specialty of central Portugal, on the beach at sundown is a good way to wrap up the day.

Nazaré

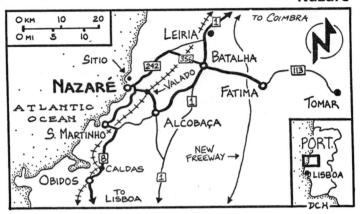

Orientation (tel. code: 062)

Nazaré faces its long beach, stretching from the new harbor north to the hillcapping old town of Sitio.

Sitio, which feels like a totally separate village sitting quietly atop its cliff, is reached by a frequent funicular (85$). Go up at least for the spectacular view (at Mirador de Suberco); there are some good eateries, shops, and quieter streets (read "fewer tourists"). Sitio stages Portuguese-style bullfights on Saturday (from 2,000$ tickets at the kiosk in Praça Sousa Oliveira, mid-July–early September, usually at 22:00) and has a new water park called NorParque with a pool, slides, and Jacuzzi (open June–September).

Down to earth, in central Nazaré, a flea market pops up near the town hall every Friday (9:00–13:00) and the colorful produce market bustles daily (8:00–13:00, off-season closed Sunday, kitty-corner from the bus station). Fish aficionados might enjoy the auction every weekday evening at 20:00 at the harbor (30-minute walk, explain you're a *turista*, bidders have to pay an entrance fee).

Tourist Information: The tourist office is on the Avenida da República, the main beachfront street (daily October–March 9:30–13:00 and 14:30–18:00; open until 20:00 April–September; tel. 062/56-11-94). Ask about the bullfights in Sitio and folk dancing at the Casino and Mar Alto (four performances weekly in the summer).

Arrival in Nazaré: Leaving the bus station, turn right (on Avenida Vieira Guimaraes), and walk 1 block to the waterfront. Cross the street. You'll see the cliffs, funicular to Sitio, and the road kinking toward the sea. The building (on the kink) with the yellow balconies is the Ribamir Hotel, next to the Turismo office. Just beyond the Ribamir are the main square (Praça Sousa Oliveira, with banks and ATMs) and most of my hotel listings.

Sleeping and Eating in Nazaré
(170$ = about $1, tel. code: 062, zip code: 2450)

You should have no problem finding a room, except in July and August, when the crowds, temperatures, and prices are all at their highest. You'll find plenty of hustlers meeting each bus and Valado train, and waiting along the promenade. Even the normal hotels get into the act during the off-season. I've never arrived in town without a welcoming committee inviting me to sleep in their *quartos* (rooms in private homes). It's the cheapest option—they're everywhere and charge from 2,000$ to 5,000$ per room, depending on the season.

Your best home base is the town center directly below the Sitio near the high cliffs, as close to the water as you can afford. I list a price range for each hotel: the lowest is for winter, the sky-highest for July and August. In spring and fall, expect to pay about midrange.

Residencial A Cubata, a friendly place on the waterfront on the north end (dwarfed by the cliffs of Sitio), is my favorite waterfront hotel value. Its rooms are clean and comfortable and prices affordable (Sb-3,500–7,000$, Db-4,000–12,000$ with great sea view, includes breakfast, CC:VMA, Avenida da República 6, tel. 062/56-17-06, fax 062/56-17-00, SE).

Ribamir Hotel Restaurant has a prime location on the waterfront, with an Old World, hotelesque atmosphere, including dark wood and four-poster beds (Sb-3,000–7,000$, Db-6,000–12,000$, includes breakfast, TV, balconies, attached restaurant, CC:VMA, Rua Gomes Freiren 9, tel. 062/55-11-58, fax 062/56-22-24, some English spoken). Look for the yellow awnings and balconies.

Casa dos Frango has two tidy, homey, and spacious *quartos* above their shop, with kitchenettes and sea views (Db-3,000–6,000$, Praça Dr. Manual Arriaga 20, tel. 062/55-18-42). The owner, friendly Sr. Leonardo (his son speaks English and dreams of visiting the U.S.A.), also has three apartment-like flats in another building on the square. A little worn but comfortable, each can accommodate up to five people (three rooms, two double beds, a dinky extra bed, bathroom, tiny kitchenette) for 6,000–10,000$, regardless of the number of people.

Albergaria Mar Bravo is on the corner where the main square meets the waterfront next to Ribamir. Though it lacks character, it's modern, bright, and fresh, with air-conditioning and a restaurant downstairs (Sb-7,000–14,000$, Db-12,000–19,500$ with sea view, elevator, CC:VMA, Praça Sousa Oliveira 67-A, tel. 062/55-11-80, fax 55-39-79, SE).

Hotel Mare, just off the Praça Sousa Oliveira, is a pre-dictably comfortable American-style hotel with prices to match (Sb-6,000–11,000$, Db-7,500–14,500$, includes breakfast, balconies, elevator, CC:VMA, popular with tour groups off-season; Rua Mouzinho de Albuquerque 8, 2451 Nazaré Codex, tel. 062/56-11-22, fax 062/56-17-50, SE). The dinners are mediocre—eat out.

Restaurante "O Navegante" offers frumpy rooms and cheap beds (S-2,500$, D-4,000–5,000$, CC:VMA, exit left from the TI, take first left, walk inland about 4 blocks, Rua Adrião Batalha 89-A, tel. 062/55-18-93, NSE). Its restaurant serves decent food (daily 11:00–15:00 and 18:00–02:00) and is classier than its rooms. The specialty is *arroz de marisco* (rice with seafood).

Nazaré is a fishing town, so don't order *hamburguesas*. Fresh seafood is great all over town, more expensive (but affordable) along the waterfront, cheaper in holes-in-the-wall farther inland. The family-run **Oficina** serves home-style seafood dishes, nothing fancy but filling, in a friendly setting that makes you feel like you're eating at someone's kitchen table (daily 12:00–15:00 and 19:00–22:00, Rua das Flores 33, off Praça Dr. Manual Arriaga). Chicken addicts can get roasted chickens-to-go at **Casa dos Frango** (Praça Dr. Manual Arriaga 20) and picnic gatherers should head for the covered *mercado* across from the bus station. I like the restaurants near the base of the funicular. Seriously consider dining up in Sitio with a panoramic view. Try a glass of the local *amendoa amarga* (like amaretto).

Sleeping in São Martinho do Porto
(170$ = about $1, tel. code: 062, zip code: 2465)
São Martinho (sow mar-TEEN-yo) do Porto, a small village 8

miles south, gets you smaller crowds and the warmest water on Portugal's west coast, with a good beach arcing around a nearly landlocked (and fairly polluted) saltwater lake. Regular bus and train service from Nazaré (nine buses and seven trains daily, 20 min) make this village a convenient alternative for public-transport users in search of peace. The Turismo is on the northern part of the beach promenade on Avenida Marginal (Monday–Friday 9:00–19:00, weekends 10:00–13:00 and 15:00–18:00, tel. 062/98-91-10). Wander up and into São Martinho's Old Town for the best food prices and the town's covered *mercado*.

Pensão Americana, with simple rooms, is a block from the beach (Sb-2,500–4,000$, Db-4,500–7,000$, includes breakfast, CC:VM, Rua D. José Saldanha 2, tel. 062/98-91-70, NSE). Plenty of *quartos* rent doubles through the Turismo for around 4,000$ in the summer.

Transportation Connections—Nazaré

Nazaré's train station is at Valado (3 miles toward Alcobaça, connected by semi-regular 150$ buses and reasonable, easy-to-share 700$ taxis). To avoid this headache, consider using intercity buses. If you're heading to Lisbon, trains and buses work equally well. While the train station is 3 miles from Nazaré, it serves Lisbon's very central Rossio station (with a quick transfer at Cacem), where you'll be a short walk from most of my listed hotels. Lisbon's bus station is a Metro (or taxi) ride away from the center.

Nazaré/Valado by train to: Coimbra (6/day, 3.5 hrs, change at Figueira da Foz; see bus info below), **Lisbon** (7 trains/day, 3 hrs). Train info: tel. 062/51172.

Nazaré by bus to: Alcobaça (stopping at Valado, 13/day, 20 min), **São Martinho** (9/day, 20 min), **Batalha** (8/day, 1 hr, change at Alcobaça), **Óbidos** (6/day, 1 hr; bus is better than train), **Fatima** (3/day, 1.5 hrs), **Coimbra** (6/day, 1.75 hrs; bus is better than train), **Lisbon** (5/day, 2 hrs).

Day-tripping from Nazaré to Alcobaça, Batalha, Fatima, or Óbidos: Traveling by bus, you can see two towns in a day, Alcobaça and Batalha. Alcobaça is easy to visit on the way to or from Batalha (and both are connected by bus with Óbidos). Ask at the bus station for schedule information and be flexible. Fatima has the fewest connections and is farthest away. To see Fatima on a tight schedule, rent a car in Nazaré for the day and see Batalha and Alcobaça as well. Without a car, for most, Fatima is not worth the trouble. A taxi from Nazaré to Alcobaça is about 1,500$.

Car rentals: M.M. Viagens e Turismo, right on Nazaré's waterfront at Avenida da República 28, handles Hertz rentals (daily 9:30–18:00, later in summer; 10,000$/day in peak season, 6,500$ off-season, includes 17 percent VAT tax, lower prices off-season, reserve a day in advance, tel. 062/56-25-71). Avis has similar prices (Mare Viagens e Turismo, Albuquerque 10, tel. 062/56-21-90).

BATALHA'S MONASTERY OF SANTA MARÍA

The only reason to stop in the town of Batalha is to see its great monastery or abbey. Considered Portugal's greatest architectural achievement and a symbol of its national pride, the Batalha (which means "battle") abbey was begun in 1388 to thank God for a Portuguese victory that kept it free from Spanish rule. The greatness of Portugal's Age of Discovery shines brightly in the royal cloisters, which combine the simplicity of Gothic with the elaborate decoration of the Manueline style, and in the chapter house with its frighteningly broad vaults. The ceiling was considered so dangerous to build (it collapsed twice) that only prisoners condemned to death were allowed to work on it. Today unknowing foreign tourists are allowed to wander under it. It's the home of the Portuguese Tomb of the Unknown Soldier. The refectory holds a small museum of World War I memorabilia, and the long hall dotted with architectural scraps used to be the monks' dorm.

Hang on to your ticket to see the Unfinished Chapels (exit from first cloister outside to a square, follow signs to the right; WC is to the left). The chapels were started for King Duarte around 1435 to house the tombs of his family and successors. Never finished, the ornate building is open to the sky. Across from the elaborate doorway are the tombs of King Duarte and his wife, their recumbent statues hand-in-hand, blissfully unaware of the work left undone.

Visit the Founder's Chapel (near church entrance) and its many royal tombs, including Henry the Navigator's. Tucked in the wall, Henry wears the church like a crown on his head.

The Founder's Chapel and church are free. The rest of the monastery costs 400$ (daily 9:00–18:00; until 17:00 off-season; helpful, free English pamphlet; tel. 044/96497).

The Turismo, located across from the monastery, has free maps and information on buses (daily 10:00–13:00 and 15:00–16:00 in summer, shorter hours off-season, tel. 044/96180). Batalha's market day is Monday.

If you take the bus to Batalha, you'll be dropped off within a block of the monastery and TI. There's no official luggage storage, but you can leave luggage at the monastery's ticket desk while you tour the cloisters.

Transportation Connections—Batalha

By bus to: Nazaré (7/day, 1 hr, change in Alcobaça), **Alcobaça** (4/day, 30 min), **Fatima** (3/day, 45 min), and **Lisbon** (5/day, 2 hrs).

FATIMA

On May 13, 1917, the Virgin Mary, "a lady brighter than the sun," visited three young shepherds and told them peace was needed. World War I raged on, so on the 13th day of each of the next five months, Mary dropped in again to call for peace. On the 13th of October, 70,000 people witnessed the parting of dark storm clouds as the sun wrote "God's fiery signature" across the sky. Now, on the 13th of each month, thousands of pilgrims gather at the huge neoclassical basilica of Fatima (evening torchlit processions on the 12th and 13th). In 1930 the Vatican recognized Fatima as legit, and on the 50th anniversary, 1.5 million pilgrims—including the Pope—gathered here. Fatima welcomes guests.

The impressive Basilica do Rosário stands in front of a mammoth square lined with parks. Surrounding the square are a variety of hotels, restaurants, and tacky souvenir stands. Visitors may want to check out the **Museo de Cera de Fatima** (650$), a wax-museum story of Fatima, and the **Museu-Vivo Aparicões** (650$) for a high-tech sound and light show that recreates the apparition (both daily 9:30– 19:00, modest dress for the basilica). Turismo tel. 049/53-11-39.

Apart from the 13th of each month, cheap hotel rooms abound. Buses go from Fatima to **Leiria** (15/day 50 min), **Batalha** (3/day, 45 min), and **Lisbon** (5/day 3 hrs).

ALCOBAÇA

This pleasant little town is famous for its church, the biggest in Portugal and one of the most interesting. Across the square from the church is the multilingual Turismo (daily May–October 10:00–19:00; off-season weekdays 10:00–17:00, weekends 10:00–13:00 and 15:00–17:00, tel. 062/42377).

If you arrive in Alcobaça by bus, exit right from the station (on Avenida Manuel da Silva Carolino), take the first right, and continue straight (on Avenida dos Combatentes) to the town center and monastery. It's a five-minute walk.

Sights—Alcobaça

▲▲**Cistercian Mosteiro de Santa María**—This abbey church is the best Gothic building in Portugal, a clean and bright break from the heavier Iberian norm. Don't miss the 14th-century sarcophagi of Portugal's most romantic and tragic couple, Dom Pedro and Dona Inês de Castro. They rest feet-to-feet in each transept, so that on Judgment Day they'll rise and immediately see each other again. Pedro, heir to the Portuguese throne, was in love with the Spanish aristocrat Inês. Concerned about Spanish influence, Pedro's father, Alfonso V, forbade their marriage. You guessed it—they were married secretly. Alfonso, in the interest of Portuguese independence, had Inês murdered. When Pedro became king (1357), he ripped out and ate the hearts of the murderers, and even more interesting, he had Inês' rotten corpse exhumed, crowned it, and made the entire royal court kiss what was left of her hand. Now that's *amore*. The carvings on the tomb are just as special. Like religious alarm clocks, the attending angels seem poised to wake up the couple on Judgment Day.

Near the king's tomb is the entrance to Hall of Tombs and more deceased royalty. Past the high altar is the sacristy. In the round room decorated with painted wooden sculptures, the little glassed-in hollows in the statues and beams hold relics (tiny bits of bones or clothing) of the monks who died in the monastery. Look out the window of the sacristy's hall to see the rerouted stream heading toward the kitchen (free admission to church and sacristy).

The abbey and cloisters cost 400$ (and the English leaflet for 200$ is worthwhile). Highlights include the Grand Hall, with statues of most of Portugal's kings and tiled walls telling the story of the building of the monastery. The kitchen's giant three-part oven, which roasted six to seven oxen simultaneously, puts General Electric to shame. The kitchen has been equipped with running water for centuries—

the industrious monks rerouted a tributary of the River Alcoa through the kitchen.

Cistercian monks built the abbey in 40 years, starting in 1178. Monks of the order inhabited it until the 19th century (when the Portuguese king disbanded all monasteries). Cistercian monks spent most of their lives in silence and were allowed to speak only in the parlatory and chapter room when given permission by the abbot. Most of the rooms are empty now, and the cloisters are still silent. Fill them with six centuries of thoughts unspoken (daily 9:00–19:00, until 17:00 off-season, tel. 062/43469).

▲Mercado Municipal—The Old World is housed happily here under huge steel-and-fiberglass domes. Inside, black-clad, dried-apple-faced women choose fish, chicks, birds, and rabbits from their respective death rows. You'll also find figs, melons, bushels of grain, and nuts—it's a caveman's Safeway. Buying a picnic is a perfect excuse to drop in (9:00–13:00, closed Sunday, best on Monday). It's a five-minute walk from the TI or bus station, ask a local, *"Mercado municipal?"*

▲▲Museu Nacional do Vinho—A half-mile outside Alcobaça (on the road to Batalha and Leiria, right-hand side), the National Museum of Wine offers a fascinating look at the wine of Portugal (Tuesday–Sunday 9:00–12:30 and 14:00–17:30, closed Monday and off-season Sundays, tel. 062/42222, your car is safer parked inside gate). Run by a local cooperative winery, the museum teaches you everything you never wanted to know about Portuguese wine, in a series of rooms that used to be fermenting vats. With some luck you can get a tour—much more hands-on than French winery tours—through the actual winery. You'll see mountains of cetrifuged, strained, and drained grapes—all well on the road to wine. Ask if you can climb to the top of one of 20 half-buried, white 80,000-gallon tanks, all busy fermenting. Look out. I stuck my head into the manhole-sized top vent, and just as I focused on the rich, bubbling grape stew, I was walloped silly by a wine-vapor punch.

Transportation Connections—Alcobaça
By bus to: Lisbon (5/day, 2 hrs), **Nazaré** (12/day, 30 min), **Batalha** (4/day, 30 min), **Fatima** (1/day, 75 min; more frequent with transfer in Batalha). A taxi to the Valado train station costs 700$, to Nazaré 1,500$.

ÓBIDOS

This medieval walled town was Portugal's "wedding city"—
the perfect gift for a king to give to a queen who has everything. (Beats a toaster.) Today it's preserved in its entirety as
a national monument surviving on tourism. Óbidos is
crowded all summer, especially in August. Filter out the
tourists and see it as you would a beautiful painted tile. It's
worth a quick visit.

Postcard perfect, the town sits atop a hill, its 40-foot-
high 14th-century wall corralling a bouquet of narrow lanes
and flower-bedecked, whitewashed houses. Óbidos is ideal
for photographers who want to make Portugal look prettier
than it is. Walk around the wall, peek into the castle (now an
overly-impressed-with-itself *pousada*, Db-28,000$, CC:VMA,
tel. 062/95-91-05, fax 062/95-91-48), and lose yourself for a
while in this lived-in open-air museum of medieval town
non-planning. Wander the back lanes, study the centuries-
old houses, and drop by the churches. St. Mary's church, on
the town square, gleams with lovely 17th-century *azulejo*
tiles. The small Municipal Museum, also on the square, is
not worth the 250$ unless you enjoy stairs, religious art, and
Portuguese inscriptions. Outside the town walls are a 16th-
century aqueduct, a windmill, and a small produce market.

Óbidos is tough on the average tourist's budget. Pick up
your picnic at the small grocery store just inside the main
gate (on the street heading downhill), the larger grocery near
the TI on Rua Direita, or at the tiny market just outside the
town wall.

Orientation (tel. code: 062)

Tourist Information: There are two Turismos almost next to
each other in the middle of town on the main street, Rua
Direita. The Região de Turismo do Oeste covers the region,
and a few doors down, the Turismo specializes in the town
(daily 9:30–13:00 and 14:00–19:00, tel. 062/95-92-31).

Arrival in Óbidos: Ideally take a bus to Óbidos, and
leave by either bus or train. If you arrive at the train station,
you're faced with a 20-minute uphill hike into town (a killer
with luggage). The bus drops you off much closer (go up the
steps and enter the archway on the right). There's no place to
store luggage, and hotel prices are steep, so Óbidos is best for
a day trip.

Sleeping in Óbidos

Spend the night, and enjoy the town without tourists. Two good values in this sterilized and overpriced toy of a town are the hotelesque **Albergaria Rainha Santa Isabel** (Sb-8,000–10,000$, Db-9,000–12,000$ with breakfast; add 1,500$ in August, CC:VMA, on the main one-lane drag, Rua Direita, 2510 Óbidos, tel. 062/95-93-23, fax 062/95-91-15, SE) and **Casa do Poço**, with four dim, clean rooms around a bright courtyard (Db-9,000$ with breakfast, Travessa da Mouraria, 2510 Óbidos, in old center near castle, tel. 062/95-93-58, NSE).

For less expensive intimacy, try a *quarto*. As you walk through town, older women will probably ask you if you need a *quarto* or *chambre*. If not, ask around.

Transportation Connections—Óbidos

To: Nazaré (6 buses/day, 1 hr), **Lisbon** (5 buses/day, 2 hrs, transfer in Caldas de Rainha; 2 trains/day, 2 hrs, transfer in Cacem), **Alcobaça** (3 buses/day, 1 hr), **Batalha** (3 buses/day, 2 hrs). The new highway will likely speed up these travel times for buses.

Route Tips for Drivers in Central Portugal

Coimbra to Batalha to Nazaré (60 miles): You'll cross Santa Clara Bridge and follow signs to Lisbon and Leiria. You'll see Batalha, proud and ornate, on the left of the highway, in 90 minutes. From Batalha, it's a pleasant drive down N356, then N242 into Nazaré.

Alcobaça side trip from Nazaré: Leaving Nazaré, you'll pass women wearing the traditional seven petticoats (trust me) as they do laundry at the edge of town on the road to Alcobaça (follow signs, then right at unmarked intersection). Within a few minutes you'll be surrounded by eucalyptus groves in a world that smells like a cough drop.

Nazaré to Óbidos to Lisbon (60 miles): Follow N242 south from Nazaré, passing São Martinho, and catching scenic N8 farther south to Óbidos. Don't drive into tiny, cobbled Óbidos. Ample tourist parking is provided outside of town. From Óbidos, take the no-nonsense direct route—N115, N1, and E3—into Lisbon. For arriving and parking in Lisbon, see that chapter.

APPENDIX

Iberian History

The cultural landscape of modern Spain and Portugal was shaped by the various civilizations that settled on the peninsula. Iberia's warm and sunny weather and fertile soil made it a popular place to call home.

The Greeks came to Cádiz around 1100 B.C., followed by the Romans, who occupied the country for almost 1,000 years, until A.D. 400. Long after the empire crumbled, the Roman influence remained, including cultural values, materials, building techniques, even Roman-style farming equipment, which was used well into the 19th century. And, of course, wine.

Moors (711–1492)

The Moors—North Africans of the Moslem faith who occupied Spain—had the greatest cultural influence on Spanish and Portuguese history. They arrived on the Rock of Gibraltar in A.D. 711 and moved north. In the incredibly short time of seven years, the Moors completely conquered the peninsula.

They established their power and Moslem culture—but in a subtle way. Non-Moslems were tolerated and often rose to positions of wealth and power; Jewish culture flourished. Rather than brutal subjugation, the Moorish style of conquest was to employ their more sophisticated culture to develop whatever they found. For example, they encouraged the making of wine, although for religious reasons they themselves weren't allowed to drink alcohol.

The Moors ruled for more than 700 years. Throughout that time, pockets of Christianity remained. Local Christian kings fought against the Moors whenever they could, whittling away at the Moslem empire, gaining more and more land. The last Moorish stronghold, Granada, fell to the Christians in 1492.

The slow, piecemeal process of the *Reconquista* (Reconquest) split the peninsula into the two independent states of Portugal and Spain. In 1139, Alfonso Henriques conquered the Moors near present-day Beja in southern Portugal and proclaimed himself king of the area. By 1200, the Christian state of Portugal already had the borders it does today, making it the oldest unchanged state in Europe. The rest of the peninsula was a loosely knit collection of smaller kingdoms. Spain's major step toward unity was in 1469, when Fernando II of Aragon married Isabel of Castilla. Known as the "Catholic Monarchs," they united the other kingdoms under their rule.

The Golden Age (1500–1700)

The expulsion of the Moors set the stage for the rise of Portugal and Spain as naval powers and colonial superpowers. The Spaniards, fueled by the religious fervor of their Reconquista of the Moslems, were interested in spreading Christianity to the newly discovered New World. Wherever they landed, they tried to Christianize the natives—with the sword, if necessary.

The Portuguese expansion was motivated more by economic concerns. Their excursions overseas were planned, cool, and rational. They colonized the nearby coasts of Africa first, progressing slowly around Africa to Asia and South America.

Through exploration (and exploitation) of the colonies, tremendous quantities of gold came into each country. The aristocracy and the clergy were swimming in money. It was only natural that art and courtly life flourished during this Golden Age.

Slow Decline

The fast money from the colonies kept Spain and Portugal from seeing the dangers at home. Great Britain and the Netherlands also were becoming naval powers, defeating the Spanish Armada in 1588. The Portuguese imported everything, didn't grow their own wheat anymore, and neglected their fields.

During the centuries when science and technology in other European countries developed as never before, Spain and Portugal were occupied with their failed colonial politics. In the 18th century, Spain was ruled by the French Bourbon family. (This explains the French Baroque architecture that you'll see, such as La Granja near Segovia and the Royal Palace in Madrid.) Endless battles, wars of succession, revolutions, and counterrevolutions weakened the countries. In this chaos there was no chance to develop democratic forms of government. Dictators in both countries made the rich richer and kept the masses underprivileged.

During World Wars I and II, both countries stayed neutral, uninterested in foreign policy as long as there was quiet in their own states. In the 1930s, Spain suffered a bloody and bitter civil war between fascist and democratic forces. The fascist dictator Francisco Franco prevailed, ruling the country until his death in 1975.

Democracy in Spain and Portugal is still young. After an unbloody revolution, Portugal held democratic elections in 1975. After 41 years of dictatorship, Spain finally had elections in 1977.

Today socialists are in power in both countries. They've adopted a policy of balance to save the young democracies and fight problems such as unemployment and foreign debts—with moderate success. Spain recently joined the European Economic Community. In the 1980s, Spain's economy was among the fastest-growing in Europe.

Art

The "Big Three" in Spanish painting are El Greco, Velázquez, and Goya.

El Greco (1541–1614) exemplifies the spiritual fervor of much Spanish art. The drama, the surreal colors, and the intentionally unnatural distortion have the intensity of a religious vision.

Diego Velázquez (1599–1660) went to the opposite extreme. His masterful court portraits are studies in realism and cool detachment from his subjects.

Goya (1746–1828) matched Velázquez's technique but not his detachment. He let his liberal tendencies shine through in unflattering portraits of royalty and in emotional scenes of abuse of power. He unleashed his inner passions in the eerie, nightmarish canvases of his last, "dark" stage.

Not quite in the league of the Big Three, Murillo (1618–1682) painted a dreamy world of religious visions. His pastel, soft-focus works of cute baby Jesuses and radiant Virgin Marys helped make Catholic doctrine palatable to the common folk at a time when many were defecting to Protestantism.

You'll also find plenty of foreign art in Spain's museums. During its Golden Age, Spain's wealthy aristocrats bought wagonloads of the most popular art of the time—Italian Renaissance and Baroque works by Titian, Tintoretto, and so on. They also loaded up on paintings by Rubens, Bosch, and Brueghel from the Low Countries, which were under Spanish rule.

In this century Pablo Picasso (don't miss his mural *Guernica* in Madrid), Joan Miró, and surrealist Salvador Dalí have made their marks. Fans wishing to say, "Hello, Dalí," should check out his museum in the town of Figueres, north of Barcelona.

Architecture

The two most fertile periods of architectural innovation in Spain and Portugal were during the Moorish occupation and in the Golden Age. Otherwise, Spanish architects have marched obediently behind the rest of Europe.

The Moors brought Middle Eastern styles with them, such as the horseshoe arch, minarets, and floor plans designed for mosques. Islam forbids the sculpting or painting of human or animal figures ("graven images"), so artists expressed their creativity with elaborate geometric patterns. The ornate stucco of Granada's Alhambra, the elaborate arches of Sevilla's Alcázar, and decorative colored tiles are evidence of the Moorish sense of beauty. Islamic and Christian elements were blended in the work of Mozarabic (Christians living under Moorish rule) and Mudejar (Moors living in Spain after the Christian reconquest) artists.

As the Christians slowly reconquered the country, they turned their fervor into stone, building churches both in the heavy, fortress-of-God Romanesque style (Lisbon's cathedral) and in the lighter, heaven-reaching, stained-glass Gothic style (Barcelona, Toledo, Sevilla). Gothic was an import from France, trickling into conservative Spain long after it swept through Europe.

The money reaped and raped from Spain's colonies in the Golden Age (1500–1650) spurred new construction. Churches and palaces were built using the solid, geometric style of the Italian Renaissance (El Escorial) and the more ornamented Baroque. Ornamentation reached unprecedented heights in Spain, culminating in the Plateresque style of stonework, so called because it resembles intricate silver filigree work. In Portugal the highly ornamented style is called Manueline. Lisbon's Belém Tower is its best example.

In the 18th and 19th centuries, innovation in both countries died out. Spain's major contribution to modern architecture is the Art Nouveau work of Antonio Gaudí early in this century. Most of his "cake-left-out-in-the-rain" buildings, with asymmetrical designs and sinuous lines, can be found in Barcelona.

Bullfighting—Legitimate Slice of Spain or Cruel Spectacle?

The Spanish bullfight is as much a ritual as it is sport. Not to acknowledge the importance of the bullfight is to censor a venerable part of Spanish culture. But it also makes a spectacle out of the cruel killing of an animal. Should tourists boycott bullfights? I don't know.

In the 1990s, bullfighting is falling out of favor with the locals. As this trend continues, bullfighting will survive more and more as a tourist event. Ultimately it will be our tourist dollars rather than the local culture that keep bullfighting alive. As that happens (even though for 20 years I have promoted tourists seeing bullfights in Spain), I have to agree with those who say bullfighting is immoral, and it is wrong for tourists to encourage it by buying tickets. Consider the morality of supporting this dated aspect of Spanish culture before buying a ticket. If you do decide to attend a bullfight, here is what you'll see.

While no two bullfights are the same, they unfold along a strict pattern. The ceremony begins punctually with a parade of participants around the ring. Then the trumpet sounds, the "Gate of Fear" opens, and the leading player— *el toro*—thunders in. An angry half-ton animal is an awesome sight, even from the cheap seats.

The fight is divided into three acts. Act I is designed to size up the bull and wear him down. The *matador* (from the word *matar*—to kill), with help from his assistants, attracts the bull with the shake of the cape, then directs the animal past his body, as close as his bravery allows. After a few passes the *picadors* enter, mounted on horseback, to spear the swollen lump of muscle at the back of the bull's neck. This lowers the bull's head and weakens the thrust of his horns.

In Act II, the matador's assistants (*banderilleros*) continue to enrage and weaken the bull. The unarmed *banderillero* charges the charging bull and, leaping acrobatically across the bull's path, plunges brightly colored barbed sticks into the bull's vital neck muscle.

After a short intermission during which the matador may, according to tradition, ask permission to kill the bull and dedicate the kill to someone in the crowd, the final, lethal Act III begins.

The matador tries to dominate and tire the bull with hypnotic capework. A good pass is when the matador stands completely still while the bull charges past. Then the matador thrusts a sword between the animal's shoulder blades for the kill. A quick kill is not always easy, and the matador may have to make several bloody thrusts before the sword stays in and the bull finally dies.

Throughout the fight, the crowd shows its approval or impatience. Shouts of "*¡Olé!*" or "*¡Torero!*" mean they like what they see—whistling or rhythmic hand-clapping greets cowardice and incompetence.

After an exceptional fight, the crowd may wave white handkerchiefs to ask that the matador be awarded the bull's ear or tail. A brave bull, though dead, gets a victory lap from the mule team on his way to the slaughterhouse. Then the trumpet sounds, and a new bull barges in to face a fresh matador. A typical bullfight lasts about three hours and consists of six separate fights—three matadors fighting two bulls each. For a closer look at bullfighting by an American aficionado, read Ernest Hemingway's classic *Death in the Afternoon*.

The Portuguese bullfight is different from the Spanish bullfight. For a description, see the Lisbon chapter. In Portugal, the bull is not killed in front of the crowd (though it *is* killed later).

Fiestas

Iberia has many regional and surprise holidays. Regular nationwide holidays are as follows:

Portugal—January 1, April 25, May 1, June 10 (national holiday), August 15, October 5, November 1, December 1, December 8, and December 25.

Spain—January 1, January 6, March 19, May 1, June 24, June 29, July 18, July 25, August 15, October 12, November 1, December 8, December 25, Good Friday and Easter, and Corpus Christi (early June).

Spain and Portugal erupt with fiestas and celebrations throughout the year. Semana Santa (Holy Week) fills the week before Easter with processions and festivities all over, but especially in Sevilla. To run with the bulls, be in Pamplona the second week in July. For more information, call or write to the Spanish or Portuguese National Tourist Office (see Introduction).

Let's Talk Telephones

Smart travelers use the telephone every day—for making hotel reservations, calling tourist information offices, and phoning home. In Europe, card-operated public phones are speedily replacing coin-operated phones. Each country sells telephone cards good for use in its country. Get a phone card at any post office. To make a call, pick up the receiver, insert your card in the slot in the phone, dial your number, make your call, then retrieve your card. The price of your call is automatically deducted from your card as you use it. If you have phone-card phobia, you'll usually find easy-to-use "talk now—pay later" metered phones in post offices. Avoid using hotel-room phones, which are major rip-offs for anything other than local calls and calling-card calls (see below).

Calling-Card Operators

Calling home from Europe is easy from any type of phone if you have a calling card. From a private phone, just dial the toll-free number to reach the operator. Using a public phone, first insert a small-value coin or a Spanish or Portuguese phone card. Then dial the operator, who will ask you for your calling-card number and place your call. You'll save money on calls of three minutes or more. When you finish, your coin should be returned (or, if using a card, no money should have been deducted). Your bill awaits you at home (one more reason to prolong your vacation). For more information, see Introduction: Telephones and Mail.

	AT&T	MCI	Sprint
Spain	900-99-00-11	900-99-00-14	900-99-00-13
Portugal	05-017-1288	05-017-1234	05-017-1877

Dialing Direct

Calling Between Countries: First dial the international access code, then the country code followed by the area code (drop the first digit, usually a 0, but in Spain it's a 9), then dial the local number.

   Calling Long Distance Within a Country: First dial the area code (including its initial digit), then the local number.

   Some of Europe's Exceptions: A few countries lack area codes, such as Denmark, Norway, and France. You still use the above sequence and codes to dial, just skip the area code.

International Access Codes
When dialing direct, first dial the international access code of the country you're calling from.

Austria:	00	France:	00	Norway:	00
Belgium:	00	Germany:	00	Portugal:	00
Britain:	00	Ireland:	00	Russia:	810
Czech Rep.:	00	Italy:	00	Spain:	07
Denmark:	00	Latvia:	00	Sweden:	009
Estonia:	800	Lithuania:	810	Switzerland:	00
Finland:	990	Netherlands:	00	U.S.A./Canada:	011

Country Codes
After you've dialed the international access code, then dial the code of the country you're calling.

Austria:	43	France:	33	Norway:	47
Belgium:	32	Germany:	49	Portugal:	351
Britain:	44	Ireland:	353	Russia:	7
Czech Rep.:	42	Italy:	39	Spain:	34
Denmark:	45	Latvia:	371	Sweden:	46
Estonia:	372	Lithuania:	370	Switzerland:	41
Finland:	358	Netherlands:	31	U.S.A./Canada:	1

Dial Away . . .
U.S. to Spain: 011/34/area code (without the long-distance prefix 9)/number

U.S. to Portugal: 011/351/area code (without the long-distance prefix 0)/number

Spain to U.S.: 07/1/area code/number

Portugal to U.S.: 00/1/area code/number

Spain to Portugal: 07/351/area code (without the long-distance prefix 0)/number

Portugal to Spain: 00/34/area code (without the long-distance prefix 9)/number

Long distance within Spain: area code/number

Long distance within Portugal: area code/number

Directory assistance: In Spain, dial 003 for local numbers and 009 for international numbers; in Portugal, dial 13.

(Note: In Spain a 908 area code indicates a mobile phone.)

Public Transportation Routes

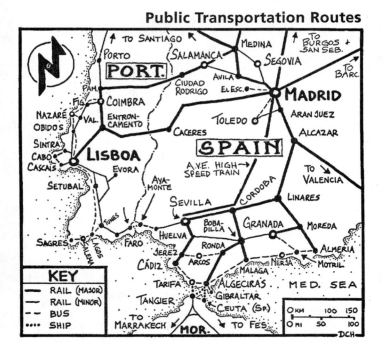

Numbers and Stumblers

• Europeans write a few of their numbers differently than we do: 1 is *1*, 4 is *4*, 7 is *7*. Learn the difference or miss your train.

• In Europe dates appear as day/month/year, so Christmas is 25-12-98.

• Commas are decimal points, and decimals are commas. A dollar and a half is 1,50 and there are 5.280 feet in a mile.

• When pointing, use your whole hand, palm downward.

• When counting with fingers, start with your thumb. If you hold up your first finger to request one item, you'll probably get two.

• What we Americans call the second floor of a building is the first floor in Europe.

• Europeans keep the left "lane" open for passing on escalators and moving sidewalks. Keep to the right.

Metric Conversion (approximate)

1 inch = 25 millimeters
1 foot = 0.3 meter
1 yard = 0.9 meter
1 mile = 1.6 kilometers
1 centimeter = 0.4 inch
1 meter = 39.4 inches
1 kilometer = .62 mile

32 degrees F = 0 degrees C
82 degrees F = about 28 degrees C
1 ounce = 28 grams
1 kilogram = 2.2 pounds
1 quart = 0.95 liter
1 square yard = 0.8 square meter
1 acre = 0.4 hectare

Climate

First line, average daily low temperature; second line, average daily high; third line, days of no rain.

	J	F	M	A	M	J	J	A	S	O	N	D
PORTUGAL Lagos/ Algarve	57	50	52	56	60	64	65	62	58	52	48	47
	61	63	67	73	77	83	84	80	73	66	62	61
	19	20	24	27	29	31	31	28	26	22	22	22
Lisbon	47	49	52	56	60	63	64	62	57	52	47	46
	58	61	64	69	75	79	80	76	69	62	57	56
	20	21	23	25	28	30	30	26	24	20	21	22
SPAIN Madrid	35	40	44	50	57	62	62	56	48	40	35	33
	47	51	47	64	71	80	87	86	77	66	54	48
	22	19	20	21	22	24	28	29	24	23	20	22
Barcelona	42	44	47	51	57	63	69	69	65	58	50	44
	56	57	61	64	71	77	81	82	67	61	62	57
	26	21	24	22	23	25	27	26	23	23	23	25
Costa del Sol	47	48	51	55	60	66	70	72	68	61	53	48
	61	62	64	69	74	80	84	85	81	74	67	62
	25	22	23	25	28	29	31	30	28	27	22	25

Basic Spanish Survival Phrases

Hello.	**Hola.**	**oh**-lah
Do you speak English?	**¿Habla usted inglés?**	**ah**-blah oo-**stehd** een-**glays**
Yes. / No.	**Sí. / No.**	see / noh
I don't speak Spanish.	**No hablo español.**	noh **ah**-bloh ay-spahn-**yohl**
I'm sorry.	**Lo siento.**	loh see-**ehn**-toh
Please.	**Por favor.**	por fah-**bor**
Thank you.	**Gracias.**	**grah**-thee-ahs
Goodbye.	**Adiós.**	ah-dee-**ohs**
Where is a...?	**¿Donde hay un...?**	**dohn**-day ī oon
...hotel	**...hotel**	oh-**tel**
...youth hostel	**...albergue de juventud**	ahl-**behr**-gay day hoo-behn-**tood**
...restaurant	**...restaurante**	ray-stoh-**rahn**-tay
...supermarket	**...supermercado**	soo-pehr-mehr-**kah**-doh
Where is the...?	**¿Dónde está la...?**	**dohn**-day ay-**stah** lah
...train station	**...estación de trenes**	ay-stah-thee-**ohn** day **tray**-nays
...tourist information office	**...Oficina de Turismo**	oh-fee-**thee**-nah day too-**rees**-moh
Where are the toilets?	**¿Dónde están los servicios?**	**dohn**-day ay-**stahn** lohs sehr-**bee**-thee-ohs
men / women	**hombres / mujeres**	**ohm**-brays / moo-*heh*-rays
How much is it?	**¿Cuánto cuesta?**	**kwahn**-toh **kway**-stah
Write it?	**¿Me lo escribe?**	may loh ay-**skree**-bay
Cheap(er).	**(Más) barato.**	(mahs) bah-**rah**-toh
Is it included?	**¿Está incluido?**	ay-**stah** een-kloo-**ee**-doh
I would like...	**Quería...**	keh-**ree**-ah
We would like...	**Queríamos...**	keh-**ree**-ah-mohs
...a ticket.	**...un billete.**	oon bee-**yeh**-tay
..a room.	**...una habitación.**	**oo**-nah ah-bee-tah-thee-**ohn**
...the bill.	**...la cuenta.**	lah **kwayn**-tah
one	**uno**	**oo**-noh
two	**dos**	dohs
three	**tres**	trays
four	**cuatro**	**kwah**-troh
five	**cinco**	**theen**-koh
six	**seis**	says
seven	**siete**	see-**eh**-tay
eight	**ocho**	oh-choh
nine	**nueve**	**nway**-bay
ten	**diez**	dee-**ayth**
At what time?	**¿A qué hora?**	ah kay **oh**-rah
now / later	**ahora / más tarde**	**ah-oh**-rah / mahs **tar**-day
today / tomorrow	**hoy / mañana**	oy / mahn-**yah**-nah

Basic Portuguese Survival Phrases

Hello.	**Olá.**	oh-**lah**
Do you speak English?	**Fala inglês?**	**fah**-lah een-**glaysh**
Yes. / No.	**Sim. / Não.**	seeng / now
I'm sorry.	**Desculpe.**	dish-**kool**-peh
Please.	**Por favor.**	poor fah-**vor**
Thank you.	**Obrigado[a].**	oh-bree-**gah**-doo
Goodbye.	**Adeus.**	ah-**deh**-oosh
Where is...?	**Onde é que é...?**	**ohn**-deh eh keh eh
...a hotel	**...um hotel**	oon oh-**tehl**
...a youth hostel	**...uma pousada de juventude**	**oo**-mah poh-**zah**-dah deh zhoo-vayn-**too**-deh
...a restaurant	**...um restaurante**	oon rish-toh-**rahn**-teh
...a supermarket	**...um supermercado**	oon soo-pehr-mehr-**kah**-doo
...the train station	**...a estação de comboio**	ah ish-tah-**sow** deh kohn-**boy**-yoo
...tourist information	**...a informação turistica**	ah een-for-mah-**sow** too-**reesh**-tee-kah
...the toilet	**...a casa de banho**	ah **kah**-zah deh **bahn**-yoo
men / women	**homens / mulheres**	**aw**-maynsh / mool-**yeh**-rish
How much is it?	**Quanto custa?**	**kwahn**-too **koosh**-tah
Cheap(er).	**(Mais) barato.**	(mīsh) bah-**rah**-too
Is it included?	**Está incluido?**	ish-**tah** een-kloo-**ee**-doo
I would like...	**Gostaria...**	goosh-tah-**ree**-ah
...a ticket.	**...um bilhete.**	oon beel-**yeh**-teh
...a room.	**...um quarto.**	oon **kwar**-too
...the bill.	**...a conta.**	ah **kohn**-tah
one	**um**	oon
two	**dois**	doysh
three	**três**	traysh
four	**quatro**	**kwah**-troo
five	**cinco**	**seeng**-koo
six	**seis**	saysh
seven	**sete**	**seh**-teh
eight	**oito**	**oy**-too
nine	**nove**	**naw**-veh
ten	**dez**	dehsh
At what time?	**A que horas?**	ah keh **aw**-rahsh
now / soon / later	**agora / em breve / mais tarde**	ah-**goh**-rah / ayn **bray**-veh / mīsh **tar**-deh
Today.	**Hoje.**	**oh**-zheh
Tomorrow.	**Amanhã.**	ah-ming-**yah**

For 336 more pages of survival phrases for your next trip to Iberia, check out *Rick Steves' Spanish & Portuguese Phrase Book and Dictionary*.

Faxing Your Hotel Reservation

Most hotel managers know basic "hotel English." Faxing is the preferred method for reserving a room. It's more accurate and cheaper than telephoning and much faster than writing a letter. Use this handy form for your fax. Photocopy and fax away.

One-Page Fax

To: _____ @ _____
           hotel   *fax*

From: _____ @ _____
              name   *fax*

Today's date: ____ /_____ /____
                day   *month*   *year*

Dear Hotel _____,

Please make this reservation for me:

Name: _____

Total # of people: _____   # of rooms: _____   # of nights: _____

Arriving: ____ /_____ /____   My time of arrival (24-hr clock): _____
           day   *month*   *year*   (I will telephone if I will be late)

Departing: ____ /_____ /____
             day   *month*   *year*

Room(s): Single___ Double___ Twin___ Triple___ Quad___

With: Toilet___ Shower___ Bath___ Sink only___

Special needs: View___ Quiet___ Cheapest Room___

Credit card: Visa___ MasterCard___ American Express___

Card #: _____

Expiration date:_____

Name on card: _____

You may charge me for the first night as a deposit. Please fax or mail me confirmation of my reservation, along with the type of room reserved, the price, and whether the price includes breakfast. Thank you.

_____
Signature

_____
Name

_____
Address

_____
City   **State**   **Zip Code**   **Country**

Road Scholar Feedback for Spain & Portugal 1998

We're all in the same travelers' school of hard knocks. Your feedback helps us improve this guidebook for future travelers. Please fill this out (attach more info or any tips/favorite discoveries if you like) and send it to us. As thanks for your help, we'll send you our quarterly travel newsletter free for one year. Thanks! **Rick**

I traveled mainly by: ___ Car ___ Train/bus tickets
___ Railpass Other (please list _____)

Number of people traveling together:
___ Solo ___ 2 ___ 3 ___ 4 ___ Over 4 ___ Tour

Ages of traveler/s (including children):

_____

I visited _____ countries in _____ weeks.

I traveled in: ___ Spring ___ Summer ___ Fall ___ Winter

My daily budget per person (excluding transportation):
___ Under $40 ___ $40–$60 ___ $60–$80 ___ $80–$120
___ over $120 ___ Don't know

Average cost of hotel rooms: Single room $_____
Double room $_____ Other (type _____) $_____

Favorite tip from this book:

_____

Biggest waste of time or money caused by this book:

_____

Other Rick Steves books used for this trip:

_____

Hotel listings from this book should be geared toward places that are:
___Cheaper ___More expensive ___About the same

Of the recommended accommodations/restaurants used, which was:

Best _____

    Why? _____

Worst _____

    Why? _____

I reserved rooms:

____from USA   ____in advance as I traveled

____same day by phone   ____just showed up

Getting rooms in recommended hotels was:

____easy   ____mixed   ____frustrating

Of the sights/experiences/destinations recommended by this book, which was:

Most overrated _____

    Why? _____

Most underrated _____

    Why? _____

Best ways to improve this book:

_____

I'd like a free newsletter subscription:

___ Yes   ___ No   ___ Already on list

_____

Name

_____

Address

_____

City, State, Zip

_____

E-mail Address

Please send to: ETBD, Box 2009, Edmonds, WA 98020

INDEX

Rick Steves' Phrase Books

Unlike other phrase books and dictionaries on the market, my well-tested phrases and key words cover every situation a traveler is likely to encounter. With these books you'll laugh with your cabby, disarm street thieves with insults, and charm new European friends.

Each book in the series is 4" x 6", with maps.

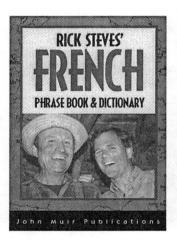

RICK STEVES' FRENCH PHRASE BOOK & DICTIONARY
U.S. $5.95/Canada $8.50

RICK STEVES' GERMAN PHRASE BOOK & DICTIONARY
U.S. $5.95/Canada $8.50

RICK STEVES' ITALIAN PHRASE BOOK & DICTIONARY
U.S. $5.95/Canada $8.50

RICK STEVES' SPANISH & PORTUGUESE PHRASE BOOK
& DICTIONARY
U.S. $7.95/Canada $11.25

RICK STEVES' FRENCH, ITALIAN & GERMAN PHRASE
BOOK & DICTIONARY
U.S. $7.95/Canada $11.25

Books from John Muir Publications

Rick Steves' Books

Asia Through the Back Door, 400 pp., $17.95

Europe 101: History and Art for the Traveler, 352 pp., $17.95

Mona Winks: Self-Guided Tours of Europe's Top Museums, 432 pp., $18.95

Rick Steves' Best of Europe, 576 pp., $18.95

Rick Steves' France, Belgium & the Netherlands, 320 pp., $16.95

Rick Steves' Germany, Austria & Switzerland, 272 pp., $15.95

Rick Steves' Great Britain & Ireland, 336 pp., $16.95

Rick Steves' Italy, 256 pp., $14.95

Rick Steves' Russia & the Baltics, 160 pp., $9.95

Rick Steves' Scandinavia, 208 pp., $13.95

Rick Steves' Spain & Portugal, 256 pp., $14.95

Rick Steves' Europe Through the Back Door, 512 pp., $19.95

Rick Steves' French Phrase Book, 192 pp., $5.95

Rick Steves' German Phrase Book, 192 pp., $5.95

Rick Steves' Italian Phrase Book, 192 pp., $5.95

Rick Steves' Spanish & Portuguese Phrase Book, 336 pp., $7.95

Rick Steves' French/Italian/German Phrase Book, 320 pp., $7.95

Adventures in Nature Series

Alaska: Adventures in Nature, 408 pp., $18.95

Belize: Adventures in Nature, 400 pp., $18.95

Guatemala: Adventures in Nature, 392 pp., $18.95

Honduras: Adventures in Nature, 360 pp., $17.95

City•Smart™ Guidebooks

City•Smart Guidebook: Albuquerque, 224 pp., $12.95 (avail. 4/98)

City•Smart Guidebook: Anchorage, 224 pp., $12.95

City•Smart Guidebook: Austin, 224 pp., $12.95

City•Smart Guidebook: Calgary, 216 pp., $12.95

City•Smart Guidebook: Cincinnati, 224 pp., $12.95 (avail. 5/98)

City•Smart Guidebook: Cleveland, 208 pp., $14.95

City•Smart Guidebook: Denver, 256 pp., $14.95

City•Smart Guidebook: Indianapolis, 224 pp., $12.95

City•Smart Guidebook: Kansas City, 248 pp., $12.95

City•Smart Guidebook: Memphis, 224 pp., $12.95

City•Smart Guidebook: Milwaukee, 224 pp., $12.95

City•Smart Guidebook: Minneapolis/St. Paul, 232 pp., $14.95

City•Smart Guidebook: Nashville, 256 pp., $14.95

City•Smart Guidebook: Portland, 232 pp., $14.95

City•Smart Guidebook: Richmond, 224 pp., $12.95

City•Smart Guidebook: San Antonio, 216 pp., $12.95

City•Smart Guidebook: St. Louis, 224 pp., $12.95 (avail. 5/98)

City•Smart Guidebook: Tampa/St. Petersburg, 256 pp., $14.95

Travel+Smart™ Guidebooks

Alaska Travel+Smart, 240 pp., $14.95

American Southwest Travel+Smart Trip Planner, 256 pp., $14.95

Carolinas Travel+Smart, 240 pp., $14.95

Colorado Travel+Smart Trip Planner, 248 pp., $14.95

Deep South Travel+Smart, 352 pp., $17.95

Eastern Canada Travel+Smart Trip Planner, 272 pp., $15.95

Florida Gulf Coast Travel+Smart Trip Planner, 224 pp., $14.95

Hawaii Travel✦
Smart Trip Planner,
256 pp., $14.95
Kentucky/
Tennessee Travel✦
Smart Trip Planner,
248 pp., $14.95
Michigan Travel✦
Smart Trip Planner,
232 pp., $14.95
Minnesota/
Wisconsin
Travel✦Smart Trip
Planner, 232 pp.,
$14.95
Montana, Wyoming,
& Idaho Travel✦
Smart, 272 pp.,
$16.95
New England
Travel✦Smart Trip
Planner, 256 pp.,
$14.95
New York State
Travel✦Smart Trip
Planner, 256 pp.,
$15.95
Northern California
Travel✦Smart Trip
Planner, 272 pp.,
$15.95
Ohio Travel✦Smart,
240 pp., $14.95
(avail. 5/98)
Pacific Northwest
Travel✦Smart Trip
Planner, 240 pp.,
$14.95
Southern California
Travel✦Smart Trip
Planner, 232 pp.,
$14.95
South Florida and
the Keys Travel✦
Smart Trip Planner,
232 pp., $14.95
Texas Travel✦
Smart, 256 pp.,
$15.95
Western Canada
Travel✦Smart, 272
pp., $16.95

Kidding Around™ Travel Titles

Kidding Around
Atlanta, 144 pp.,
$7.95
Kidding Around
Austin, 144 pp.,
$7.95
Kidding Around
Boston, 144 pp.,
$7.95
Kidding Around
Chicago, 144 pp.,
$7.95
Kidding Around
Cleveland, 144 pp.,
$7.95
Kids Go! Denver,
144 pp., $7.95
Kidding Around
Indianapolis,144
pp., $7.95
Kidding Around
Kansas City, 144
pp., $7.95
Kidding Around
Miami, 144 pp.,
$7.95
Kidding Around Mil-
waukee, 144 pp.,
$7.95
Kidding Around
Minneapolis/St.
Paul, 144 pp., $7.95
Kidding Around
Nashville, 144 pp.,
$7.95
Kidding Around
Portland, 144 pp.,
$7.95
Kidding Around San
Francisco, 144 pp.,
$7.95
Kids Go! Seattle,
144 pp., $7.95
Kidding Around
Washington, D.C.,
144 pp., $7.95

Other Terrific Travel Titles

The 100 Best Small
Art Towns in Amer-
ica, 256 pp., $15.95
The Big Book of
Adventure Travel,
400 pp., $17.95
The Birder's Guide
to Bed and Break-
fasts: U.S. and
Canada, 416 pp.,
$17.95
Costa Rica: A Nat-
ural Destination,
416 pp., $18.95
Indian America, 480
pp., $18.95
The People's Guide
to Mexico, 608 pp.,
$19.95
Ranch Vacations,
632 pp., $22.95
Understanding
Europeans, 272 pp.,
$14.95
Watch It Made in the
U.S.A., 400 pp.,
$17.95
The World Awaits,
280 pp., $16.95

Ordering Information

Please check your
local bookstore for
our books, or call
1-800-888-7504
to order direct and to
receive a complete
catalog. A shipping
charge will be added
to your order total.

Send all inquiries to:
**John Muir
Publications
P.O. Box 613
Santa Fe, NM 87504**